WHO KILLED MARTIN LUTHER KING?

Second Edition

Library of Congress Cataloging-in-Publication Data

Ray, James Earl, 1928-
Who Killed Martin Luther King?
the true story by the alleged assassin
James Earl Ray
288 pp. 15.25 cm x 22.85 cm
Includes index
ISBN 0-915765-93-4: $21.95
1. Ray, James Earl, 1928-
2. Assassins--United States--Biography.
3. King, Martin Luther Jr., 1929-1968--Assassination.
I. Title HV6248.R39A3   1991
364.1'524'092--dc 20   91-34847
CIP

The publisher gives special thanks to Michael Dolan, F. Tupper Saussy, William R. Saussy and H.B. Saussy. This book is based in part on *Tennessee Waltz (1987)* by James Earl Ray.

PRINTED IN THE UNITED STATES OF AMERICA

WHO KILLED MARTIN LUTHER KING?

The True Story
by the Alleged Assassin

by James Earl Ray

National
Press
Books

Washington, D.C.

Table of Contents

Foreword by Jesse Jackson 5

Preface by Mark Lane 9

Part I: Early Years

1. Family 17
2. The Army 22
3. Civilian Life 24
4. In and Out and In Again .36

Part II: Freedom

5. Breaking Out 45
6. Raoul 61
7. Back in the USA 69
8. Mexico Again 74
9. Los Angeles Revisited 80

Part III: The Road to Memphis

10. Events Accelerate 89
11. Abroad 102

Part IV: Caught in the Web

12. Midnight Sunstroke 115
13. Music City Prisoner 135
14. Brushy Mountain 141
15. Shifting Around 149
16. The 100-Mile Farce 158
17. Media Madness 165
18. The Select Committee 173
19. Another Escape 205
20. The Ray Brothers 213
21. Alexander Eist 222
22. Knives in the Library 226

Part V: Conspirators

23. Randy Rosen........................... 237
24. The FBI Connection 243
25. David Graiver and the Parole Board 252
26. Spica's Payoff 259
27. Talking Mustangs and Courts of Last Resort . .262

Appendix 269
Index 279

Foreword

by Jesse L. Jackson

Dr. Martin Luther King Jr. believed and often said "Truth crushed to Earth will rise again. The arc of the universe is long, but it bends toward justice."

No thoughtful person, after reviewing the evidence, can believe that this one man, James Earl Ray—who had bungled virtually everything he had ever tried, including criminal activity—acting alone, killed Martin Luther King, escaped during the evening traffic rush in Memphis on April 4, 1968, traveled to Canada and England with international passports, avoided an international network in search of him, and was only caught sometime later. Such a scenario strains the imagination, not to mention the reasoning process.

I have never accepted the "one crazy man" theory of political assassinations. I certainly do not accept such a theory with regard to James Earl Ray and Dr. Martin Luther King Jr. I have always believed that there was a conspiracy involved in Dr. King's assassination. I have always believed that the government was part of a conspiracy, either directly or indirectly, to assassinate him.

I have never ruled out the government's *direct* involvement because there were many in the government—J. Edgar Hoover among them—who had an intense, visceral and deep emotional hatred and fear of Dr. King.

Dr. King was projected by Director Hoover as a threat to our national security. Mr. Hoover felt Dr. King threatened the interests of the military-industrial complex and the ideology and mentality of the Cold War warriors. Thus, Dr. King faced the economic and political opposition of those interests. These elements, along with the government, and their pawns and sympathizers in the press, unabashedly attacked him.

The Johnson administration saw his moral stance against the Vietnam War as a threat to its corrupt foreign policy. His moral stance against the war was a patriot missile to an ill-conceived war full of scud missiles. Members of the administration sanctioned and wiretapped him. The President raised questions about his motives. Mr. Hoover called him a "damned liar" when he spoke of the FBI's lack of pursuit of the killers of Schwerner, Goodman and Chaney, the three civil rights activists slain in Philadelphia, Mississippi in 1964.

But even if the government was not directly involved, it was *indirectly* involved by helping to set a climate in which someone might think that they were doing the country a favor and acting in the national interest to do away with him.

James Earl Ray may or may not have been part of the conspiracy. I have no proof or facts one way or the other, nor am I in a position to know. Read his story and draw your own conclusion about him.

I only contend that there are some things you *sense* before you *know*. During the struggles of the 60s we sensed that the government was against us, but we did not *know* that it had a program to destroy our movement until later investigations revealed that it did.

What *is* known *now* is that *the government,* under the direction of FBI Director Hoover, *did* have a COINTELPRO program—i.e., a domestic counter intelligence program—to discredit, disrupt and destroy the Black movement and to prevent the rise of a Black Messiah (i.e., a Black leader who could unify and move the masses). We now know that they were not only afraid of someone who could rally the African-American masses, but the African masses as well. Such a connection had the potential of affecting America's racist foreign policy.

Thus, while I do not know, I have a strong sense that there was a government conspiracy to kill Dr. Martin Luther King Jr.

Where I do agree with James Earl Ray is that he deserves a full and fair trial, and the American people deserve to know the truth to the best and fullest extent possible. We have appointed independent special prosecutors for less important crimes. Denying James Earl Ray a trial and sealing the evidence to the year 2027 does not seem to me the best way for justice to be served. Justice delayed is justice denied.

The death of our great leader is at least of the magnitude of the Iran-Contra scandal, and other cases where a special prosecutor was appointed. We surely do not expect the Justice Department and the FBI to investigate themselves. The cover-up must be exposed. The sealed FBI files must be unsealed and the truth revealed.

An independent special prosecutor may more likely lead us to that truth. Like the Phoenix, we need the truth to rise from the ashes of deceit and end the cover-up that has protected the conspirators. The nation and justice have suffered long enough.

Over a decade ago, Congressman Louis Stokes (D., Oh.) chaired the House Select Committee on Assassinations which investigated the death of Martin Luther King Jr. In its report, which was released in 1979, the Committee concluded James Earl Ray fired the shot that killed Dr. King. [It should be noted that its conclusions were not based on ballistic evidence since the rifle allegedly used in the shooting was not test-fired.] However, on the basis of circumstantial evidence available to it, the Committee also concluded that there was a likelihood that the assassination of Dr. King was the result of a conspiracy.

In 1958, Dr. King was stabbed in the chest by a deranged woman. The doctors said the wound was so near his heart that if he had sneezed he would have died. Yet Dr. King said of this deranged woman "Don't do anything to her; don't prosecute her. Get her healed."

If Dr. King had been wounded and lived through the assassination attempt in Memphis on April 4, 1968, I believe that he would have been the first to call for a full and complete investigation. I believe that he would have been the first to demand a fair trial for James Earl Ray. I believe he would have been the first person seeking justice for his alleged assaulter. Surely the American people and its government can settle for nothing less.

Preface
by Mark Lane

[Mark Lane served as the Director of the Washington, D.C. based Citizens Committee of Inquiry, an organization committed to investigate the murders of Dr. Martin Luther King and President John F. Kennedy. Lane, an attorney and former member of the New York legislature, is the author of nine books, including the number one best seller Rush to Judgment and most recently Plausible Denial.]

Who Killed Martin Luther King? by James Earl Ray is a remarkable book. In an isolation cell, which a court has declared to be unfit for inmates, Ray has created an historic document.

Ray has been subjected to brutal treatment, was the victim of a murder attempt in prison, and was badly mistreated and tortured by the authorities. Had these events transpired against an American in a foreign country of which the U.S. president does not approve, they might constitute the basis for a covert attempt to overthrow the authorities there or to launch a full-scale invasion.

Ray, sentenced to 99 years in prison, has been incarcerated for more than two decades for a crime that I am convinced he did not commit. A personal and human drama lurks on each page and increases in tempo and volume with each chapter. Much of the drama is unspoken and unwritten but it thunders at the reader, who must contemplate how this man, America's most notorious political prisoner, maintains his sanity, not to say his apparent calm, as his life is spent in a cement tomb. Yet Ray writes with humor, that while touched with bitter irony never devolves into self-pity.

If a skilled, experienced investigator and writer with newspaper morgues, libraries and other archives at his command aided by a secretarial staff equipped with transcribing machines, word processors and editorial assistance produced this book, it would be noteworthy and commendable. That Ray, devoid of a support system, relatively uneducated in the formal sense, pecking away surreptitiously in his cell, has achieved such a result is monumental.

Yet Ray has found a way to tell the story and it is an intriguing one filled with inconvenient facts and insights compelling uncomfortable conclusions for those who come to it with an open mind.

Ray recounts his early years, a petty theft, a robbery, his service in the U.S. Army and his confinement in various prisons. Primarily what distinguishes this work from other prison works is the fact that Ray was subsequently arrested, extradited and sent to prison for 99 years for the murder of Dr. Martin Luther King Jr.

And what distinguishes Ray from other political prisoners is that, Catch-22-like, he was sentenced before the trial, indeed, instead of a trial.

Ray was arrested in England by agents of Scotland Yard. The case presented to the British authorities by the U.S. attorney rested almost entirely upon an affidavit of Charles Q. Stephens.

The crime took place on April 4, 1968; the extradition hearing in Bow Street Magistrate's Court in London on June 27, almost three months later. Due to domestic and international concerns the FBI, the Memphis police and other law enforcement agencies conducted an intensive investigation to locate any evidence that might link Ray to the crime. The Stephens affidavit constituted all the discoverable evidence.

Stephens was a notorious drunk who lived on skid row in Memphis with his wife, Grace. The room they occupied shared a wall with the bathroom from which the shot that killed King was apparently fired.

According to Mrs. Stephens, on April 4, 1968 her husband was drunk. He pounded on the locked bathroom door to no avail and stumbled down the stairs to urinate in the bushes behind the rooming house. Then she heard a shot, and almost immediately after that she saw the killer as he walked with a package in his hand, past her door.

Later Charles Stephens stumbled into the room, unaware that a stranger had been in the rooming house and oblivious to the shooting.

Very likely the only eyewitness of value in the rooming house was Mrs. Stephens. When photographs of James Earl Ray were shown to her she unequivocally stated that he was not the man who had emerged from the bathroom just after the shot was fired.

She was threatened by FBI agents and local police and told to cooperate. She was offered a substantial "reward" if she would identify Ray. She said she would be glad to cooperate and if they ever caught the right man she would readily identify him.

In violation of the laws of Tennessee Mrs. Stephens was surreptitiously sent to a mental institution. She had never before been to such an institution and had no history of mental illness. She was illegally incarcerated there for ten years until I was able to organize a public campaign to seek her freedom. The campaign included active participation from black and white religious leaders in Memphis, led by Rev. James Lawson, a close friend and colleague of Martin Luther King. That movement, together with motions filed in court, secured her transfer to a half-way house in Memphis. From there, at her request, I spirited her out of that city to Los Angeles, where she resided with my family. I returned to Memphis and challenged authorities to take action against me—they declined.

The federal authorities, having disposed of the inconvenient and truthful testimony of Mrs. Stephens, then approached her husband. Told of a $100,000 reward, he signed an affidavit saying Ray was the killer. Immediately the attorney general of Memphis had Mr. Stephens arrested, claiming that he was a drunk. This prevented reporters and investigators from interviewing Stephens for a considerable period of time. As Ray comments: "The prospects of winning a hundred thousand bucks, and all the fermented grapes it would buy, sharpened Stephens' recollections considerably about what he had seen in the flophouse on April 4."

Clearly, Ray could not be tried. The state had not a shred of credible evidence linking him to the murder. Stephens would collapse as a witness (later, incidentally, when shown pictures of Ray, he said that that was not the man he saw in the rooming house) and the testimony of Mrs. Stephens would destroy what remained of the state's allegations.

Therefore, the federal and state authorities arranged for the case not to be tried. A detailed description of how this was accomplished forms the centerpiece and, in my view, the most chilling portion of this book. It defines the abrogation of the judicial system in a civilized society.

Months of torture in a specially designed cell in which Ray was subjected to sensory deprivation, bright lights focused on him 24 hours a day, together with threats to imprison his elderly father and above all the selection of a lawyer who betrayed his interests, combined to deny Ray his day in court and brought a coerced plea of guilty. Later, when Ray again demanded a trial the Tennessee court system, which had already unlawfully imprisoned Mrs. Stephens, unlawfully denied him a trial.

Ray is clearly the primary victim of federal and state lawlessness in this matter. However, the American people and those throughout the world who care to know who killed Martin Luther King and why he died that day in Memphis are also victims. The truth became a target of the intelligence operations that suppressed the facts, suborned perjury, imprisoned witnesses and tortured the defendant.

I join in James Earl Ray's call for the appointment of an independent federal special prosecutor to investigate the FBI's involvement in the plot to kill Martin Luther King. The facts are clear that former FBI officials removed King's defenses just before he was killed, transferred potential witnesses the day before the murder and tampered, "lost" and destroyed key evidence. FBI written memos provide undisputed evidence that the bureau targeted King for harassment and "removal" from the scene. This documentary evidence alone is enough to establish probable cause that the bureau, Director J. Edgar Hoover and his underlings conspired to assassinate the civil rights leader. Together with the testimony of former agents and Memphis police officers I am convinced that a federal grand jury presented with relevant evidence by an honest special prosecutor would conclude that Hoover and other FBI officials were responsible for the assassination of Dr. King.

If you are going to read just one book this year, read James Earl Ray's *Who Killed Martin Luther King?* You will learn more about our flawed judicial and intelligence systems than you may have cared to know.

Part I

Early Years

Chapter One

Family

I was born on March 10, 1928, in Alton, Illinois, a small town of the sort familiar to readers of Mark Twain's books about life on the Mississippi River. Alton is 20 miles upriver from St. Louis, Missouri, closer to Tennessee than Chicago. Today, the suburbs of the larger city mesh with the smaller, but when I was a boy, Alton was its own little place, home to about 40,000 people.

Like many towns along the Mississippi, Alton had a number of factories: steel mills, an Owens-Illinois glass plant and others. Most of the streets were wide, and the town was hilly. The main street, Broadway, ran the length of Alton from the river to the factories, with hotels, apartment houses and small businesses all along it. My maternal grandmother and her sister lived on Broadway.

My mother's maiden name was Lucille Maher. Her family was of Irish stock. My father, George Ellis Ray, was descended from Scots and Welsh immigrants who'd come to America after the Revolution. He'd grown up in Quincy, Illinois, another Mississippi River town 145 miles north of St. Louis, and had come to Alton to work in one of the factories and try to stay out of trouble. In 1925, he'd been convicted of robbery and sent to Fort Madison Prison in Iowa, but he'd escaped a year later and didn't want to call any attention to himself. Besides factory work, my father sometimes drove a cattle truck, using a driver's license he'd gotten by using a phony name.

My parents met in Alton and married in 1926. We were nominal Catholics. I was one of seven children. Eventually my brothers John, Jerry and Frank and sisters Marjorie and Carol joined the family. Marjorie was killed at age eight when her clothing caught fire as she was playing with matches. Frank died in a car wreck when he was 19.

We didn't have elaborate lives. My father sometimes took me and my older brother fishing. Once in a while one of my uncles would invite me on a trip to St. Louis to see the Browns play baseball.

In 1934 my parents enrolled me in first grade at St. Mary's Elementary School, but I didn't finish out the year. My father's brother Earl saw to that by using our address—we lived on Seventh Street—in a failed forgery scheme that got us run out of town. We moved 120 miles northwest to Ewing, Missouri, a village of 350. To avoid being caught up in another of his brother's schemes, my father changed the family name to "Rayns." When it came time to enroll in school, I was James Earl Rayns, and I was in the first grade for the second time.

I was an average student, and didn't have any favorite subjects. My siblings and I were close, but as the oldest I was freer to spend my playtime in places forbidden to the younger children, such as the area near the Fabie River about a mile behind our house. Sometimes my father would take me and my brothers to the river. I stayed in the Ewing School until the eighth grade, when I quit to go to work.

Since Ewing was only 20 miles from Quincy, I spent most of my idle time there with my father's parents, Jim and Lillian Ray, who lived at 413 Vermont Street. Their neighborhood was on the north side of town, and its residents were a mixture of working and middle class people. Ted Crowley, who lived across the street from my grandparents, was a local godfather.

Uncle Earl often stayed with my grandparents when he wasn't in jail or trying to evade the police. Earl, who had a taste for whiskey, tended to try criminal ventures that weren't very successful. Once he decided to rustle cows. He'd been drinking, as usual. He was wearing a new $10 white linen suit and Panama hat when he borrowed a truck and set out for a farm he'd cased earlier.

Once in the barnyard my uncle got a noose over a calf's head, but in the dark he'd misjudged how big the animal was, and when it bolted Earl wound up being dragged across the manure-laden ground for several minutes until he could get the upper hand. He showed up at our house with the calf to see if my dad wanted to buy it. After Earl's check forging escapade had nearly gotten him caught as a prison escapee, my father shied away from his brother's shenanigans. This time, though, he paid Earl a few bucks for the calf, meaning that with the destruction of his suit and hat Earl's brief career as a rustler only cost him $7 or $8. It was this sort of behavior that attracted the police to our family, and often wound up with us moving, as we did several times, or with us children staying with our grandparents and our folks only coming by to visit under cover of darkness, to avoid being noticed.

Quincy had fewer factories and people than Alton, but more night life, which drew mainly out-of-town visitors and farmers looking for a big night off the tractor seat. The town occupies a bluff overlooking the Mississippi. In the 1930s about 35,000 people lived there, roughly half of Irish background and half of German descent. The Irish concentrated on the north side. The south side, which was mostly German, was called Calf Town because nearly every yard had a cow tied up in it. Quincy was the seat of Adams County, Illinois, but its biggest industries were whoring and gambling. At night the north side glowed red, lit by the taverns that sat on nearly every corner. Following river town tradition, the whorehouses clustered on the streets nearest the river—First, Second, and Third—with prices reflecting location. The $3 houses were furthest inland.

A little farther from the river, between Fifth and Sixth Streets, City Hall and the county courthouse took up an entire block bordered by Vermont Street on the south and Broadway on the north. The police and politicians didn't have to travel very far to collect their fair graft.

Grandfather Jim operated a tavern on Fifth Street, just off Broadway, a half block or so from City Hall. During the 1920s, he'd been a bootlegger. When Congress repealed Prohibition in 1934, he merely bought a beer license. Another attraction was a back-room poker game run by a gambler named Tom Maddix. I spent many evenings watching Maddix shuffle and deal.

When Uncle Earl was around we had regular visits from Dick Pursell, a policeman who knew where to look after my uncle had crossed the line, often in a dispute with a pimp. Earl disliked pimps.

When I reached my early teens, Earl sometimes took me with him on his barroom excursions, which usually ended at a whorehouse on the corner of Third and Vermont. The place was run by Big Marie. When she and the girls were particularly busy, they'd sometimes ask me to run errands, like getting something from the drugstore. On one such run I entered the girl's first-floor room as she was between customers, and noticed an open window right by the chair where a john probably would hang his pants. A couple of nights later I decided to see what I could score by reaching into that window from the passageway beside the building.

I staked out in a bush under the window until the light went on in the room. I saw a pair of trousers slung over the back of the chair. I made my move—but not without being noticed. No sooner had I grabbed the pants than a man shouted at me to drop them. Instead, I took off running, with him right behind. We both were knocking over garbage cans as we tore through the alley. I dropped the trousers, then realized he wasn't behind me anymore. I slowed my pace to a cautious walk, relieved that I hadn't been caught, with or without the goods.

The next day, I returned to see if by chance the object of the foot race was still on the ground. No such luck. But I did see why my pursuer might have stopped chasing me. Wrenched from its pole, there was a clothes line dangling near the ground. I'd been small enough to run beneath, but a taller man would have run right into the line and gotten tangled.

World War II had started, and I lost my guide to the Quincy underworld when Earl was jailed for assault. I also stopped hanging out at Big Marie's. After my gimmick with the window she viewed me with a jaundiced eye suspecting I was the culprit.

Not every citizen of Quincy was as wild as Earl, but many people had ties of one sort or another to the less legitimate businesses of the day. Another uncle of mine, Frank Fuller, made a living in the rackets, collecting cash from slot machines owned by the local mob. Frank never frequented the red-light district, but he knew it well. The route he followed emptying nickel and dime slot machines took him to all the joints. Sometimes I'd be able to persuade him to take me along.

Besides collecting and recording the take on the machines, Frank had the responsibility of keeping them working. Often customers would "slug" a slot, substituting a worthless piece of punched metal for a genuine coin. Slugs are usually very soft, which tends to cause them to stick in the innards of a slot machine. A jammed slot machine isn't making money for anybody, and the operators of the joints were always calling Frank to come over and straighten them out. He'd collect the slugs and save some of them for me. I'd take them to the slot machine at Grandfather Jim's place and have a ball, running the slugs through the slots and keeping piles of real coins. Of course, eventually the machine would jam, and my grandfather would have to call Frank. He'd fix the problem and always ask me when I was going to start splitting my take with him.

Chapter Two

The Army

In May 1944 I reached 16 and quit school for good, then moved back to Alton to live with my grandmother, Mary Maher, and my uncle, William "Hoss" Maher. With WWII still in full cry, there were plenty of jobs, and I landed one at the International Shoe Company in Hartford, Illinois, about ten miles south of Alton. I worked in the dye shop, where hides got their color, making 60 cents an hour plus overtime.

That job lasted until December 1945. With the war over, the plant was cutting back, and I was laid off. A few months later, in March 1946, I enlisted in the Army, signing up for a three-year term. The recruiters told me I'd be able to choose whichever specialty I wanted. I asked for the Quarter Master Corps. However, once you're in, you're in, whether they give you what you want or not.

After basic training at a signal corps base near Joplin, Missouri, I was transferred in July to Camp Kilmer, New Jersey, and that same month to Bamberg, Germany, and soon after to a base near Nuremberg.

I suppose I didn't carouse as much as the average GI. German bars were off-limits, and the only beer available to us was weak stuff sold by an Army-sanctioned club near the base.

I couldn't drive, but that didn't stop the Army from assigning me to a trucking company. I spent a few months with that unit, then was transferred again, this time to a post in nearby Bremen, where I finally learned to drive. I spent a year with a military police company, shuttling guards by Jeep to and from their posts.

As 1947 was ending, tensions were high in Germany. The Russians were tightening the noose around Berlin, and the United States was responding by increasing its military strength. I and hundreds of other servicemen in non-combat roles were conscripted into a new combat unit, the 18th Infantry Regiment, under the First Infantry Division.

In April 1948 my battalion moved to Regimental Headquarters in Bad Neuheim. We spent the summer on maneuvers at Grafenhor, a training area near the Czechoslovakian border. When autumn came, we moved to winter quarters in the outskirts of Nuremberg, where we all had to stand guard for lengthy periods. One day when I was supposed to be on guard duty I got sick and missed my shift. This got me confined to quarters pending an investigation. Instead of lying low, I hitchhiked into Nuremberg. While there, a sweep by the MPs caught me and several other soldiers who were where they weren't supposed to be.

My ill-conceived excursion resulted in a special court martial, a conviction for breaking arrest of quarters and a sentence of three months in the stockade. I spent my sentence in a fortress-like structure, the Palace of Justice, where the war crimes trials of prominent Nazis had taken place a few years before. After six weeks in the stockade, my sentence was suspended, and I was shipped home out of Bremerhaven. I returned to Camp Kilmer, where, on December 23, 1948—two days before my enlistment was up—I received a discharge "under honorable conditions." This was a slap in the face—if the Army had wanted, it could have let me stay a soldier another 48 hours and muster out with a standard honorable discharge.

Chapter Three

Civilian Life

As soon as I was out of uniform for good, I left New Jersey for the Midwest traveling by train. My family was living in Quincy again. I stayed there a while.

In the spring of 1949, I moved to Chicago. There weren't any jobs, so I enrolled at a school downtown and took some high school classes. My education was taken care of by the GI bill. In the warm months Chicago was all right, but as soon as that cold wind started coming in off Lake Michigan in September I decided I wanted to live in a more hospitable climate. My finances being what they were, I had little choice of transportation. It was ride the rails or nothing, so I rode the rails, headed for Southern California.

My first night in the trainyards I looked around for an empty boxcar that seemed to be headed the proper way, and climbed aboard. I was right about the direction, though the route was less than direct. For three weeks I rode freights, meandering through the western states, and actually working briefly in Colorado as a laborer.

I was on the outside of some little town, watching the tracks and waiting for a California-bound train, when a migrant labor recruiter offered me a chance to make some money. He hauled me and a few other recruits to a barracks-like building. All but two or three of us were Mexicans.

The barracks was a headquarters for migrant farm workers. In the early morning hours a truck would take crews to the fields. I and a few others stayed behind. Our job was to build another barracks. The foundation was complete. Carpenters were framing up and starting on the roof. I mainly carried lumber.

At night the place went crazy, everyone staying up until two or three in the morning drinking and fighting. Some Mexicans had their girlfriends along, which contributed to the turmoil. The girls sometimes stayed around the premises during the day. While their paramours were toiling in the fields, they'd get in some different work with those of us on the building crew, myself included.

That was the end of my building days. Soon after enjoying my first noonday acquaintanceship I began to notice that I was getting a lot of dirty looks from the Mexicans. I decided it was time to move on. When payday came, I collected my week's wages, walked into town, and that night caught a freight. A few days later I arrived in Los Angeles, sitting atop a boxcar.

First Civilian Arrest

My Colorado wages covered a few days' rent on a room in a flophouse on lower Broadway. I spent my evenings in a nearby honky-tonk, continuing a habit I'd started in the Army.

One night I got loaded, either from drink or a goofball slipped into my glass by one of the hostesses. All I know is that one minute I was in the bar, the next I was waking up in a hallway in some building where I'd never been. There was a character shaking me and yelling about me breaking into his place. We started to argue, but when he mentioned the police I shook the cobwebs out and started walking rather hastily.

The next day a policeman stopped me. The guy from the previous night's hallway argument ran up and exclaimed that I was the one he'd complained about. He claimed I'd tried to rob his office. The cop handcuffed me and loaded me into his squad car. At the Los Angeles County Jail, I was charged with burglary and attempted theft of office equipment.

In December 1949 I pleaded guilty to the burglary charge, but because it was my first arrest, I got off light, drawing three months in jail, followed by two years' probation—provided that as soon as my jail term was up, I returned to Illinois, my last place of official residence.

I got out of the county jail in March 1950, 15 or 20 pounds lighter and somewhat wiser about the workings of the legal system. Otherwise, nothing much had changed, especially my financial status. I spent my first day out looking for something to steal so I could eat and pay my way out of town.

I had enough money for a bowl of chili, which I saw advertised in the window of a Chinese restaurant. When I sat down to order, I saw that there was an opening over the back door that housed an exhaust fan so big that a fellow could squeeze in between the blades—especially if the fellow had been on a jailhouse diet.

I ate my chili, paid my bill, and left, walking to the trainyards to wait until sunset. When it was dark, I returned to the restaurant and eased in between the fan blades. Once inside I had a scare—there was a dog sleeping in the kitchen. But he didn't wake up, even though I rummaged around the place collecting some groceries and rifling the cash register, netting a few rolls of coins.

I went out the back door and returned to the yards, where I caught a freight that wound up in Las Vegas. There I played boxcar roulette, winding up in a car that was detached from the train on a desert siding in Arizona. During the heat of the day I sat in the shade of the boxcar, living on the groceries from the restaurant and hoping a train would come by. By the time a train did pick up the boxcar I was dehydrated.

When we got to the next town I hopped off and found a restaurant. I found out how dry I was when I opened my mouth to order a cola and some ice cream from the waitress—my throat was so parched I had trouble speaking.

Finally I latched onto a boxcar bound for Salt Lake City, where I moved up a class in transportation, hitching a ride on a passenger train by running alongside and grabbing onto the steps of a ladder on the side of a coach.

Unfortunately the train headed north into the mountains. The temperature dropped precipitously, and there was a freezing rain. I had no choice but to cling to that ladder until the next stop, but at least passenger trains move faster than freights, and I was soon hopping off again.

I kept on moving that way, and by April I was in Iowa, almost to my court-ordered destination of Illinois. But while passing through Cedar Rapids early one morning the train stopped briefly, and a deputy sheriff rousing hobos spotted me crouched in my boxcar. I was still carrying a coin roll from the Chinese restaurant, arousing the deputy's suspicions. But I wasn't in the mood to explain anything, so I spent a month in the local jail, which had the L.A. County Jail beat, at least as far as cuisine went. I'd nearly regained the weight I'd lost in Los Angeles and was thinking of sticking around until the weather improved before making any noises about getting sprung. However, I didn't get the chance to experience warm weather in the Cedar Rapids Jail, which looks out onto the Iowa River as it flows through the city.

Although he'd run a blank on the coin roll, the deputy who'd busted me offered me a choice: I could go before the judge, plead guilty to vagrancy and receive a suspended one-year sentence and a bus ticket out of town—or I could plead not guilty and spend a year in the workhouse.

The next day, I appeared before the judge and pleaded guilty to vagrancy. The deputy immediately took me to the bus station and bought me a one-way ticket to Chicago, with my roll of stolen coins.

Chicago, Again

I got to Chicago in May 1950. The Korean War was on, and once again jobs were plentiful. I found a job in a factory and bought a black 1949 Buick.

I lived alone on Fullerton Avenue. My social life included occasional visits to the local bars. Once in a while I caught a Cubs game.

I generally stayed inside the law in Chicago until the winter of 1951-52, when an acquaintance told me he'd started casing a liquor store and bar on the city's Near North Side. He'd noticed that the owner was running a bookie operation and kept large amounts of cash in a back room.

We decided to hold up the place. We had a .38 revolver, but we needed a getaway car to use right after the robbery. Once we'd pulled the heist, we'd race for my Buick, which I'd park a few blocks away. We figured the easiest way to steal a getaway car would be to hold up a taxi driver, then use his car for the robbery.

I was elected to grab the cab. Since he knew the layout of the joint in question, my cohort would handle the holdup. On the appointed night, I parked the Buick on State Street, leaving my accomplice in it. Then I walked a ways, getting as far as Clark Street before I flagged down a taxi. I gave the driver an address three or four blocks to the east. Once we arrived, I pulled my gun.

I announced a holdup, telling the driver I wanted the keys. He yanked the keys out of the ignition and either flipped them out the window or under the seat. With the hijacking of the taxi foiled I reached onto the front seat and grabbed his cash bag, then bailed out of the cab and took off at a dead run for State Street, now two or three blocks away. I wasn't alone. A passerby had seen the action in the cab and followed me, stopping a police car and pointing me out to its occupants.

I made it to State Street with the pedestrian and the squad car in hot pursuit. When I passed my Buick, my partner took off in the opposite direction.

After crossing State I cut down an alley, intending to double back and get to my car. But the alley turned out to be a dead end, and with shouts of "Halt, police!" coming close behind me I broke a basement window and jumped into the darkness, landing on all fours. I felt a tingle on the side of my face but got up, stuck the gun into one of my back pockets and ran for a partially lit doorway—the same one the police were using to enter the basement, guns drawn. I collided with one of the cops, who accidentally shot me in the arm.

The policemen took me around to State Street. One of the officers ducked into a bar and called for a paddy wagon. His partner had a hammer lock on me. A couple came out of a nearby bar, and the woman noticed that my head was bleeding badly—the result of a cut suffered when I dove into the basement, I suppose. She'd obviously had a few drinks and began accusing the cops of beating me up. Her protests were so strong that they tried to calm her down, which kept them from searching me before the Black Maria arrived. Without patting me down, the policemen handcuffed me and stuck me inside, where I managed to wrestle the revolver out of my pocket and shove it under the seats, reducing the charge against me from armed to unarmed robbery.

This time around I wasn't treated leniently. Despite the lightness of the charge, the judge sent me up for one to two years. I entered the Illinois prison system at Joliet, then was moved to a medium security institution near Pontiac.

I was assigned to the farm outside the compound, where I spent the next 18 months working in the kitchen. About 20 of us occupied a two-story dormitory; I helped cook the evening meal and spent my spare time playing softball or lifting weights using a set of barbells that had been made at the prison.

I got out of Pontiac on March 12, 1954. Along with my release papers I got $25, my turnout suit and a bus ticket to Quincy, 130 miles away.

Quincy hadn't changed much. The girls were still operating along the riverfront streets. But my Uncle Frank's line of work had disappeared. The slot machine operators were no longer in business.

After a few days in Quincy I moved on to Alton, where my uncle, Hoss Maher, hired me as a part-time painter. Uncle Hoss had a contract with Miller's Mutual Insurance Co. to paint its sign on barns. He paid farmers to let him put the signs on their barns where passersby could see the ads. I helped my uncle until August, when the Alton police arrested me. The charge was a burglary involving a dry cleaning store.

Dominic Tadaro, who owned a nightclub in town, agreed to post my bail. I was to reimburse him in monthly installments and hire his lawyer to represent me. The deal was that his lawyer would delay the trial until I'd paid Tadaro off entirely. But like my Uncle Earl, I'd gotten on the wrong side of the Alton police. Two weeks after Tadaro posted my bail, they grabbed me again, this time for "suspicious behavior." I was taken before the chief of police. He called in 14 of his officers, as well. With them surrounding us, the chief pointed at me.

"Arrest this bastard whenever you see him on the street," he told them. "Right now book him for vagrancy."

I would have stayed in jail until my trial for the burglary if Tadaro, who now had a financial interest in my staying outside, hadn't paid my bail a second time. Once he did, I headed back for the more tolerant confines of Quincy.

Leavenworth

In Quincy I was scraping by, trying to stay even on my monthly payments to Tadaro. I had to steal to make ends meet, living in cheap hotels.

In the course of hanging around the usual joints, I met Walter Rife, a petty thief and part-time pimp. Uncle Earl, who was then out of jail, tried to warn me off the acquaintance, but I ignored him. One day Rife told me he'd broken into the U.S. Post Office in his home town of Kellerville, Illinois. He'd made off with a stack of money orders and the official stamp to validate them.

Rife made me an offer: if I'd drive him to Florida to cash the paper, he'd make it worth my while. Then we'd part company.

I was strapped, and Tadaro was leaning on me. I said I'd do it. We left in March 1955, stopping briefly in St. Louis, where Rife took me down on Skid Row and showed me how to buy identification papers from winos. You could buy a man's identity for a few bucks. We collected several sets of papers.

Once we had ID paper we set out for Florida, stopping now and again so Rife could cash a postal order. He was a glib type, better at that sort of thing than I. We'd stop somewhere, he'd fill out and stamp a money order, and then we'd cash it at a clothing store or whatever was handy. Eventually, we arrived in Jacksonville, where we checked into a motel.

We needed more ID with which to write postal orders, so Rife went out to find the wino district and do some identity shopping. I waited in the motel. He returned empty-handed, but said he'd found a joint where he thought we could score. It was a freak joint—a bar frequented by homosexuals. I followed Rife's directions, and parked outside the little hole in the wall. Inside, there wasn't much except a small bar and three or four tables off in the darkness.

We sat at the bar near the door and ordered drinks. After a few minutes, Rife got up and followed a customer to the men's room. I figured he was going to sound the guy out about buying his identification. Things were quiet in the john for a long time, but suddenly a commotion erupted. There were shouts and curses, even screams. Then Rife and his quarry burst out into the bar, wrestling and scratching.

Rife had picked a male impersonator to mug. In the tussle he'd pulled her wig off. Now he was trying to break away, but she was all over him, and I realized that the place was full of dykes, all of whom started screaming. To distract them, I threw a stool into the crowd, enabling Rife and me to charge out into the night and get away.

"What the hell was going on in there?" I asked once we were safely away.

"The bitch refused to sell me her ID papers," Rife said. "So I tried to strong-arm her, but she kicked me in the balls and started screaming."

It was time to get out of Jacksonville. We left at once on a seven-state, two-week trip, during which Rife passed most of the forged money orders. Then we headed back for Quincy.

We made it as far as Mark Twain's hometown, Hannibal, Missouri. There, about 20 miles south of Quincy, the Highway Patrol stopped us. While searching my Pontiac, the cops found evidence connecting us to the stolen money orders. They arrested us and held us for the postal inspectors, who charged us with forgery and transporting stolen documents across state lines, then had us shipped to a federal jail in Kansas City, Missouri. There, Rife admitted that when we'd first gotten to Hannibal he'd phoned a girlfriend in Quincy. He thought she'd given us up to the police.

Again I played the legal shell game, this time in the Kansas City U.S. District Court. Rife and I pleaded guilty on all counts. He drew three years. I got three years and nine months, to be served in the federal penitentiary at Fort Leavenworth, Kansas.

"Leavenworth" has come to mean "hard time," and for good reason. In 1955, inmates there had a choice: submit to the rules or rot in solitary confinement. My fellow prisoners were bank robbers, drug traffickers, mobsters, Communists convicted for failing to register as Party members, and bent labor leaders like Lawrence "Larry" Callahan, the St. Louis Steamfitters Union president, who was serving time for extortion. Callahan had gotten caught up in a federal crime investigation engineered in part by an ambitious Capitol Hill lawyer named Robert Kennedy, who ran similar investigations in several states, including Tennessee. There, a state criminal court judge named Raulston Schoolfield was indicted for accepting a $20,000 bribe to fix a case in which 13 members of the Teamsters International Union were acquitted of charges involving labor violence. Schoolfield was absolved by the Tennessee state Senate but lost his seat on the bench.

Leavenworth is just another jail. I lived in a dorm on medium security due to my relatively short sentence. I worked from 4:00 p.m. to midnight in the bakery. I would roll out dough with a rolling pin and later help bake bread.

Prison Life

To understand prison culture, it's important to remember that in many ways prison life is like life on the outside. You have a place to live, a place to eat, a job to do, rules to follow and people you have to get along with. The people you don't get along with—or with whom you want nothing to do—you stay away from. The people whose company you prefer, or can a least tolerate, you gravitate toward.

Anything you can get on the outside, you can get in prison. The only difference is the sanctions for violating the rules. If a prisoner cheats a guard or an administrator, the price could be a stint in the hole, as solitary confinement is called. If the prisoner cheats another prisoner, the price could be his life.

In jail inmates usually are there for only a brief period, during which they're locked up, so there's not a lot of action. But a prison is like a small city. Many institutions have "prison industries"—commercial-grade shops where they make license plates, furniture, shoes, clothing or materials needed to keep up the place. At many prisons, inmates grow vegetables, bake bread and prepare food consumed in the dining hall. Prisoners are often walking to or from these jobs.

Prison isn't a very relaxing environment. There's a lot of noise—televisions, boom boxes, shouting, banging, screaming. You can get relief in the library (prisons usually have good libraries, particularly of law books collected by inmates trying to research their cases) or in the exercise yard.

A lot of prisoners spend their spare time working out—running, lifting weights, doing calisthenics. Staying fit is very important, both for keeping a positive attitude and as a way to stay out of trouble. Even though prison isn't as depicted in the movies and on television, with big mean guys always picking on little weak guys, it often comes down to who's going to yield and who's going to prevail, no matter what the dispute. That's why a lot of prisoners join gangs—usually organized along racial lines, or set up to maintain a structure from the outside, like the Cosa Nostra. A lot of prisoners carry shanks, which are homemade knives fashioned out of scrap metal or whatever is available. All that's required is a piece of metal and an object to sharpen it with. If you don't want to make a shank, you can buy one. I've tried to avoid shanks because getting caught with one can mean as much segregation time as a prisoner can get for attempting to escape.

There's considerable violence in most prisons—beatings, stabbings and occasionally rapes. The authorities like to maintain a certain level of awareness of what's going on in the prison, so they recruit informants, particularly sex offenders, and reward them with whatever commodity applies: cushy jobs, and sometimes a pat on the head. If the informant has a taste for kinky sex, his controller, usually a prison official, will arrange for a new kid—provided he's weak—to be placed in the informant's cell for him to rape. Or if the informant's tastes run in the other direction, he'll be provided with someone to dominate him. Informants are about the lowest life form in the prison food chain. When they're found out, they often have to be transferred to another institution or kept in protective custody.

Prison escapes get a lot of attention in the press, but not every prisoner is itching to go over the wall. A lot of inmates simply want to get through their sentences and get out. Any attempt at escape brings down a lot of heat on the general prison population, with cells being searched, sections being put into lock-down (when everyone is kept in his cell) and more guards than usual working the hallways. For a lot of prisoners, the idea of trying to escape is frightening, and they want nothing to do with it. For others, the outside wall is a challenge they can't resist. It isn't a matter of heroism or bravery—they don't have a choice. They have to try.

I was in good shape, able to work an eight-hour shift in the bakery doing whatever needed doing. I usually teamed up with another prisoner to roll out dough on a big table; we'd flatten the dough, then shape it into rolls and leave them to be baked by the day shift. The clean-up chores were handled by Mafia types who preferred their own company and spoke only in Italian.

During the day I played handball and lifted weights. When you're behind bars you need to be in good condition, if only to be able to outrun an attacker. I could look around and see the despair of those who'd sunk into drugs, and realized that if I made it out of Leavenworth alive, I wanted to get out of the United States entirely.

I had no disciplinary problems while in the prison and thanks to the "good time" I'd accumulated in the bakery, was released from Leavenworth in April 1958. But I wasn't completely free. I was on "conditional release," a form of parole, which meant I'd have to postpone my plans to leave the country until I didn't have anybody to report to.

Chapter Four

In and Out and In Again

I walked out of Leavenworth in my turn-out suit—a dark-colored outfit made in a prison by prisoners to be worn by ex-prisoners until they could get some real clothes—with a $50 stake, courtesy of my bakery work for the U.S. government, and a bus ticket to Kansas City. That was where I'd been sentenced, so that was where I had to live until my conditional release expired in December. However, the rules permit a prisoner to ask his parole officer to transfer him to the location where his family lives, provided the parole officer there is willing to add the prisoner to his caseload.

There were three or four of us on the bus from Leavenworth. When we got to the Kansas City terminal we had the usual reception committee waiting: a pawn shop operator who could recognize the cut of a turn-out suit. As was his custom, he offered us each ten dollars, a T-shirt and a pair of dungarees in exchange for our suits. Two of the guys went for the deal, changing clothes in the lavatory.

I declined the offer and checked into a flophouse on East Ninth Street, from which I reported directly to my parole officer—as it happened, he was the same bureaucrat who, three years earlier, had conducted my pre-sentencing investigation. Neither of us showed much enthusiasm for renewing the acquaintance. He told me to check in with him daily, in person or by phone, and give details of my efforts to find a job.

Later that day I went to the bakers' union, coming clean about where I'd learned to make bread and pastries. A union official treated me with courtesy. He said to stay close to my hotel in case he phoned there with a possible job. He did call the next day, with an offer from a local bakery, but I was out—seeing my parole officer to explain what I was doing to find work. That job went to somebody else, and the union never called again.

After a couple of weeks I could see that if I didn't transfer to St. Louis, where my mother was now living, I'd be right back in Leavenworth. I used what money I had left to buy the makings of a hot-wire—large alligator clips and a few feet of heavy-duty electrical wire.

After dark, I found a used car lot in a secluded area, hot-wired a clunker, and headed for St. Louis, 130 miles away.

At daybreak, five miles short of my destination, the car's engine went. I hoofed it into town to my mother's home. I then found the local federal parole officer and made my pitch. He authorized a transfer. Then I got to my mom's house. She lent me a little cash, and I moved into an apartment house on Mississippi Street, not far from where the winos hung out.

For a few months I worked part-time as a baker and cook. But the jobs slacked off, and I continued in my grandfather's footsteps after a fashion, becoming a bootlegger.

On Sunday, Missouri state law prohibited the sale of alcoholic beverages. This makes it tough on the city's winos, who rarely stock up on Saturday night for that long dry spell the next day. At the end of the week, I'd stock up on fifths of muscatel, hold them until the package stores closed, and then on Sunday offer my wares at inflated prices. With the stores closed I could get $1 for a fifth that cost only 55 cents the rest of the week.

I kept up this practice until the end of December 1958, when my conditional release expired. Now I could get out of St. Louis, Missouri, and out of the United States. I figured to go to a port city and enroll in a seaman's school, then ship out on a freighter. That would require more money than I could amass as a Sunday bootlegger. I needed one more score.

I hoped to better my situation semi-legitimately, by gambling illegally, and possibly by robbing whoever was running the game. If I won, so much the better. If I lost and had to pull a heist, I didn't expect to be followed, since professional gamblers tend not to call the police when they're robbed.

I had a 1949 Pontiac sedan, a stake of about $200 and a pistol. Just before Christmas, I drove over to Madison, Illinois, and found State Street, which ends across from the railyards in a long line of bars, whorehouses and gambling joints. I checked out several bars, returning near closing time to a place at the edge of the district, where traffic was minimal.

There was a dice game going on a pool table in a side room. I decided to try my luck. It was just me and the guy running the game, and within minutes the house had all my money. As I left, I could see that the sharpie with the dice and the bartender were the only ones left in the joint.

I went to my car and got my gun, then walked to a rear window where I could look in on the bar. The sharpie came my way. I stopped him by shoving my pistol into his ribs. We went back inside, where the bartender filled a cloth sack with the evening's receipts, about $1,300. I ran for the car, and drove back across the Mississippi.

While it's true that those who live outside the law don't like to call the cops, they don't mind obtaining justice in their own way, so I cleaned out my apartment and headed for New Orleans, figuring to find a school for apprentice merchant seamen. If I could get seaman's papers, I'd have a way out of the country without having to spend every cent I had. But once I got to New Orleans I found that the seamen's school wasn't enrolling students. I drove around the Texas coast to Brownsville and crossed the border into Matamoros, Mexico, where I acquired a Mexican visa, which was all I needed to travel in that country.

I continued on to Veracruz, where I rented a room and made the rounds of the sailor's bars. One night I met an American merchant seaman. He was broke. I bought a few rounds. He returned the favor by inviting me to his ship the next day for a meal.

My new friend turned out to be the ship's steward, which meant he knew the ins and outs of signing on with a freighter. I asked if this was possible without papers. No, he said, it wasn't.

I gave up on Veracruz, and made for Acapulco. Things were no better there. In fact, because most of the ships in the harbor were tourist vessels with tighter controls on their crews, Acapulco offered even fewer possibilities than my last port of call.

By February 1959, I was back in St. Louis, bootlegging again. One of my steady customers was a guy who went by the nickname "Dirty John." No one knew his real name. He claimed to be about 30, but he looked far older, and no one could accuse him of not living up to his moniker. But Dirty John was always steering customers my way, and I tried to look out for him.

Months passed. I was doing well enough to have bought another car—a black 1949 Lincoln—and thought I might have found a calling. But then Dirty John let me down by pulling an armed robbery in East St. Louis, using my old car. He and a buddy robbed a supermarket owner but were spotted by the police, who chased them down a dead-end street, where they abandoned the automobile. The other guy escaped. Dirty John froze, holding the bread knife he'd used in the heist. The cops held their guns on him until he dropped the knife, then arrested him and confiscated the car. When they searched it they found papers linking it to me.

Within days St. Louis police officers were crashing into my mother's house in the wee hours, looking for me. But I wasn't around. I was at father's house. When I got wind of the raid, I headed for Montreal until the heat died down. I rented a room near the train station and spent a lot of time on the east side of the St. Catherine district, in the French Quarter. It was a familiar setting: an old town at the side of a river, full of gamblers, prostitutes and bunco artists. I looked for a job, but to get work in Canada you need to hold the Canadian equivalent of a U.S. Social Security card. I still had my goal about expatriating, but by summer I was back in St. Louis, trying to avoid a welcome-wagon visit from the cops.

I ran into James Owens, an ex-con I'd met before through a mutual acquaintance. Owens was just out of Missouri State Prison at Jefferson City, living at Preacher Jim's Mission, a North St. Louis flophouse run by a minister who'd taken over an abandoned moviehouse and offered cots and a meal to anybody, including Owens and some other ex-cons who'd been paroled to the reverend's custody.

The ex-cons had jobs in the city and turned over part of their earnings to the mission, which had two distinguishing features. Every day at 6 a.m., rain or shine, anyone who'd stayed the night and wanted breakfast had to fall out in front of the building for prayers and hymns. The other feature was less uplifting: thanks to the guys paroled to Preacher Jim's custody, the mission occasionally was used as a hideout by hold-up artists. They'd pull a robbery, run for the old theater, and hide among the bums and winos until the police sirens had died down.

Eventually the ring was busted up, but by then Owens had moved on. He had an eye for the hustle and was tired of those dawn patrol hymn sessions. I was looking for funds, too, which brought me to fall into regular contact with Owens, leading to our arrest for robbing a couple of grocery stores.

We both were picked up on the morning of October 19, 1959. In court, I pleaded not guilty to the first robbery, while Owens pleaded guilty to one charge of robbery. The jury found me guilty, and the judge sentenced me to 20 years in state prison. I appealed—the case still hasn't been resolved (see *State v. Ray*, No. 48583, Missouri Supreme Court, March 1983).

On the second robbery charge, I did plead guilty, after the district attorney offered to let the seven-year sentence on that charge run concurrently with my earlier 20-year sentence. Owens got seven years total.

In March 1960, I was transported by train to Jefferson City, site of Missouri's maximum security prison. Located only seven blocks from the state capitol building, Jefferson City prison was known as "the bloodiest 47 acres in the United States," thanks to a 1954 riot that got five prisoners killed and others injured, along with several guards. The incident began in E Hall, the maximum-security section, with prisoners feigning illness and ambushing their guards. The violence quickly spread across the grounds and lasted 15 hours, with several buildings burned to the ground before the Highway Patrol and the guards restored order. Afterward, a Highway Patrol sergeant, E. V. Nash, was appointed warden. He'd led a detachment into the riot zone and later headed the inquiry into the causes of the violence.

Jefferson City prison sits on a bluff overlooking the Missouri, surrounded by the suburbs of the state capital, which goes by the same name as the penitentiary. The original compound was the first prison built west of the river. It started out as a wooden stockade, and grew through the 19th century into a massive collection of stone buildings. The main compound sits on high ground. It contains the cellblocks, called "halls." As space was needed to build plants to house the prison industries—small factories making brooms, license plates, soap, tobacco, furniture, gloves, shoes and clothing, along with a dry cleaning plant and a shop for manufacturing fences and other items used around the prison—another section was constructed. This is the lower yard, which is down a steep slope from the original prison and contains the industries buildings and the recreation yard. The halls and the lower yard are are connected by an iron gate knocked out of the original gray stone wall.

As is customary, I spent my first 30 days at Jefferson City—known inside as "JeffCity"—in isolation. Prison officials decided I'd get a cell in K Hall and assigned me work in the dry cleaning plant. After I was released into the general prison population, I made my first trip to the recreation area, where many of the 1,700 or so convicts were hanging out. Immediately I saw that JeffCity had a live-and-let-live attitude. In the rec area, you could get into a poker game or buy and rent magazines or books of any kind.

Such tolerance didn't stem from any desire to coddle convicts. Rather, Warden Nash and his assistants had figured out after the 1954 riot and a number of escape attempts that it would be easier to placate the prison's population by allowing gambling and other "recreational activities" than to keep everyone in a constant state of tension.

And Nash wasn't a rule freak, either. Many prison administrators publish a steady stream of memos listing all the trivial do's and don'ts—not Nash, who in those days was dealing mostly with professional criminals convicted of robbery, burglary and so on, for whom getting caught and doing time was a cost of doing business. They just wanted to tear dates off the calendar and get through their sentences, and Nash felt the same way.

After I'd been on the yard about two hours, a whistle sounded, ending recreation period. We lined up. Another whistle blew, signaling meal time. The dining room was old-style, with rows of iron benches for tables and shorter benches for seating. The benches were partitioned: one section was for white prisoners, the other was for blacks. A roped-off subsection at the back of the room was reserved for homosexual prisoners. Another, at the front of the room, was for snakes who'd been exposed. These informants were referred to as "Russell's Rangers," for the guard who escorted them to and from the dining room. Silence was supposed to reign during meal time, but there were always insults being shouted at the homosexuals and informants.

Part II

Freedom

Chapter Five

Breaking Out

After about seven months at JeffCity, I was ready to try an escape. My job in the dry cleaning plant offered a reasonable opportunity for such an undertaking. That and my 20-year sentence were all the encouragement I needed to plan an escape.

Not every prisoner thinks this way. For a lot of guys, even the idea of trying to escape is too frightening. For others, the heat that comes down when somebody else tries a breakout only adds to the generally high level of aggravation brought on by prison life. I was doing my best to be seen by the authorities as cooperative. If you're not cooperative you wind up in the hole, from which nobody escapes.

There were no guards in the dry cleaning plant. Only myself and six other convicts. And I didn't have to report for head count until 8 p.m. In the late fall and winter months, that would give me about two hours of weak light in which to pull off an escape before I'd be missed.

The walls of the cleaning plant were lined with long wooden shelves on which we stacked supplies. I could see being able to fashion a ladder out of the shelving.

But I had to be wary of informers, especially as I was forming my plan. It's easy to keep track of the guards, but snitches are stealthy, always prowling around for some morsel of information they can take to the authorities in exchange for a favor.

With no guards on duty in the dry cleaning plant, it was almost a certainty that the administration had an informant among the convicts working there, so I kept my escape ideas to myself.

By November 1961, I was ready. I had my route figured, I had my tools in place. One evening I decided the time had arrived. Six o'clock had come and gone, and with it all but one of the other cleaning plant workers. I hid behind some boxes at the back of the plant until I heard the last convict walk out. If he'd been the snitch, all he could say was that the plant was empty when he'd gone for the day.

The lights were out, but I could see well enough to begin dismantling shelves. The boards were oak, which made for tough nailing. But I persisted, connecting four 2x6s to make a long plank, with narrow strips nailed along its length to act as steps.

I finished the ladder and dragged it behind me as I crawled out of the cleaning plant and toward the clothing shop 50 feet away. The guard in a tower overlooking my route didn't spot me. Once in the shadows of the clothing shop, I pulled the ladder down a narrow passage between the clothing plant and the license plate plant. This put me within 20 feet of the wall.

To reach the base of the wall, I had to risk being seen by another tower guard. I scuttled across the open space unseen. It took me a few seconds to hoist the ladder into place and begin climbing.

I was about halfway to the top when the ladder began creaking and then collapsed at one of the points where I'd spliced the 2x6s together. Despite the racket, the tower guard didn't seem to notice, so I gathered up the pieces and returned to the cleaning plant. I had another plan.

I stowed the broken pieces of ladder near the base of the wall and moved on to my alternative—a ladder made of pipe taken from the yards of metal racks on which the drycleaning crew hung clothing to dry. These racks were made of ordinary plumbing parts, and I was able to screw together another ladder in jack time.

I repeated my high-tension crawl, set the rickety assembly against the stone barrier, and started my second climb of the evening. This time I made it two-thirds of the way to the top before my ladder gave way. I landed in a heap, and a section of pipe crashed onto my head, but still the tower guard didn't stir.

This time, when I returned to the cleaning plant, several guards with flashlights were coming toward me. They arrested me, and my escape attempt landed me in long-term segregation for six months.

Long-term segregated prisoners stayed on the upper floor of E-block, a two-story brick building and one of the prison's oldest structures. When I checked in, a guard gave me a canvas bag about six feet long. He sent me on to a room containing straw, where I was ordered to fill the bag. One of Russell's Rangers stitched it closed, and that was my mattress for the duration. For the first several nights, until my weight flattened it, the mattress was so round that I'd roll off onto the floor while sleeping.

The straw mattress and one blanket were the only furnishings in my cell. I was permitted to order 35 cents' worth of extra food per week from the commissary—enough for five or six candy bars.

Long-term segregation was full of head cases, who would harass the guards, provoking them into shooting tear gas into the offending parties' cells. Of course, the gas would spread over the whole area. The only way to escape the fumes was to lie on the floor and try to suck fresh air through rusty cracks where the plumbing entered your cell. The gas never lasted long, though. The window frames were loose enough that birds could enter through gaps in them, as could winter cold so fierce that prisoners had to stay in bed clutching their single blankets to feel the slightest bit of warmth.

But in segregation you at least knew one thing: when your time was up. Nash didn't permit extensions of original sentences. So in May 1962, I returned to the general prison population. When I got to the lower yard I noticed a large spotlight atop the clothing plant was aimed at the stretch of wall I'd tried to scale.

I went to work in the "spud room" peeling some of the millions of potatoes that went into prisoners' meals. The administration reserved spud duty for its least favorite inmates. My companions on the potato line were sex offenders—not exactly my cup of tea, either.

The only way out of the spud room was refusing to work. The penalty for that was ten days in the hole—solitary confinement with only one meal a day. I refused to peel potatoes, and did my ten days in the hole.

Custom held that once you'd served that penalty time you wouldn't be reassigned to the spud room. I helped tradition along with a $10 donation to one of the convict clerks. This guaranteed that I could pick my job. I knew the chief cook, Neil Abey—his brother Aubrey and I had met while we were both in Leavenworth—and asked if I could sign on with one of his crews. He said he'd have the civilian steward assign me to work in the bakery, which was where I spent the next three years.

During this time my younger brother Frank was killed when the car in which he was riding jumped the guard rail on the bridge leading over the Mississippi from Quincy.

There was a streak of racial violence inside the prison. Black prisoners successfully petitioned to integrate F and G Halls. The administration went along, partly to get men out of A Hall, which was ancient and overcrowded. To discourage trouble between the newcomers and white prisoners who disliked the change, a squad of guards escorted the blacks to and from the hall. The truce held for two weeks.

The fight occurred on the evening of June 9, 1964. Inmates from F and G were coming in from the yard when a dozen men wearing pillowcases over their heads attacked them with shanks. Several prisoners were stabbed, one fatally. Led by the guard supervising the project, the goon squad leaders and inmates ran for the control center at the end of the tunnel, where an electrically-controlled gate offered sanctuary. One of those fleeing the fighting had a shank sticking out of his back.

The next day, Nash ordered all prisoners, black and white, into the yard. In each tower stood a pair of guards armed with shotguns and automatic weapons. Down below we were hearing that if another riot broke out, the guards would open up indiscriminately. Later, a white gang leader made a deal with one of the black gang leaders: things would revert to the old ways. No one was ever charged in the assaults.

JeffCity underwent other turmoil. In December 1964, during the prison staff's annual Christmas party, Warden Nash shot himself to death. That November Thomas Hearns had been elected governor of Missouri, partly by vowing to clean up the prison system. He appointed a pair of ex-federal wardens to key jobs.

Fred Wilkinson, who was Hearns' director of corrections, had run federal penitentiaries all around the country. He'd also done some work for the Central Intelligence Agency. In February 1962, he'd escorted captured Russian spy Rudolph Abel across no man's land to exchange him for U-2 pilot Francis Gary Powers. In 1963, he'd helped ship the last 250 prisoners out of Alcatraz. At Jefferson City, he kept the nickname "Friendly Fred" that he'd gotten at one of his earlier postings.

Hearns' choice for warden at JeffCity was Harold Swenson, another ex-fed—he'd run pens for more than 25 years—who liked to talk about humane treatment for prisoners. However, as soon as he was in command, he had the goon squad round up 30 or 40 of the hardest cons for confinement in segregation—a simple gesture designed to show who was in charge.

In 1965, I'd been in Jefferson City for five years. It had been nearly four years since my last attempt to get over the wall, and I was ready to try again. I transferred from the bakery to a clean-up crew in K Hall, which enabled me to roam outside my cell until as late as nine in the evening.

There were no bars on the windows in K Hall. You'd still have to scale a wall to get out, but at least you didn't have to saw your way through the first stage of the game. But I soon found a severe drawback: even though it would be relatively simple to scale a portable scaffold and climb out a window, the window ledge was 30 feet above rocky ground. I asked for and got a transfer to J Hall, still doing clean-up and free to roam. There was only one guard on duty most of the time, and I thought I could see a way to use that situation to my advantage. I began collecting tools—hacksaw blades and a long pole with a hook at the end used to open hard-to-reach casement windows—and watching for my chance.

On weekend nights movies were shown in an old brick building next to F Hall. Until the 1954 riot, the prisoners could watch movies in Garner Hall, which had a real theater, complete with marquee. It was burned down during the disturbance.

Movie night could be quite tense. The darkness was an excellent cover in which to exact revenge, and we hardly ever got through both reels without somebody getting shanked or knocked in the head with a rock picked up by a convict crossing the 20 feet of open space between F Hall and the jerry-rigged moviehouse.

Before the lights went down, all the extra guards on that shift congregated around the movie hall to discourage the inevitable. The attackers often hit the wrong guy. If someone knew he was in for trouble, he'd take his seat conspicuously and wait for the lights to dim, then scoot to another spot, leaving his hapless neighbors to deal with what came down. The four or five guards prudently stayed off to one side until the hit took place, then flipped on the lights to a chorus of catcalls and complaints, and hauled away whoever had gotten hurt.

One movie night I skipped the show and eased around to the rear of J Hall, where I'd arranged for the cleaning crew to set up a scaffold so we could wash the higher windows. I'd made sure my window hook was nearby before we knocked off work for the day. About 20 feet above the floor, a small window covered with a thick wire screen led out onto the roof of a covered passageway linking several buildings behind J Hall. The scaffold was right beneath the window.

Pushing my broom as nonchalantly as I could, I got to the bottom of the scaffold and climbed up to where I could get at the window. I'd brought along a hacksaw blade and used it to saw away enough of the screen that I could crawl onto the passageway roof, after shoving the window pole out in front of me.

Dragging the window pole, I crawled about 100 feet, following the leftward curve of the tunnel until I reached the roof of a low-lying building that led another 40 feet to the main administration building's south wall. I planned to hook the window pole to one of the gutters on the administration building and pull myself onto the roof, then cross over the top and drop down the outside of the wall onto the road that passed the prison.

Everything went smoothly until the gutter gave way. I fell about 15 feet, injuring my right arm. As I collected my thoughts, I spied a shack on the roof where I lay. Its door was padlocked, but there were air-vent slats in the door. I pulled them loose, squeezed inside and pushed the slats back into place to cut the risk of being found out.

Inside there was only a small generator—nothing to require a guard's attention during daylight hours. I figured I could hole up until nightfall, sneak down into the lower yard and make another ladder. It was March, the foggy season. Maybe the weather would break my way.

I waited until around 3 a.m., then slipped out of the shack, once again taking care to replace the vent slats. I hadn't traveled 50 feet when guards surrounded me. They hustled me to the hospital. While my arm was being bandaged, I met Warden Swenson, who ordered the guards to throw me into the hole.

After several days, I got out so I could be charged with attempting to escape. The usual punishment was six months hole time plus six months in segregation. But I only had four or five years to serve, so instead of following custom Swenson wanted me tried so I'd get another half-decade as his guest.

But I refused to plead guilty and demanded a trial. The judge appointed an attorney to represent me, and he turned out to have some creative ideas. He suggested to the judge that I might not have been in possession of all my faculties when I allegedly tried to escape.

The judge had been around the block, and he knew what to do. He had me transferred to the Missouri Hospital for the Criminally Insane in Fulton, to be tested to see if I was mentally competent to stand trial. I made the trip to Fulton in September 1966, in the company of another prisoner who was working hard on his performance, complaining about hearing voices and noises emanating from the trunk of the squad car in which we were being transported.

At the bughouse, we were taken to the maximum security ward. The other guy kept rambling about these voices he was hearing.

When our paperwork was finished, the guards had attendants take us to our cells, which were across the hall from one another. Instead of iron bars, the doors were solid metal, open only near the floor, where a mesh grate covered a small hole.

The attendants locked me into my cell and took the other guy across the hall. He was still raving. I crouched on the floor, squinting through the mesh and listening while the attendants talked to him.

"Gonna give you a chance to straighten up," one of them said. "Anytime we hear you say, 'Yassuh, boss!' we gonna stop."

Then they commenced to whacking him. The attendants didn't say anything more, but I could hear a lot of thudding noises and the other guy hollering and screaming. I figured that even though I hadn't tried to cop a nut plea the way he had, I was next. After the thudding and hollering ended, though, the attendants moved on. I found out later that the treatment they'd given my fellow traveler was an informal way of diagnosing the severity and reality of a prisoner's mental symptoms.

But even if the attendants' fists worked a miracle cure, you still had to go through two months of testing. The first morning, I lined up with the other patients in a hallway to be interviewed by a psychiatrist. As the line moved toward his office, it passed a door that had a window in it, through which I saw a patient strapped to a table with wires taped to his head. He was flopping around like a fish on a dock—undergoing shock therapy.

This had an unsettling effect, and I instantly lost interest in trying to convince anybody I was mentally ill. I came clean with the shrink, and he told me to mind my own business and I'd have no problems while I was at the hospital. That was fine with me.

After two months I was certified as competent to stand trial for the attempted escape. My lawyer said we could ask to have an outside doctor give a second opinion on my mental state, which we did. The state agreed to foot the bill for another assessment, but a budget crunch sent my second opinion up in smoke.

But the charges of attempting to escape were dismissed, and I eased back into the boring stream of prison life, this time as part of a crew building an auditorium to replace the one that had burned in 1954. This was rough work, and after a few months I asked to go back into the kitchen, where I latched onto an assignment pushing the hospital diet cart.

The hospital menu was heavy on items that we didn't see much in the regular prison. To boost patients' strength, they got eggnog and a lot of beef—and so did the guys who pushed the cart. This was ideal. After my most recent stint in segregation I was run down, and pushing the cart let me sample the high-protein meals served prisoners on the mend after an illness or injury.

I wanted to be in good shape. Who knew when the next opportunity to escape might present itself, or when somebody might come after me?

The prison hospital at JeffCity had been built in the 1930s by the Works Progress Administration. It was an old-fashioned place, with one resident physician, Hugh Maxey. He was in his 70s, and relied on several prisoner technicians to handle most of the medical care. What they mainly did was prescribe tranquilizers, often donated by drug companies as a way to obtain information on products still in the research phase. The technicians also had to take over for Dr. Maxey in the operatory when his hands cramped up during surgery, as often happened.

One of the prisoners I got to know while working in the hospital was a St. Louis guy named John Paul Spica, who was doing life for conspiracy to commit murder. He was said to have heavy mob connections.

Once I'd gotten myself back into shape, I quit the diet cart job and returned to the bakery, where it looked as if I had another chance of breaking out.

A guy who worked there had figured out what looked like a fine escape plan. It seemed simple. Each morning, a 6x6 truck with a canvas roof over the cargo bed would arrive from the prison farm to pick up a big wooden box full of bread for the farm crew's meals. My man had realized that a guy could arrange to be in the small room near the bake shop where the bread was stored. When the farm-bound breadbox came up from the loading dock to be filled, he could slip into it and hide at the bottom while somebody filled the rest of the box with loaves. The accomplice would take the box down on the elevator and out onto the dock, where he'd wheel it onto the back of the farm truck.

The truck had to pass through a tightly guarded tunnel, where every vehicle coming and going was searched. If he got past that checkpoint, all the guy in the breadbox had to do was to gauge when the truck was halfway to the farm, which was about eight miles from the main prison, and jump off.

The prisoner who'd thought up the plan decided not to try it himself, but he was willing to let me in on it because I had more seniority.

I saw a few rough edges in the plan. To keep from being discovered by the tunnel guard, I built a false bottom out of heavy cardboard and cut some vent holes near the bottom of the breadbox to keep from suffocating. And if I had to jump out of the truck, I'd need a change of clothes so my prison uniform—dark green pants with a black stripe down each leg—wouldn't give me away. I got a pair of black pants from a member of the prison band.

The other problem wasn't so easily solved. Anytime more than one prisoner plots an escape, it's usually not long before another prisoner hijacks the idea or informants learn of the plan and expose it to the administration. I thought we'd been turned in when a shakedown in the breadroom uncovered civilian pants hidden on the shelves where the bread cooled.

But my getaway pants had been hidden in a hollowed-out loaf. The second pair of trousers must have been stuck there by someone who'd gotten wind of our idea and was preparing to try it himself. However, the guard who'd found the other pants gave them to me and suggested I get rid of them, which I did. These developments speeded up our schedule, which also called for a phony story fed to a known informant.

We agreed that if I made it out of the prison, my accomplice would "reveal" that I actually was hiding somewhere inside, much as had occurred during my previous attempt. If the informant and the administration bought this, the search for me would stay inside the wall for hours, giving me a good head start.

At about 8 a.m. on April 23, 1967, I entered the kitchen. As a member of the kitchen crew, I normally ate breakfast there rather than in the dining room. Not knowing when I'd see my next meal, I ate about a dozen eggs and waited for my accomplice's signal to enter the bread storage room.

He appeared and gave me the high sign. Everything was ready. I climbed into the breadbox, set the false bottom into place, and my man stacked 60 or so loaves on top of me. It was a tight squeeze, and I was uneasy until I could feel the box moving onto the cart, then down in the elevator, and onto the loading dock. Someone shoved the breadbox onto the back of the truck, which immediately started down the tunnel toward the checkpoint.

The tunnel was a cage with an iron gate at either end. When a vehicle entered, both gates were closed while a guard made his search, then waved the car or truck through if everything was jake.

It took the truck a couple of minutes to reach the cage. I heard the breadbox lid being raised, then dropped. The outside gate creaked open, and the truck began moving again, picking up speed as it got onto open road.

I shoved the false bottom up as hard as I could. At first the loaves compressed and the lid wouldn't yield, but I pushed harder and bread crumbs showered down into my face. Suddenly the breadbox lid popped free and the loaves flew. I stood, up to my knees in mangled loaves, and peeled off my prison trousers. By the time I had slipped into the bandsman's pants, the truck had passed every traffic light between the prison and the farm. We were on the bridge spanning the river, which meant there would be no more stops until we reached the farm.

This posed a problem. Did I have the nerve to jump out at 45 miles per hour, or would I sit tight and be busted at the farm?

My dilemma was resolved by a minor traffic jam. The truck driver paused at the gravel road leading to the farm to let oncoming cars pass. When he slowed down, I jumped, quickly standing up straight and pretending to be a civilian hitching a ride. I even waved to the driver, who may or may not have seen me when he let in the clutch and continued on toward the farm.

As soon as the truck was out of sight I crossed to the opposite side of the road and began walking along a path back to the bridge. I came upon an old junkyard strewn with wrecked automobiles and chose one to hole up in until night fell 11 hours later. With the advent of darkness I walked two more hours to a set of railroad tracks. I began following them, headed in a northwesterly direction.

Besides my prison pants, now stuffed in a paper sack, I had some bread, a few candy bars, a small transistor radio and I had about $250 hidden in my shoes. I tuned the radio to a local station to listen for reports of my escape, but there were none. (Later I learned that our bogus story had gone down without a belch. The informant went to the guards, the guards scoured the yard and every prison building and I got the head start I'd hoped for.)

My first night out I stayed on the railroad right of way and put as much distance as possible between myself and the prison. At dawn I hid in the bushes and napped. I was out in the middle of nowhere. The only sound was the rush of water from a creek that ran alongside the rails. When I got thirsty, I drank from it.

I kept up this routine for three days. On the third day I ran out of food. But the tracks had veered closer to the banks of the Missouri, and I came upon a fishing shack, where I found some fresh eggs that I boiled in a can over a fire made from twigs and small branches. There was also a half-empty bottle of wine. After eating the eggs and washing them down with the wine, I fell asleep beside the shack, dozing until it began to rain. I got up and moved on.

I reached a stretch where the train tracks ran parallel to Highway 63, but the occasional sound of traffic barely intruded on the tranquillity. As I walked I saw foxes playing. Sometimes I'd pause and sit on the river bank, soaking up the solitude. The prison yard seemed very far away.

Only once did I see other people. One day a thunderstorm came up quickly. I climbed beneath a trestle seeking shelter and started a fire to dry out my clothes. I was standing as close as I could to the flames without getting burned when I heard voices up on the rails.

Two men climbed down the hill.

"Say, what's going on down here?" one of them asked.

"I was walking along the rails when the storm came up," I said. "I got soaked, so I came down here and made a fire to dry off."

They turned out to be railroad inspectors, checking the ties and rails using an old-fashioned handcar. They seemed to buy my explanation, said they were sorry to have disturbed me and climbed back up. The last I heard of them was the wheels of their handcar rolling down the line.

On the sixth day, I came to a small town. I waited until sundown, then walked in through the railyard. I found a combination pool hall and lunchroom, where I loaded up with food. The counterman told me I was in New Franklin, about 50 miles northwest of Jefferson City.

I returned to the trainyard and fell asleep, but soon awoke to the sound of a passing freight. A train shakes the ground so much you don't hear it as much as you feel it. I jumped up, lunged for the ladder on a coal car, and crawled aboard.

The freight was headed opposite to the direction I'd been taking, but that would get me to St. Louis, which was okay with me. When the train reached St. Louis, I jumped off and spent the rest of the night at the edge of the yards. At daybreak I headed for the south side, to find an ex-con I knew. His name was Jack Gawron, but he called himself "Catman," in honor of his alleged talents as a burglar. Catman was about 65, and a bit deaf. He walked with a limp that he claimed to have acquired when he fell from a telephone pole during a second-story job.

I found his place, but he wasn't home, so I caught a taxi to East St. Louis. From there I caught another cab to Edwardsville, about ten miles out in the countryside, where I boarded a Trailways bus bound for Chicago. Fearing a police stakeout at the ticket window, I waited until I was boarding the bus to pay the driver for a ticket.

In Chicago I rented a room in the 2700 block of North Sheffield Avenue. My ankles were badly swollen, but otherwise I was none the worse for wear. I began watching the classifieds in the *Chicago Tribune,* and on May 3, 1967, applied to work as a dishwasher at the Indian Trails restaurant in Winnetka, Illinois, one of Chicago's wealthier suburbs. I used the name "J.R. Rayns," for which I had a Social Security number. I was making $100 a week. My rent was $11 a week.

I tried to save as much as possible so I could buy a car. If I had the title to a car, I could use that piece of paper to obtain other ID. I was feeling very good.

It took me a month or so to accumulate the $100 I needed to purchase a white 1960 Chrysler that I brush-painted dark blue. Car title in hand, I took and passed a driver's license examination. Toward the end of the test my examiner got a little cranky, so I slipped him a ten-spot to improve his attitude. Once I had my temporary driver's permit, I felt safe. If someone asked for proof of my identity, I had it.

Reviving my notion of living abroad, I rented a post office box. Using the box as a return address, I wrote to the Canadian consulate in Chicago requesting information on emigrating to that country. I got back several brochures on the subject.

I also phoned my brother Jerry, who was living in nearby Northbrook and working as a watchman at a country club. He told me to meet him at a bar on Howard Street, which divides Chicago from Evanston. Over beers Jerry told me agents from the Federal Bureau of Investigation had questioned him as to my whereabouts. It didn't occur to me that it might be unusual for the FBI to involve itself in so petty a matter as the escape from a state prison of a two-bit career criminal like myself. We talked for an hour, then said good-bye.

By June, I had enough ID and cash to get to Canada. I'd moved up to cook at the Indian Trails, but quit. The restaurant made a practice of holding a departing worker's last paycheck for a week. To pass that time, I cleared out of my rented room and drove down to Quincy, where a hotel room cost only $1.50 a night. I stayed first at the Milnor, on the corner of Third and Oak, then at the Gem, which my grandparents' old neighbor Ted Crowley, local godfather, still owned. I told him I'd been paroled. Crowley had done some time himself, and having any connection to a fugitive would get him into big trouble. Inflation had hit Third Street. The girls had raised their rates from $3 to $5. I couldn't spare that much, so it was a slow week.

After ten or 12 days of bumming around, I drove back to Winnetka and collected my final paycheck, stayed in Chicago a few days and then headed for East St. Louis. I planned to ask Catman Gawron to have my brother John rent a mail box under an assumed name so I could contact him by mail without arousing the curiosity of anyone who might be searching for me.

On the way the Chrysler started acting up. I made it to East St. Louis, but the car was beyond repair. On July 14, I sold it to a gas station in East St. Louis for $40. At a nearby used car lot, I spent $200 for a red 1962 Plymouth two-door sedan.

I arranged to meet Catman at a bar. He agreed to help with my scheme, as well as to do another, riskier favor. Buying the Plymouth had left me short of cash. I wanted to pull a heist so I'd have enough cash to make it to Canada, but to do that I needed a gun. I figured to repeat my old gimmick of robbing someone who operated outside the law.

I asked the Catman to get me a pistol from a mutual acquaintance—a fence who dealt in stolen merchandise out of Madison, on the outskirts of East St. Louis. The Catman came through with a .38.

That night I left East St. Louis, stopping to sleep in a hotel in Indianapolis and the next day passing through Detroit and on into Windsor, Ontario.

Chapter Six

Raoul

I'd made it to Canada, but I was still low on funds. My first couple of nights in the country, I slept in my car, moving north by day until I reached Dorion, a town on the outskirts of Montreal. On July 17, 1967, I checked into a motel there. That evening, I drove into the big city to revisit the French-speaking area and its whorehouses, which I'd gotten to know back in 1959 on my first trip north of the border.

The red-light district was about the same. I parked the Plymouth and hit the street, moving from bar to bar in hopes of being picked up by a woman with that commercial air. It didn't take long.

A dark-haired working girl in her 30s suggested that I accompany her to her apartment in a taxi. She had a second-floor flat. When we got there, she asked me for $25, whereupon she left for a few minutes—no doubt to give the money to her pimp.

She came back, we concluded our transaction and we talked briefly as we were getting dressed. She said she worked St. Catherine East steadily. I buttoned up and left, stopping outside to write down the address of the apartment building before heading back to the motel in Dorion.

In the morning, I checked out and drove into Montreal again. I rented an efficiency at the Har-K Apartments in the 2500 block of East Notre Dame, as "Eric S. Galt," the first time that I used this alias.

I had figured out where I was going to get the money I needed. The World's Fair, Expo '67, was on, and Montreal was crawling with tourists. Illegal operators such as pimps would be flush. That evening I returned to St. Catherine East, parking the Plymouth a couple of blocks from the apartment of the whore I'd met the previous night. I went back to the club where that had happened; she was at the bar. After drinks we caught a cab to her place, but instead of giving her another $25 I pulled my pistol and told her I'd walk her to her pimp.

She led me there and knocked on his door. When he unlatched the door, I pushed it open far enough that he could see my piece. He was small, swarthy—and cooperative, once he realized what I had in my hand besides his girl.

"I want the money," I said.

He took a few bills out of his pocket.

"All the money."

He shrugged and stepped to a nearby cabinet. He took out a tin can, removed a roll of bills and handed it over. I shoved it into my pocket.

I knew I had to get downstairs without a lot of screaming, but I figured once I got onto the street I could make it to the Plymouth and get away in safety. Throughout all this, the girl had been silent. I asked her to pull off one of her stockings and tie up the pimp. She did as I asked. To play it safe, I had her get under a cot that stood against one wall. I told her to keep quiet and took off running down the hallway.

Not wanting to risk driving through the French area to my apartment on East Notre Dame until the holdup dust had settled, I went the opposite way, into the English section of Montreal, where I spent the night sitting in my car in a parking lot. Next morning, back at the Har-K, I tallied my take: $1,600 or $1,700 in American and Canadian currency.

Now I had the capital I needed to put my plans into action. I didn't want to use the name "John L. Rayns," under which I'd bought the Plymouth. I decided to keep the Galt alias for my trip abroad. I'd first get papers identifying me as a Canadian citizen, then I'd work some angle that would get me on board a cargo ship as a merchant seaman, and I'd be seeing the last of North America for a good long while. To while away the evenings I bought a television set. I also walked a lot: after being in prison it felt good to be outside.

I called a travel agency to ask how to get a Canadian passport. Easy, said the agent. If I didn't have a birth certificate, all I needed was a sworn affidavit from a Canadian citizen attesting that he'd known me to be a Canadian citizen for the past two years.

This sounded too complicated, as well as risky. I started hanging out at waterfront bars, hoping to roll a drunken seaman and relieve him of his papers, then use them to catch a ship to Australia or some other distant country.

One place on my list of regular haunts was the Neptune Tavern, at 121 West Commissioners Street. Appropriate for its clientele, the Neptune had heavy oak tables on the floor and pilot wheels hanging on the walls. One afternoon, I stopped by and met an individual who seemed to be in his mid-30s. He was about 5'8", weighed 140 pounds or so and had slightly wavy dark red hair that might have been the result of a dye job. He sat down at my table, ordered a drink and made small talk in what sounded to me like a Spanish accent, then introduced himself as "Raoul." He never mentioned his last name. I figured if he wanted me to know it, he'd tell me, and didn't press the matter.

Raoul seemed to wrap himself in mystery. He spoke in loose terms and he answered questions with generalities or not at all. His conversation drifted like a cool fog. I thought he might be a junkie. He wore long-sleeved shirts or jackets, a fashion style favored by addicts trying to hide needle marks.

But I wasn't interested in making a lifelong friend, I was trying to make sure I didn't wind up back in the Missouri penitentiary, and Raoul's personality wasn't of much interest to me. Besides, his pose was one familiar to me. I'd used it myself, especially in prison, where a request for the simplest information, whether from an official or a cellmate, was sure to have a second or even third purpose, and no one goes around telling the whole truth and nothing but the truth. I'd known guys like Raoul for years. Sometimes I was one—as now, in my guise as Eric Galt, innocently inquiring about how to obtain travel documentation without having to deal with the bother of official sources.

As we talked and drank, I sensed that I had a potential ally. Over the next few days I often returned to the Neptune and met with Raoul, each of us trying to keep the other at arm's length but finally striking a bargain: he'd help me get travel documents if I'd assist him in moving some material across the border into the U.S.

I wasn't wild about going into the contraband business. I had more than enough trouble waiting for me stateside without being busted for smuggling. But what else could I do? I decided to roll with Raoul's program and keep thinking about other ways to obtain papers.

One other approach occurred to me: What if I would strike up a relationship with a lady who'd be willing to file the affidavit I needed to get a passport? This seemed a better—or at least less risky—bet than the wager Raoul was offering, so I contacted a travel agency and found out that a lot of single women vacationed at a resort called Greyrocks, 50 miles or so north of Montreal, near Saint Jovite in the Laurentian Mountains.

I made reservations there and aimed the Plymouth in that direction. My car wasn't exactly gigolo material, but I tried to compensate by blowing some of my whorehouse booty on new clothes.

My room had a terrific view. The windows opened onto a series of swimming pools with the Laurentians rising in the distance—quite a sight for eyes accustomed to the drab perspective of a penitentiary. It was five days before I met a woman at a bar and we took a liking to each other. However, with time growing short, I didn't think I'd feel comfortable asking her to sign an affidavit. Before I left she gave me her address in Ottawa. I looked forward to meeting her again to build on our friendship. (I must admit that I have been very protective of this woman's identity, which I have only revealed to my attorneys and investigators.)

As I drove back from Greyrocks, Raoul's offer was looking better and better. Some days after I got back to Montreal, I stopped into the Neptune. Raoul was there, and ready to talk specifics.

Raoul's deal was this: we'd meet in Windsor, he'd hand over the contraband and leave, then I'd carry his package down to Detroit, where we'd hook up again. I'd travel alone to Mobile, Alabama. Raoul would meet me there for a trip to the Mexican border, where we'd repeat the smuggling routine.

I said that sounded fine, except that I had a better place to meet in Alabama. Birmingham was bigger than Mobile, which meant it would be easier to remain anonymous there.

Raoul said Birmingham would do. It didn't matter to me. I wasn't going to set foot in either place. As soon as I had a Canadian passport, I was going to hotfoot it back to Montreal and use it to depart for Australia or Europe.

Raoul said he'd arrange for our trip, and on August 17, 1967, I checked out of the Har-K. I stuck the TV in the back seat of the Plymouth and drove down to Windsor several days earlier than planned. I still hadn't given up on the lady I'd met at Greyrocks, who lived not far from where I was supposed to make my debut as a smuggler.

I found a motel in Ottawa and checked in, then called my lady friend. If I could keep the romance going, maybe I wouldn't have to participate in Raoul's scheme.

She seemed glad to hear from me, and we met for dinner. We had a romantic everning but I didn't spend the night at her place because she had children at home. The next day we went for a drive around Ottawa. At one corner she had me stop the car.

"That's where I work," she said, pointing to a big office building with the Canadian flag flying on a pole out front. It was a government agency. So much for my passport scam. I kept my disappointment to myself and enjoyed the next couple of days. When I left I told her I'd call her soon, and headed for my appointment with Raoul. Just before I got to Windsor, I stopped along the side of Highway 401 and buried the revolver I'd used in the whorehouse robbery.

I was to meet Raoul outside the railroad station at 3 p.m. on a prearranged date in late August. I showed up on time, and so did he, carrying a briefcase. He got into the Plymouth and directed me to a side street.

I parked the car. Raoul got into the back seat and pulled out the back cushion. He took three plastic bags, each roughly three inches by six inches, out of his briefcase. He stowed the packages down among the springs and replaced the cushion. Raoul rejoined me in the front seat and gave me directions to the tunnel leading to Detroit.

Before we got there, Raoul had me stop the car so he could get out.

"I'll take a taxi across," he said. "Meet me on the far side of the American customs building."

I gave him time to catch a cab and get ahead of me, then drove through the tunnel. There were no other cars in the lane, and the border officials waved me on into the United States.

When I passed the customs house, I spotted Raoul standing off to the side. I picked him up, then continued on the road into Detroit.

"Pull in here," he said suddenly, pointing to a side street. He got into the back seat and retrieved his packages. He seemed to be satisfied.

"Let's go downtown," he said, giving me directions that took us to the bus station.

"Next time we'll use the bridge, not the tunnel," he said, referring to the above-ground connection between Windsor and Detroit. He got out at the bus station and told me to meet him back on the other side at the train station.

I recrossed the border and found Raoul as advertised, briefcase in hand. We repeated the business with the seat cushion and the drop-off, but when I hit the bridge there was a line of cars in the far right lane. American customs men were conducting inspections. I remembered the TV set. Rather than risk anything, I decided to declare it. When my turn came with the inspectors, I did that, and the official waved me into the search lane.

The Plymouth got a meticulous going over. The inspector raised the hood and checked the engine compartment, then began working his way toward the back of the car. However, just before he reached the back seat a second officer came up and told the first that he'd complete the search. The first inspector walked away. The second abruptly ended the search without checking the back seat or trunk except to note the television and assess me a $4 import tax on it. He made out the receipt to "John L. Rayns," as per my auto registration.

I was relieved that my first try at smuggling hadn't landed me back at Leavenworth. When I picked up Raoul, he asked about the delay. I described the shakedown, showing him the $4 import tax receipt. If Raoul, who knew me as "Eric Galt," noticed the Rayns name, he gave no indication.

This time I knew the drill without being told. We found another side street where Raoul could pull the packages out of the back seat. This time he seemed quite satisfied—until he got back into the front seat. His look got very serious.

"Something's come up," he said. "I'm having more trouble than I expected getting that passport."

I complained that I'd been counting on getting that passport. He said he just couldn't get it, then abruptly switched to the topic of money.

"Here's some cash to tide you over," he said, handing me a stack of bills. "Get down to Birmingham. As soon as you're in town, go to the general delivery window at the main post office. There'll be some mail waiting for you."

I counted the wad of bills he'd given me. There was about $1,500 American.

"I'll have the passport by then, and we'll buy a better car," Raoul said as he was getting out at the bus terminal. "Here's a number where you can reach me. It's in New Orleans."

Chapter Seven

Back in the USA

There was little point in returning to Canada. Birmingham looked like my best bet. But before heading south I wanted to see my brother Jerry in Chicago. He was working at Sportsman's Country Club in Northbrook. I called him there and asked him to meet me in a bar near the old Biograph movie theater on Lincoln Avenue. Our visit was brief—after all, I was on the lam and seeing me could set him up for charges of harboring a fugitive.

We met as arranged. I asked him if the police had been around—he said "no." After talking for a while I handed over the keys to the Plymouth. Jerry drove me to the train station in Chicago, where I boarded a sleeper bound for Birmingham.

The trip to Birmingham was uneventful. I thought about what Raoul had planned for me. But I decided I would just have to wait and see what his specific plans involved.

When I arrived in Birmingham I checked into a hotel near the train station. In the morning I picked up a newspaper in the lobby and started looking for rooms to let. I found one at 2608 Highland Avenue. The landlord, Peter Cherpes, was an easy-going middle-aged fellow of Greek extraction who didn't ask a lot of questions.

One reason I picked his place was that when he showed me the room, I noticed a side window opening onto a passage leading to the back of the building—a handy escape route if the occasion demanded. The rent was about $15 a week, which included one meal per day. There was a pay phone in the lobby.

I let a few days pass, then went to the main post office and found the general delivery window.

"You might have some mail for me," I told the clerk. "My name is Eric Galt."

The clerk checked a cubbyhole, and asked, "What's your middle initial?"

"S."

He handed me a letter from Raoul. I read it as I left the building. It said that I was to meet him at a certain time and date at a bar near the post office. I walked to the Starlight Club and found Raoul sitting at a table with a beer in front of him.

After some small talk Raoul said, "We'll need a good set of wheels. But I don't want to spend more than a couple of thousand. Can you take care of that?"

"Sure," I said.

We agreed to meet again in a few days. I watched the classifieds and found a likely possibility: a 1966 Ford Mustang. I called the number and got hold of the owner, William Paisley. He gave me directions to his house, where I checked out the car. It was in good shape and painted a color Ford called "Springtime Yellow," a very pale yellow. I told Paisley I'd be in touch, and when my date with Raoul came up I told him about the car. He said the deal sounded okay but didn't show much enthusiasm for the color.

"Let's meet here tomorrow morning," he said. "I'll have to get the money."

The next day he handed me $2,000. We agreed to meet at the Starlight once I'd completed my transaction. I called Paisley, who gave me the address of his bank, where he sold the Mustang to Eric S. Galt. As I'd done in Chicago, I figured to use the car registration papers to get a driver's license. I was still holding the license issued to "John L. Rayns" back in Illinois.

The drive to the Starlight was pretty edgy, but I picked up Raoul without incident and we proceeded toward my apartment. Raoul liked the car, and when I told him my driver's license had expired and I had to get another, he seemed quite interested. We discussed our trip into Mexico.

"There are some things I want you to buy," Raoul said. "Here's a list, and some money."

He handed me $500 and a sheet of paper on which he'd written what he wanted: a super-8 movie camera and a telephoto lens to go with it.

"Get these items and have them with you when we go into Mexico," Raoul said. "I'll need a set of keys to the car."

I gave him the spare set of Mustang keys, one for the ignition and one for the doors and trunk.

I asked for living expenses and Raoul gave me another $1,000.

Just before Raoul left me, he asked me for the number of the phone in the lobby at my apartment house.

"I've got another number you can use besides the one in New Orleans," he said. "It's in Baton Rouge—the guy there will take a message if you can't get through in New Orleans. Be sure to check in regularly so I know what you're up to. I expect we'll be hitting Mexico in about two months. Keep checking with general delivery. I may send you a letter or two."

I had several matters to take care of. Besides rounding up the camera gear, I needed that driver's license for Eric Galt. My landlord was a big help. Someone applying for a license can't drive his own car to the test area—a licensed driver has to be at the wheel. Mr. Cherpes did me that favor, and Eric S. Galt passed with flying colors. The driver's license enabled me to get additional ID in that name.

I also needed a safe place in which to store my Rayns identification and some of my stash of cash. On August 28 I rented a safe deposit box at Birmingham Trust National Bank. I also set about buying a gun—who knew what might happen in Mexico? A .38 would be nice. I found a snubnose in the classifieds and paid $50 or $75 for it, then put it in the safe deposit box. I had trouble locating the movie camera and lens, finally resorting to ordering them from a Chicago mail-order house.

During this time I'd check in every few days at the number Raoul had given me. When someone answered, I'd give my name, we'd talk briefly and go over whatever was occurring at the time.

By late September, I was ready to make the run for Mexico. Raoul wrote, instructing me to call him at the New Orleans number. His intermediary answered. It sounded as if he'd been expecting my call.

"I've taken care of everything but the camera and lens," I told him. "They're on order; they ought to be in any day."

"Well, call me as soon as it gets there," he said.

The camera equipment didn't show up, so I phoned New Orleans again, this time seeking advice.

"Come on down here and pick up Raoul," the guy said. "Stay in touch while you're on the way."

On October 6 I quit the apartment and emptied the safe deposit box at Birmingham Trust, but paid up the rent on it in case I needed it again. I headed south through Alabama and Mississippi, passing through Vicksburg. In Baton Rouge, I tried Raoul's back-up number but the call didn't go through. I dialed the New Orleans number. The intermediary answered. I gave him an update.

"Raoul's already left for Mexico," he said. "You go ahead on down there. Get to Nuevo Laredo and check into [a specific] motel. Wait there until Raoul contacts you."

I had a little time to spare, and I was curious. Somewhere I'd learned how to check phone numbers by reading them backward. I sat down at a phone booth and started by checking the last two digits of the number against the last two digits of all the numbers in the directory. Then I checked the preceding two numbers, and so forth. It was tedious, but it worked, and there wasn't any other way to do it.

I wanted to see if I could get a name to go with Raoul's Baton Rouge telephone number. I sat down with a copy of the Baton Rouge directory and went to work. I found that Raoul's back-up number was the same as that listed for "Herman A. Thompson."

Knowing this made me feel a little better. So did buying a box of ammunition for the .38. It didn't look like I'd be back in Birmingham, so I mailed back the safe deposit box key.

As I headed out of Baton Rouge, I thought of a character I'd known in Leavenworth. When he wasn't in jail, Johnny Miller lived in Dallas. In prison he'd been full of stories about running dope from Mexico across the Texas border. I thought that if I could find Johnny he might be able to give me some advice about how things went south of the border, so I pointed the Mustang toward Dallas.

Then I had second thoughts. What if Miller was in jail? What if the cops had him under surveillance? That was enough to set me back on course for Nuevo Laredo, which I knew from my last visit to Mexico in 1959. On the outskirts there was an area known as "Boystown," a wide-open scene with about 35 bars that ran 24 hours except for a ten-minute break when the operators cleared the floor so someone could sweep up. I'd gotten to know Boystown pretty well on my last visit. I wondered if it was still the same wild place.

Chapter Eight

Mexico, Again

Nuevo Laredo was across the border from the Texas town of Laredo. The sun was setting as I rode over the bridge leading from the United States into Mexico. At the customs checkpoint I asked for directions to the motel, which turned out to be about two miles inside the border and atop a small hill.

An inclined 60-foot driveway led to the office. Each room had a parking stall, so guests' automobiles couldn't be seen from the street. Something odd occurred. I hadn't rushed through Texas, but I'd still gotten to Nuevo Laredo a couple of hours ahead of schedule. Even so, I'd been in my room no more than 30 minutes when I heard a knock at the door. It was Raoul.

I knew from experience not to call attention to the peculiarity of his seeming to be watching me. We said hello, and he ran down the next stage of the plan. Essentially, we'd repeat the drill we'd run in Windsor. I'd drive him to the Nuevo Laredo city square, he'd take a taxi across the border and I'd cross behind him in the Mustang, then pick him up at some distance beyond the U.S. Customs House.

It was completely dark. We left the motel in the Mustang and did as discussed. After I'd picked him up on the U.S. side, he had me drive about ten blocks north.

"Turn left here," he said.

I did, and continued on two miles or so into a slummy area. Raoul motioned me to pull over and park behind a sedan. I was no car buff and I'd been in prison for six years, so I wasn't up on makes and models, but it looked like a Chevy or Ford. There was a figure at the wheel. Raoul approached the driver, who gave him a key. Raoul went around to the trunk and opened it, removing a tire mounted on a wheel and bringing it to the Mustang's trunk, unlatching the lock with the key I'd given him in Birmingham.

Transaction completed, Raoul got back into his seat and directed me back to the border bridge.

"Stop at Mexican customs and get a visa," he said. "You'll be needing it to travel in the interior. And when the Mexicans search the car, give each of them one dollar, no more, no less."

We were nearing the Mexican customs building. Raoul had me stop the Mustang so he could get out.

"I'll wait outside while you're getting that visa," he said.

I got my papers with a minimum of questions. They ran through a slapdash search, marking the spare tire and other items in the trunk with chalk slashes, and indicated I was free to go on.

Raoul rejoined me in the street and said to go back to the motel. When we were within a couple of blocks of the place, he pointed to a street I hadn't taken before.

"Turn right here," he said, setting us off on a roundabout route that brought us across the street from the motel. The car from which Raoul had taken the spare tire was parked at the entrance to the motel driveway.

"Park here," Raoul said. "I'll be right back."

He went for the Mustang trunk and got out the tire, taking it to the other vehicle. I kept my eye on the driver. First in left profile, then frontally as he turned toward us, I saw a man with a dark complexion whose nose suggested he might have

Indian blood. Raoul got a key from him and put the tire into his car's trunk, then came back to the Mustang.

"I'll see you in the morning around nine," he said. "We'll be taking the tire to the interior. There's a customs checkpoint about 50 kilometers from here."

Then he joined the dark man in the other car, and they drove off. The next morning Raoul showed up. His tone of voice suggested that he expected me to have spent the evening in Boystown, but I'd forsaken the fleshpots. I was thinking about that passport, and the money Raoul had said I'd make on this run. I was ready to roll.

He had another guy outside waiting in a car. I couldn't tell if the car or the man were the same as I'd seen the night before, but I don't believe it was. Before leaving the motel, Raoul pulled another tire transfer, sticking the wheel back into the Mustang trunk. The customs official's chalk mark was still on it.

"Let's go," Raoul said. "You follow us out of town and down the road to the customs checkpoint. Once we get through, we'll drive a while, then stop and switch tires again."

I coasted in behind the other car, my .38 near at hand in case they had any funny ideas. Raoul got out and walked back to the Mustang. I drove straight ahead and circled back. They had the driveway blocked off.

We set out, I in the Mustang and Raoul at the wheel of the other car. The 50 kilometers went by quickly. The interior customs building looked like a former gas station, with two driveways, the innermost covered by a canopy hanging from the building. Raoul took the inside lane—I took the outside. A customs officer came over, checked the Mustang's license plate and scrutinized me. Then he waved me through.

But Raoul and associate were detained. Through the rear-view mirror I could see them sitting as the customs men went over their car. I slowed down, assuming Raoul would catch up. He did, passing me on a lonely stretch of highway and then pulling over.

"I still haven't gotten that passport," he said as he climbed inside. His voice was tense. "But here's something for the meantime."

This distressing news was softened somewhat when he handed me $2,000 in twenty-dollar bills.

"I can get you considerably more money, and will still work on your passport, if you care to join me in a future project in Mexico," he said. "What were you going to do now?"

"I was figuring to go over to Los Angeles or catch a ship" I said. "Say, what did you want me to do with that camera equipment you had me order?"

"Forget the camera. How about giving me a call once in a while?" Raoul said. "Here's another number in New Orleans. Get rid of that other one. If I need to send you anything, I'll address it to you at general delivery, same as in Birmingham."

He got out of the Mustang and went back to the other car, then drove off with his companion. I felt relieved. They could as easily have killed me.

I decided that before heading to L.A. I'd drive to Acapulco. In 1959, I'd stayed briefly at the San Francisco Motel there. I wondered if it was still in business. I drove across Mexico at a leisurely pace, taking four days, including a stop in Mexico City, to reach the Pacific Coast.

The San Francisco Hotel was still alive and well, and I was able to rent a room. I revived my thought of catching a ship but, as before, the harbor was full of tourist liners, so I packed it in. I remembered an article I'd read about Puerto Vallarta, a little beach town set between the mountains of the Sierra Madre Occidental and the Bay of Banderas. At that time it was a primitive place, not yet a big tourist attraction—and for good reason. I was traveling at the end of the rainy season, and Route 200, which led into town, was very muddy. At one point the Mustang got bogged down, and I had to flag a truck to pull it out.

The landscape was grim, a wall of trees broken only by the occasional Indian hut made of grass and clay. Suddenly, though, I could see through an opening in the forest. Below me lay Puerto Vallarta, and beyond it, the Pacific.

The road angled downhill for a few miles, leading to a customs shack at the edge of a quaint town. I found out just how unsophisticated Puerto Vallarta was: the customs men didn't demand a bribe.

I spent a while admiring the scenery, then checked into the Hotel Rio, a secluded place at the end of the main street. My room was on the second floor and overlooked a stream that surged down out of the mountains and emptied into the bay a hundred yards from the hotel. At the stream's mouth locals had stretched nets to catch fish which they cooked over fires they'd made on the banks.

It all looked idyllic, and during my three-week stay I got to like Puerto Vallarta so much I almost wound up staying. At one of the bars I struck up an acquaintance with a pimp from one of the town's several whorehouses. We palled around together. I'd let him and his girls drive the Mustang to and from the beach. He liked the car so much he offered to buy it.

But he was broke, so we discussed a swap: the Mustang for a plot of land outside town. I seriously considered the deal, thinking to throw up a lean-to and retire, living off the land and joining the fishermen on the bay. But I canceled out when the pimp said the transaction would have to be processed by the local police.

By mid-November, I could see I wasn't going to be able to secure permanent residency in Mexico. I took the gravel road out of Puerto Vallarta and got onto Highway 15, following the coastline toward California. The side of the road was full of Mexicans hitchhiking north. My last morning in Mexico, as I pulled out of Santa Ana onto Highway 2, I picked up a small fellow who spoke little English. We rode together in silence, occasionally smiling at one another.

The approach to the border was through desert. I noticed the gas gauge was sitting at "empty." I was getting nervous but then a cabin came into view. There was a 1930's-vintage car parked in the yard. We pulled in. I gestured to the hitchhiker that he should ask the owner, an old Mexican, if we could buy some fuel.

The two of them started talking and quickly got into an argument that went on for the better part of an hour. Finally, I took my partner aside and suggested he offer the old man more money. As soon as he did, we had a deal. We siphoned off a few gallons of gas, enough to get us out of the desert and into the town of Mexicali, where my friend took his leave. I continued on to Tijuana, the Mexican town adjoining San Diego, California, and a hot spot frequented by sailors from the San Diego naval base. That means an abundance of police, take-off artists and other types I wanted to avoid, so I checked into a hotel and stayed there until morning.

Crossing the border required preparation. I searched the Mustang for anything that might hang me up at customs. Lodged between the right front bucket seat and the gearbox I found a pack of cigarettes in a plastic case, into which someone had tucked a business card. The name of the business had been inked out, but I could discern the letters "L.E.A.A." At the bottom appeared a two-word phrase, perhaps the name of a city, like "New Orleans," that also had been inked out. Below and to the right of "L.E.A.A." more type had been scribbled out. On the other side, though, in what appeared to be the same ink, someone had scrawled:

> *Randy Rosen*
> *1180 Northwest River Drive*
> *Miami Florida*

I copied all this information onto a piece of paper, writing the address number "1180" backward. If I were arrested, I didn't want to make it any easier than necessary for the police to use the numbers against me.

Following the search I drove north of the border, found a motel and rested for the night.

Chapter Nine

Los Angeles Revisited

On the afternoon of November 19, 1967 I arrived in Los Angeles. I began looking for an apartment and chose one in the 1500 block of Serrano Avenue, a residential street near Hollywood Boulevard. It looked as if I might be in L.A. for a few months, so I ran ads looking for work in hotels or restaurants—places that aren't too picky about checking job applicants' papers. I also monitored the help wanted ads. I answered one that turned out to be a position helping taxpayers fill out their IRS returns. I let that one go on by.

I enrolled in a correspondence course in locksmithing, a trade for which I'd always felt an affinity. I frequented the Sultan Club, a bar in the St. Francis Hotel, about three blocks from my apartment. I struck up a casual friendship with Marie Martin, a barmaid with the dark good looks I associate with Cajun women from Louisiana. She said a cousin of hers had nieces in New Orleans. His name was Charles Stein. Sometimes Marie went by that surname as well.

In her younger days Marie had danced in nightclubs. Now she was starting to take things more seriously. Her boyfriend was in San Quentin on a narcotics conviction, and she was looking to find someone with the political connections to help spring him. I suggested that Marie begin by registering up to vote.

I hadn't forgotten about Raoul. I was checking the general delivery window, but nothing turned up. By mid-December, I was running out of money and worried that Raoul had lost interest or moved on to something else that didn't include me. I dialed the New Orleans number he'd given me at our last meeting in Mexico.

The intermediary answered. We chatted, but I said nothing of substance since I had assumed that the line was tapped. He suggested I drive to New Orleans later in the month and meet with Raoul. I said I'd do that.

When I told Marie I might be going to New Orleans, she became enthusiastic. She wanted to get her cousin's nieces out to L.A., and said Charles would help with the driving if I'd bring the girls back. I agreed.

The day before the New Orleans trip, I picked up Marie at the Sultan Club. Someone was with her—a big, swarthy, balding man in his 40s decked out in beard, beads, sandals, the whole hippie costume: cousin Charlie, who also wanted to become a voter.

With his get-up, Charlie wasn't exactly my first choice as a traveling companion, but I told him to come along. I dropped him and Marie at the voting office, then went to a nearby tire store and bought a pair of new tires. Back at the voter registration office, I sat in the Mustang for an hour before I went inside to see what was going on.

What was going on was cousin Charlie arguing with the registrar. Each registrant was entitled to a complimentary cup of coffee. Charlie wanted a refill, with cream and sugar. The registrar had said no, setting off the dispute. With visions of the police showing up and carting us both off to jail, I took Charlie aside and promised to buy him a cup of coffee when we got back to the St. Francis.

With that he, Marie and I returned to the Sultan Club. They'd both registered as members of the Independent Party, supporting Alabama Governor George Wallace for president. Later I told Marie that if she wanted to have some political influence, she should have signed on as a Republican, since that was the party in power in California.

The next day, I met Charlie as planned, stopping at my apartment so he could call his people in New Orleans to let them know we were on our way. The trip was uneventful, except that once in a while as he was driving and I was sleeping Charlie would nudge me awake and exclaim that a flying saucer had just passed the car.

We made it to New Orleans in three or four days. I dropped Charlie at his relatives' house and checked into the Provencal Motel in the French Quarter. I walked around, found a comfortable bar and called Raoul's number, reaching his man. He asked where I was, then told me to meet Raoul at LeBunny Lounge on Canal Street.

LeBunny Lounge had a bar stretching down the left side of the room, with booths on the right leading back into a darkened section. I took a seat at the bar. Raoul came in a few minutes later. After a few words, we moved on to one of the booths.

Raoul wanted to discuss another smuggling proposition: guns into Mexico, for which I'd pull $10,000 or $12,000, plus—this time for sure—the famous passport. He alluded to a trip to Cuba after the Mexican operation was wrapped up, but was characteristically vague about how we'd get in.

"I'm running out of money," I told him.

He went on some more about the gunrunning, and finally I agreed to do it, but added that I had no interest in Cuba. I again emphasized that I needed a passport and enough cash to finance an extensive one-way trip out of the United States. Raoul said he'd contact me by phone or letter during April 1968. Then we'd begin assembling the shipment for Mexico. He gave me $500 and left LeBunny.

I was ready to head back to L.A. then and there, but when I went around to the place where I'd dropped Charlie, he said he wanted to visit a little longer. That was okay with me; I'd stayed in worse places than the French Quarter.

After a couple of days, though, Charlie and I and his nieces—a pair of pretty little girls who were six or eight years old—piled into the Mustang for the trip west. We had a good time crossing the country—no police, no car trouble, no flying saucers.

We got back to Los Angeles around December 20. During my four months there, I'd tried to dodge situations or settings where I might be pegged as a fugitive. It wasn't always easy. Keeping the same residence for a long period of time while driving a car with out-of-state license plates—those on the Mustang were from Alabama—is asking for trouble from policemen or civilian busybodies.

One evening I parked the Mustang on Hollywood Boulevard and went across the street to the Rabbit's Foot Club. Inside a patron who must have seen me parking asked if I was from Alabama.

"Yes," I said.

This set him off on a tirade against Alabama politics, complaining about the status of blacks there. A young woman sitting nearby was egging him on, and I could see several black faces among the crowd in the club. I smelled the makings of a major brawl, so I eased toward the door, only to be mugged by two guys who'd followed me out. One pulled my jacket down over my arms, pinning them to my side. The other was punching at my head and grabbing for my watch. I slipped out of the jacket and ran for the Mustang to get my .38 equalizer from under the front seat. But the car keys were in my coat, now in the muggers' hands. Looking about I noticed a church up the street and sprinted up to it, hiding in the shadows for an hour or so.

After that I crossed the street back to the Rabbit's Foot, crouching between two houses by the club to see if the police showed up, and fearing that if they did, they'd tow the car. Nothing happened.

I sat watching the Mustang until dawn, then walked to my apartment—luckily, my house keys and wallet had been in one of my trouser pockets. After I'd rested a bit, I had a locksmith on Hollywood Boulevard make a new set of keys for the Mustang. It began to occur to me that I ought to be thinking about moving, especially after I met the odd couple.

They showed up in mid-January, after I'd run some ads in newsletters published by clubs promoting "creative relationships." I wasn't looking for romance—I wanted to collect some extra names and addresses in case I needed a new identity. And in the process of meeting marks, I might even recruit an ally. I used the Galt name and gave the address of a mail-drop outfit in Alhambra. My ads drew several responses, including one from a woman in Toronto! Where had she been when I needed her?

But despite using the Alhambra postal box, my Serrano Avenue address somehow got out. One evening as I left the apartment, two middle-aged characters stopped me at the front door. They were male and female, or dressed to convey that impression. The male said they hadn't been able to find the manager and asked if I knew an "Eric Galt" who lived on the premises. I said no and took off.

That was all it took to get me moving. I packed my bags and moved into the St. Francis Hotel, where Marie worked, and contemplated my situation. The question of getting a passport nagged at me. I imagined a room somewhere in Washington, D.C., filled with bureaucrats doing nothing but comparing passport photos with mug shots of wanted criminals and escaped cons.

I'd read that the most distinguishing features in a photograph are the nose and ears—also the most easily altered elements of the face. I sounded out several plastic surgeons, and in February showed up for an appointment with Dr. Russell C. Hadley at his offices on Hollywood Boulevard.

I'd also heard that the authorities urge plastic surgeons to pump potential customers for information and report any suspicious individuals, so I led Dr. Hadley to believe I was a would-be actor who thought plastic surgery on his nose would enhance his prospects of working in television commercials. We set a date for the operation—March 5—and he gave me a price for my new look: $200.

That day came, and I lay down on the operating table in the doctor's office. The procedure wasn't complicated. Dr.

Hadley used a local anesthetic, rearranged my nose and applied tape to hold the reconstruction in place until it healed. I paid him the $200 in cash. Back at the St. Francis I decided to improve on Dr. Hadley's handiwork, adjusting the tape he'd put on to add pressure to the tip of my nose and give it a more aquiline look.

I planned to see another doctor to have my ears pinned back, but before I could go under the knife again Raoul contacted me by mail. He'd moved up the date for our New Orleans rendezvous from April to March. The ears would have to wait.

I was ready for another move. At first, the St. Francis had seemed ideal—staid, with a minimum of surprises. But that was far from the truth. After a couple of weeks female residents would come knocking at my door after the bar closed, advertising their interest in some company. Apparently the barman was free with information about who lived where. In another setting I might have been glad to have such visitors, but at that time late-night callers were unnerving and I wanted out.

When Raoul sent the new schedule, I wrote to the locksmithing school, asking them to suspend the mailings for my course, and prepared to head east. On March 17, I went to the post office and executed a change-of-address form, giving my forwarding address as general delivery, Atlanta, Georgia. The next day I loaded the Mustang and set out for New Orleans.

While I was organizing my trip and leaving L.A., someone telephoned the Alabama Highway Patrol in Birmingham, identifying himself as Eric S. Galt. He claimed to have lost his driver's license and requested a duplicate copy. The clerk said to send in the 25-cent fee. When that arrived, the Highway Patrol mailed a new license to "Galt" at my old apartment in Mr. Cherpes' building on Highland Avenue. I don't know if anyone picked up the new license. By filing a change-of-address form someone could have my mail forwarded.

Part III

The Road to Memphis

Chapter Ten

Events Accelerate

My trip to New Orleans took three days. As soon as I reached the main part of the city, I called Raoul from a pay phone. His intermediary said he'd left for Birmingham and would meet me at the Starlight Club on the morning of March 23.

Before hitting the road again, I wanted to get some rest, so I checked into a motel on the eastern outskirts of New Orleans. The next day I was back behind the wheel, making it as far as Selma, Alabama, where I spent the night at the Flamingo Motel. The next morning I finished the run to Birmingham and met Raoul as instructed. He wanted to go to Atlanta, and by evening we were there.

Raoul seemed to know Atlanta's layout. He gave me directions to a section that looked like one where someone looking to rent a furnished room wouldn't have to answer too many questions.

I found an apartment house just off Peachtree Street, at 113 14th Street NE. Raoul said he'd wait in the car while I checked the place out. I found the manager, Jimmy Garner, who fit the neighborhood. When I entered his office, he and another character were well into the wine. Garner said he had a room available, but he was too far gone to fill out a receipt.

Raoul came in, irritated that I was taking so long. This inspired Garner and me to finalize our deal as best we could. Once that was done, Raoul led me around the block to a diner on Peachtree, where we had supper. After we ate, he departed. I went to the apartment and fell asleep.

The next morning, there was a knock on my door. It was Garner.

"I think I rented you someone else's apartment," he said. "You mind moving to another building?"

"That's no problem," I said.

Garner said his sister owned the second building. It had been a doctor's office, he claimed. To get inside, you passed through a front door that was usually locked into a hallway leading to numerous small furnished rooms. I settled into my new digs. Except for me and Garner's sister, everyone in the place was a drunk.

Around noon, Raoul showed up, evidently directed by Garner. We discussed the Mexican operation, with him talking generally about purchasing American-made and foreign rifles. He was more specific about Miami, saying he'd be gone for two days. When he returned, I'd drive him to Miami. He wanted to know how he could get my attention without disturbing the other roomers. The building had a side door usually kept locked from within. I said I'd unlatch it.

After Raoul left, I stuck close by the rooming house except to exchange a few hundred Canadian dollars for U.S. currency at a bank on Peachtree. To pass the time, I decided to bone up on Atlanta's street system. I bought a map and marked where I lived in relation to other sections of the city.

Raoul's two-day absence stretched into three days, then five. Not sure when we'd be leaving for Miami or how long we'd stay there, on March 28 or so I paid Garner another week's rent. On the next day Raoul appeared at the rooming house to cancel the Miami trip. But he still wanted to talk about weapons. He asked me to buy a large-bore deer rifle and scope, and to check around for a source of cheap imported rifles. Reminding him of my Alabama ID, I suggested it might be more prudent for me to take care of this business in Birmingham. Raoul thought this was a good idea. Before we headed that way, I left Garner a note in my room, telling him I'd be out of town a few days.

I buried the .38 in the cellar of the apartment building, which had a dirt floor.

Once we were in Birmingham, Raoul had me drop him at the main post office. I was to get a hotel room, then pick him up at the Starlight. After registering at the Five Points Travel Lodge, I picked him up and drove to a restaurant near the train station.

We ordered a meal and began checking a newspaper and the *Yellow Pages* for sporting goods stores, settling on Aeromarine Supply, out by the airport. I called the store and found out it stocked the sort of guns Raoul wanted. We finished eating and went back to my room, where he gave me $700 to buy the deer rifle and some ammunition.

I drove alone to Aeromarine Supply. Inside, I told the salesman, Donald Wood, that I was looking to buy a good deer rifle and scope for my brother-in-law. He showed me a .243 Winchester, suggesting it was just the ticket. I told him to wrap it, along with a box of bullets. While he was doing that, I saw some foreign-made rifles in a rack. I asked their prices. Wood said some disparaging things about them—I figured Aeromarine didn't make as much money on them as on American-made weapons.

I'd bought quite a few guns in my time, but I'd never done business with a legitimate gun dealer. I wasn't sure how much ID Aeromarine would demand. I didn't want to use the Galt alias if it wasn't necessary, so when Wood asked my name and address, I made up a street address and said my name was "Harvey Lowmeyer"—my brother Jerry had had a pal by that name, and it had always stuck in my head. If Wood asked for ID, I was ready to claim I didn't have any with me but would go get it if he'd let me take the piece—never intending to follow through. If he balked at this suggestion, I was ready to walk out and try another gun shop, using the Galt ID. But Wood didn't ask to see anything except my money.

Back at the motel, Raoul examined the weapon. He said the bore was too small—he wanted something with more punch. Wood had given me a sales brochure in which Raoul found the rifle he wanted—a Remington model 760, 30.06 caliber. From a pay phone outside the room I called Aeromarine, explained my situation, and asked if I could exchange the .243 for the 30.06. Wood said that was fine with him, but I'd have to wait until the next day. I relayed this proposition to Raoul, who said that was okay. He needed to go to New Orleans for a couple of days anyway. He instructed me to pick up the second rifle and bring it to Memphis, Tennessee, where he was to meet some prospective gun buyers. I was to check into the New Rebel Motel on Lamar Avenue in Memphis no later than April 3. Raoul would contact me there that evening.

The next day, with Raoul gone, I returned to Aeromarine Supply. Donald Wood said he couldn't understand why my brother-in-law didn't want the Winchester.

"It's big enough to bring down any deer in Alabama," he said.

I answered that my brother-in-law would be hunting in Wisconsin, where the deer were larger.

Memphis

From Aeromarine Supply, I drove up Highway 65 toward Memphis, a trip of 200 miles. It was March 30, 1968. That night, I stayed in a motel near Decatur, Alabama. On March 31, I stayed near the twin cities of Florence and Tuscumbia, at the northern corner of Alabama. I spent the evening of April 1 at a motel near Corinth, Mississippi, and on April 2 checked into the Desoto Motel on Highway 51, about two blocks south of the Tennessee border and the Memphis city limit.

The next day I checked into the New Rebel. I was able to park the Mustang right at the door to my room. Early that evening a thunderstorm blew in. It was still raining hard at around 9 p.m., when someone knocked at my door. I opened it to find Raoul, dripping wet, wearing a trenchcoat. He looked like a Hollywood spy.

He asked if I'd brought the 30.06, then briefed me on what would be happening. We'd probably be in town three or four days, and needed a place to do business, he said. He'd located an apartment near the waterfront where he could stay and we could meet with clients. He wanted to rent the place in my name. I objected—if anything went wrong, I told him, the law would come after me. I suggested we use the name "John Willard," an old alias of mine that would come easily to my tongue.

Raoul went for my idea. He wrote the apartment address on a slip of paper: 422-½ South Main Street. He added the phrase "Jim's Grill" beside the address. He said that was the name of the tavern on the ground floor, where I was to meet him at three the next afternoon. Then he left, taking the Remington, which was still in the box. He said something about "showing it to the dealers." It was still raining when he drove away.

By morning, the rain had stopped. I waited until noon to check out. With nothing to do until three, I drove to a place near the Mississippi line and had lunch.

On my way out of the restaurant, I noticed that the Mustang's right rear tire was nearly flat. I jacked up the car and put on the spare. That took about 20 minutes.

At a commercial parking lot near downtown Memphis I stowed the Mustang and asked the attendant for directions to Main Street. Once there, I asked a policeman how to get to South Main. On South Main I came to Jim's Belmont Cafe. I went into the cafe, ordered a beer and looked around for Raoul. He wasn't there, but I noticed two other characters looking me over. The one showing the most interest was dark-complected, about 30, and wearing a navy blue peacoat. After several minutes, they left. I hailed the waitress.

"Is this the same place as Jim's Grill?" I asked.

"No," she said. "That's a couple of blocks down."

I left my unfinished beer and followed her directions on foot, caught up in thinking about making connections with

Raoul. I reached Jim's Grill at around three, as Raoul had ordered. As I went in I saw that there were several empty parking spaces on the street in front of the bar. Inside, the two guys from the place up the street were sitting there. As I entered I thought, why should I pay for Raoul's tardiness? And if I moved the car I might be able to shake my two shadows.

While I thought about my next move, I ordered a beer but didn't drink it—bartenders don't appreciate non-buyers sitting around. I went out to move the Mustang and parked the car right in front of Jim's. The car ahead of mine was pale yellow, too. When I got back inside, Raoul was waiting, but the other two characters had disappeared.

Raoul asked where the car was. He was happy to learn where I'd parked it. He said our business with the gunrunners might take a little longer than he'd expected, and suggested that I rent a room upstairs. I agreed.

We went out onto the sidewalk. Raoul looked over the Mustang. I went upstairs to ask about a room. The manager of the flophouse above Jim's, a woman named Bessie Brewer, gave me a tour. The place was a typical wino habitat with no locks on the doors. In fact, there were no knobs on the doors, only leather straps nailed on for handles.

I had my choice of two rooms: a kitchenette and a sleeping room. I chose the sleeping room and gave Brewer $10 for a week's rent. She pocketed the ten-spot and led me to the front room, where I signed the registration book "John Willard." (I don't know if Raoul had rented a room there as well. I didn't see another "John Willard" in the registration book.) After this transaction I went to my new room, then back downstairs to the street. Raoul then went upstairs.

"We might be in Memphis several days," Raoul said when I got there. He urged me to remove whatever personal property I had in the Mustang and bring it to the room. Thinking of the poor security upstairs, I said no, but I did bring in my overnight case. We went upstairs. I put my suitcase on the bed. Raoul said our customers were interested in infrared binoculars for night use. He told me how to get to the York Arms Co., where I could buy a set.

I set out for that destination, but had trouble finding the gun dealer and returned for more precise directions. Raoul was still in the room, and repeated his description of the route to York Arms.

The second time around I found the place, but they didn't stock infrared devices. The salesman suggested I check with a surplus store. Instead, I bought a pair of ordinary binoculars at York and returned to the room. I tossed them on the bed, telling Raoul he or his clients could get infrared attachments for them somewhere.

It was around 4:00 p.m. The flophouse air was getting to me, and I was hungry. I went downstairs for a hamburger. Raoul stayed in the room. After eating, I went for a walk, heading north along the same side of the street as Jim's. I came to the Chisca Hotel, where I took a seat at the lunch counter and ordered ice cream. The young black waitress seemed new to the job. Several times she had to ask another employee, a white man, how to operate the cash register. I tend to notice such conversations, especially when they're on topics of interest to me. I finished the ice cream and returned to Bessie's to find Raoul still in the room. It was probably 5:00 p.m. Raoul hadn't taken his own advice. The only personal property of his that I could see were the clothes on his back and a small radio, perhaps a walkie-talkie, in his jacket pocket.

He said he was expecting visitors, representatives of the people who were to buy the guns. He wanted to meet them without me present, and suggested I take in a movie—on foot, since he'd be needing the Mustang.

I later learned from Mark Lane's investigation that at about this same time the Memphis police detail assigned to Martin Luther King was withdrawn. Two black firefighters, who were the only blacks stationed a few hundred yards away from the flophouse, were transferred elsewhere on April 3. According to Lane, these reassignments never were justified or explained.

I went back out to the car and sat in it briefly, trying to decide how to spend the next couple of hours. A movie sounded good. I got out of the car, crossed the street and walked several blocks north to a bar across the street from a couple of theaters. While sitting there and wondering if I really wanted to take in a movie, I thought of the flat tire in the Mustang's trunk. I didn't want Raoul to get stuck with another flat and no spare while trying to conduct business, so I headed back toward the flophouse. The streets were dark, deserted except for a few cars near Bessie's.

Between 5:45 and 5:50, I eased the Mustang north onto Main Street. I drove a few blocks more, reaching an intersection where there were two or three service stations. I pulled into the nearest one and asked the attendant if he could repair the tire in the Mustang trunk.

Leaving the first station, I may have driven over to an adjacent station and purchased gas. (I don't remember exactly where I filled the tank, but I did fill up in Memphis that afternoon since I drove 200 miles that evening without refueling.)

As I approached the area of Jim's Grill I noticed uniformed officers. A squad car was parked near the intersection. A cop was directing traffic, diverting vehicles from entering South Main. This forced me to turn left, away from the rooming house.

What in the hell could have brought on a roadblock, I wondered. Had the law latched onto Raoul? I switched on the radio and continued driving, intending to stop at the south end of town and phone Raoul's man in New Orleans to see if he could tell me anything. As I neared the state line, however, I heard a bulletin that Rev. Martin Luther King had been shot. Soon after the announcer said the police were looking for a suspect: a white man in a white Mustang. My car and I were too close to that description for comfort. I couldn't do anything about my skin color, but I could lose the car.

I dropped the idea of calling Raoul's contact in New Orleans. Instead, I headed for Atlanta, remembering that I'd left the .38 and my television set there and thinking that if I got caught up in a dragnet I'd better have disposed of them.

As I was placidly driving out of South Memphis, the north end of the city was the scene of a hoax. About 30 minutes after Dr. King was shot—and just before the first news bulletin went out— an unidentified citizens band radio operator announced on channel 17 that he was speeding after a white Mustang he said had been involved in the shooting. Giving his location as a street in northeast Memphis, the CB operator requested a telephone connection to the city police department. Several police cars were dispatched to the area as the anonymous tipster claimed he was being shot at by the driver of the fleeing Mustang. Later the second Mustang and the alleged chase were believed to be imaginary. A Memphis teenager named Eddie Montedonico was named by the police as the perpetrator of the hoax, but he denied the charge. He was never prosecuted for the "false" report.

In Flight

I drove through the night, stopping only to dump the camera gear in a ditch somewhere in Alabama and to wipe the Mustang's exterior clean of fingerprints. I knew that the car could be hot for some time, and I didn't want to leave any calling cards in or on the vehicle before abandoning it once I got to Atlanta.

At daybreak I stopped for gas on the outskirts of Atlanta. By 8 a.m., I'd parked the car in the lot of an apartment complex known as Capitol Homes. I wiped down the interior, collected my stuff, and hailed a taxi to take me to the vicinity of Jimmy Garner's rooming house. Alert for any unusual activity but seeing none, I went down to the basement, dug up the buried .38, and stuck it in my belt. In my room, I began filling a trashcan with everything I couldn't fit into the suitcases I'd left there before going to Memphis. I hauled the contents of the trash can outside to a receptacle, but there were still a few things lying around, such as the map I'd marked up a few weeks before, the television and a couple of pairs of Raoul's trousers.

But I wanted to be out of there, so I quit my clean-up routine and got to a phone booth, where I called Greyhound. I was trying to decide where to go next when I thought of Detroit and Windsor and crossing back into Canada. I'd be less likely to run afoul of the U.S. legal system, I still might be able to get a Canadian passport and anyway, where else did I have to go?

There was a bus leaving for Detroit that afternoon. I checked my bag at the depot, then went to a bar until departure time. When I got to the terminal I found out the bus was running late. It didn't pull out of Atlanta until 4 p.m. A two-hour layover in Cincinnati kept us from reaching Detroit until eight the next morning. That afternoon, I took a taxi into Windsor, then a train to Toronto.

From the Toronto train station I walked west, stopping along the way at several nondescript apartment houses to ask if a room was available. Finally, a couple named Szapowski—both of them spoke with heavy, Polish-sounding accents—rented me a room for $12 a week in their house at 102 Ossington Street. They didn't ask any questions—I didn't volunteer any information. I'd come to Canada looking for bogus travel documents, left for the same purpose, and now I was back, still looking.

Passport

I was down to $1,200 or so—not enough to get me as far away as, say, Australia. Last time around, I'd played it relatively safe in trying to get a Canadian passport. This time, I couldn't afford to be so cautious.

I'd read that Soviet spies operating in Canada routinely assumed the names of actual Canadians, taking them from grave markers or from birth notices in old newspapers. On April 8, I went to the reading room of the Toronto *Evening Telegram* and asked to see back issues for the year 1932. The librarian brought me a set of microfilms and helped me put them in a projector. I checked the birth notices. Among the names I copied down were "Ramon George Sneyd" and "Paul Bridgman," both born that year and so roughly my age. I might be able to use either name to apply for a passport.

On my way home a policeman stopped me for jaywalking. He asked my name and address. I had to think quickly. Back when I was collecting names from the swingers' club in California, I'd memorized the address of the Toronto woman who'd responded to my ad: 6 Condor Street. I gave that address, saying I was visiting the occupant. Then I showed him the Galt ID. He wrote out a citation, handed me a copy, and we went our separate ways.

At Szapowski's I wrote the name "Paul Bridgman" on a slip of paper and gave it to Mrs. Szapowski, hoping she'd assume that's who I was.

The next day, I phoned the police substation nearest the spot where I'd gotten the jaywalking citation and asked if the officer had filed his copy of the ticket. The answer was no, but now that Eric Galt was somewhere in the Toronto police data system—and I had a couple of prospective new aliases—I didn't need to be him any longer. In the toilet at the rooming house I tore up and burned whatever Galt ID I had, as well as some papers on which the name appeared, then flushed the ashes. I even burned the piece of paper bearing Randy Rosen's address, but before doing so memorized that information.

It was time to play detective. Over the next few days, I telephoned some of the men whose names I'd copied from the *Evening Telegram* birth records. I represented myself as an agent of the Registrar General's office conducting an inquiry into passport irregularities. Ramon George Sneyd told me he'd never applied for a passport. This meant his picture would not be on file in case someone tried to match a photo of me to recent applicants. Eventually I did apply for and receive a passport under his name. What I didn't know was that Sneyd was a Toronto policeman.

Meanwhile, several blocks over from Ossington Street, I rented another room at 962 Dundas Street from Mrs. Sun

Fung Yoo, telling her I worked nights to avoid suspicion about my absence from the premises during the evening. I used this address when asking for a copy of Sneyd's birth certificate from the Registrar General's office.

On April 16 I visited Kennedy Travel Bureau in Toronto. Introducing myself as Ramon George Sneyd, I asked the agent, Lillian Spencer, how to get a Canadian passport. She gave me the same story I'd heard before. I'd need someone who'd known me for two years to corroborate my claim of Canadian citizenship. But she also mentioned a loophole: if a guarantor wasn't available, Canada would issue a passport on the strength of the applicant's claim of citizenship. I promptly executed an affidavit and gave it to her. To explain why I couldn't produce a guarantor in Toronto, when I supposedly had been born there, I said that for several years I'd been selling used cars in Sudbury, Ontario, and had lost contact with my Toronto friends.

More than two weeks after the King assassination, on April 19, the FBI announced that suspect Eric S. Galt, actually was James Earl Ray, an escaped convict. The Bureau said that after the shooting, Memphis police found both the rifle I'd purchased in Birmingham and, lying on the sidewalk near the door to the flophouse, the overnight case I'd taken into Bessie's. The Lorraine Motel balcony where the civil rights leader was shot was about 300 feet from the back door to the flophouse. The FBI said that during examinations of the discarded items, found on the sidewalk after the shooting, agents at FBI headquarters found several fingerprints, including one on the rifle that matched mine. The FBI decided not to conduct a ballistics test on the rifle claiming that the fatal bullet was misshapen.

> *The British Broadcasting Company consulted ballistics expert Dr. Herbert MacDonnell. MacDonnell, after reviewing the land and groove markings from the bullet stated the "FBI decision not to test fire the rifle . . . is absolutely ludicrous."*

As these announcements were being broadcast across the world, I was traveling by train to Montreal, where I stayed about a week trying to book passage on a ship bound for Europe or Africa. But I couldn't find a berth I could afford, so I returned to Toronto to wait for the results of my passport application. On May 2, I called Kennedy Travel from a pay phone and learned that the Sneyd passport had been sent to their offices. I zipped over like the Road Runner and collected the document, along with a round-trip ticket to London on British Overseas Airways.

Chapter Eleven

Abroad

On May 6 I flew out of Toronto, landing at Heathrow Airport the next morning. I exchanged the return portion of the ticket for a ticket to Lisbon, Portugal, and departed that evening on a Portuguese airliner. In Lisbon I checked into the Hotel Portugal, and spent the day walking around the city like a typical tourist.

I ended up on the waterfront, where I noticed that the docks were rather informal. You could walk near some of the ships without going through a customs gate. I stopped at several shipping offices to ask about ships headed to Africa. I had in mind to get to an English-speaking nation there— perhaps Nigeria where the break-away province of Biafra was fighting for its independence. Possibly I could gain free passage there in a mercenary military unit.

After a couple of days I located a small passenger ship whose rates I could afford and that was leaving soon for the Portuguese colony of Angola. But when I tried to book passage, the ticket agent said I'd have to have a visa from the security police. Reluctantly, I went through that motion. The police said the process took seven days—the ship was sailing in three.

Besides hanging around that wharf and shipping offices looking for passage out of the country, I also contacted the Portuguese foreign ministry for information about joining a foreign military unit. I could get a free ride over, desert and light out for the bush until the fireworks died down. But Portugal wasn't in on that fight, the ministry official told me. However, between the lines of his remarks, he managed to give me the address of an outfit where I might make arrangements of the sort I had in mind.

I went outside and hailed a taxi, giving the driver the address I'd gotten from the bureaucrat. He took me to a plain-looking building. At a cubbyhole inside, a man listened to my inquiries and said, "All the way back." All the officials I met spoke good English.

I went down the corridor to the end, turned right and found a small office with two men in it. A British-accented black did most of the talking. The other man was a middle-aged white who mainly looked and listened. Both seemed skeptical of my motives, the spokesman insinuating that my real interest was journalistic. During this conversation, someone came to the door—a tall, non-English European with a military bearing and a pronounced scar running down the left side of his face to his chin. It looked as if he'd been cut with a dull knife, which leaves a coarse line. He spoke a few words in some European dialect, then left. I don't make it a practice to stare at people, but the scar drew my eye to him. He strongly resembled the late actor Robert Shaw, and I sensed that he was in charge. Shortly after he came and went our conversation ended and I left. Nothing came of this episode, though, and on May 17 I caught a plane back to London.

I checked into Heathrow House, a tourist quarters at the edge of downtown London in an area known as "Kangaroo Alley" for its popularity among Australian tourists, staying there until May 28, during which time I looked for ways to get out of England. In the London *Telegraph*, I read an article by reporter Ian Colvin about organizations that transported parties out of Europe and into the Nigerian war. I got in touch with Colvin. He suggested I look in Brussels, Belgium, for a group of this sort, and he mentioned a former British Army officer with contacts in Nigeria.

I didn't want to stay too long in one place in case the police might be looking for me in England. On May 28, I moved to New Earls Court, another Kangaroo Alley guesthouse, and on June 5 moved to the Pax Hotel. There I purchased a copy of the May 3, 1968 *LIFE* magazine, one of the main branches of the Time, Inc. publishing empire. The cover story was titled "The Accused Killer: RAY alias GALT, The Revealing Story of a Mean Kid." Looking at the cover, I got a preview of the lynch party the American press was readying for me.

Portrait of an Assassin

The magazine's cover featured a grainy black-and-white enlargement from the class photograph taken when I was ten years old and a student at Ewing School. In combination with the bright red *LIFE* logo and the screaming headline, the picture makes for a riveting image, and an outstanding example of illusion-making. (See photo insert).

Thanks to the positioning of the picture and the other elements, the reader's eye goes straight to the surly face of a boy at the middle of the page. He looks exactly like a future killer—but he isn't James Earl Ray. He's my boyhood friend, Robey Peacock, caught in an uncharacteristic glare. I don't remember Robey as being particularly evil, but in this picture his expression would delight a casting director searching for an underage sociopath. The look on Robey's face plays to the "mean kid" reference and the topic of assassination.

Try this test: hold up the reproduction of the *LIFE* cover that appears in this volume and ask a friend which face is mine. Five will get you ten that your friend picks Robey, and not the real James Earl Ray, who's to the right of the Peacock boy, all but his face and one eye obscured by another youngster's head. The look on my ten-year-old face might seem anti-social to some, but I'd call it one in which I was hiding from the camera. All but hidden against the black background is a small, deep-red arrow ostensibly intended to point me out—another round in the magazine's barrage of subtle and unsubtle messages.

As usually occurred in *LIFE's* advertising layout, that week the magazine ran a four-color ad on the back cover. This meant the art directors could have chosen any shade for the identifying arrow. Why select such a deep red?

According to the International Color Council, color has three attributes: hue, lightness and saturation. On these measures, black and red rank as nearly identical. Seen against a black background, that small, deep-red arrow appears as black to the eye—essentially invisible. (Note how in the reproduction you can't even see the arrow—the printing process sees red as black, too.)

If the art directors at *LIFE* had wanted to make my face jump off the page, they could have made their little arrow white, or used a color that has more contrast when set against black. But *LIFE's* artists didn't want to do that. They wanted to maintain that stark red-and-black-and-white aura on the cover—and in the process leave Robey Peacock's stare stuck in the reader's mind. This is illusion in its most accomplished form.

And that's not all. *LIFE* actually had its choice of Ewing School class portraits. There were two. In the other picture, everybody's face shows, and no one's eyes are closed. True, Robey Peacock is still making his "mean kid" face, but I wear an open, friendly look—your average American boy, caught in a happy moment. But this picture didn't fit into *LIFE's* idea of what an assassin should look like, so the art department found one that did.

The copy inside reflected the same slanted inaccuracy. In the article, Associate Editor William A. McWhirter, with correspondents Gerald Moore, Richard Woodbury, John Pekkanen, Frank Leeming Jr. and Ron DePaolo ruminated about my origins, describing me as "a character shaped by a mean life," then exploring alleged aberrations and illnesses in my family background. To nail down their thesis that I was a guilty "lone nut," they said my father's death in the 1940s from prolonged addiction to hard liquor had left me an anti-social loner.

But in May 1968 my father was quite alive, and would remain so for many years, dying of natural causes at 86 in April 1985. He did drink beer—if somebody else was buying—but he wasn't a bottle-hound.

The rest of the article was as rife with error and innuendo, all designed to convict me of Dr. King's murder long before I ever saw the inside of a courthouse.

Another Flight

The *LIFE* article convinced me to try Ian Colvin's contacts in Brussels. On June 8 I caught a taxi to Heathrow, planning to fly to Belgium. At the departure gate I handed the control office the Sneyd passport. He hesitated, then politely asked me to step into an anteroom. He had some questions, he said. Figuring he wanted to check my baggage, I did as he asked, entering a cell-like enclosure with a switchboard to one side, where a second officer stood waiting. He and the man from the gate seized my arms and searched me, finding the .38 I'd been carrying in my hip pocket since I left Atlanta. They said I'd be detained.

Within minutes, eight or ten plainclothes detectives were crowding into the room. One introduced himself as Superintendent Thomas Butler of Scotland Yard's "Flying Squad," a special branch of that police force. Butler said he had reason to believe my correct name to be James Earl Ray. I was wanted for questioning in the Martin Luther King Jr. murder, he told me.

I made no reply. Butler asked if I'd let my fingerprints be taken. I declined. In England, no fingerprints can be taken against the will of a suspect without a court order.

Ignoring that nicety, Butler motioned for several officers to hold me while others forcibly took my prints. When that had been done, the Yard officers took me down a set of back stairs to a police car for a ride back to London and a cell in the Cannon Row police station.

Two days later I appeared before a magistrate, who appointed counsel to represent me at an extradition hearing requested by the U.S. Justice Department. Normally, British courts select court-appointed solicitors from a rotating list of names. In this case, the court abandoned rotation to select Michael Eugene, a member of Michael Dresden & Co. (The reason for breaking tradition, the British court clerk later wrote me was that Dresden & Co. "had expertise in extradition law.")

For confinement, Scotland Yard transported me to Brixton Prison, but security there wasn't up to U.S. Justice Department standards. Assistant U.S. Attorney Fred M. Vinson asked that I be relocated to someplace more secure. Scotland Yard moved me to Wandsworth Prison south of London. The accommodations weren't significantly different from those I'd experienced in the United States. Segregation is segregation, no matter what the country.

From Wandsworth I wrote letters asking two well-known American attorneys—F. Lee Bailey of Boston and Arthur J. Hanes Sr. of Birmingham, the only two prominent lawyers for whom I could recall a city and state location—if they would consider representing me when I returned to the United States.

I was eager to engage an American lawyer. I didn't want some Justice Department bureaucrat saying I "confessed" or made incriminating statements with respect to the King case before I could obtain counsel.

Both Bailey and Hanes responded through my British solicitor, Michael Eugene. Bailey said he had a conflict of interest (in later years, he'd serve as something of a mouthpiece for the King case prosecution).

Hanes said he'd take the case. However, Eugene opposed this, saying the U.S. Embassy had told him "bringing Arthur Hanes into the Martin Luther King Jr. matter would be unwise." Despite this admonition, I agreed to see Hanes, who made three trips to London before I returned to the United States. The first time, British authorities refused to let him see me. On his second trip, he received permission to see me, but we could discuss nothing of substance about the King case because we were bracketed by a pair of prison guards stationed directly behind us, one on either side.

The only legal matters we discussed involved contracts. I gave Hanes power of attorney to sign publishing contracts with author William Bradford Huie, who said he intended to write a series of articles about the case prior to trial.

On Hanes' third trip, he advised me to waive my right to appeal an extradition order. He also said he thought the income from Huie's articles would finance my defense. I had doubts about trying to pay my legal fees by doing business with publishers, but I went along.

I went through extradition hearings on June 10 and again on June 27. The hearings were a formality. Without weighing the adequacy of the "evidence" against me, the magistrate obediently complied with a Justice Department extradition request.

While in British custody, I had no visitors except the attorneys representing me. British prison rules protect prisoners from interrogation by anyone, including police and prosecutorial authorities, unless the prisoner executes a waiver agreeing to be interviewed. The only person who formally requested to interview me was Superintendent Thomas Butler, the Scotland Yard man who'd ordered me fingerprinted against my will at Heathrow.

I declined to see him. I was wise to the Confession Game, in which prosecutors place a corrupt official or informant in the presence of a defendant. At trial, the informant takes the stand and testifies that he heard the defendant "confess" to the charge, often leading to convictions otherwise unlikely owing to a weak or nonexistent prosecution case.

I was certain this was Butler's angle. He'd already lied about me. At an extradition hearing he testified that when he confronted me in the anteroom at Heathrow, I "swooned" and fell onto a bench, saying "Oh God! I feel so trapped!"

When Butler put on this phony display, I asked a Yard man who'd been present at Heathrow—and who knew I'd neither swooned nor gotten hysterical—why Butler felt it necessary to lie about an incident in a case he didn't have to solve. The other officer finessed the question, saying that for some time Butler had been extremely distraught about his failure to catch Ronald Biggs. Biggs and accomplices had pulled off the 1963 "Great Train Robbery," hijacking a mail train and stealing about $7 million. Butler had tracked Biggs down and seen the case through to conviction, but then Biggs broke out of Wandsworth and was still evading Butler's efforts to recapture him.

But Butler's histrionics weren't the central element of the extradition proceedings. Besides statements about the alleged assassination weapon and my overnight bag, the main basis for the Justice Department request that Britain return me to the United States for trial in the King murder was a sworn statement by Charles Quitman Stephens, a resident of Bessie Brewer's flophouse at 422-½ South Main Street in Memphis. Stephens' police record ran to nearly 200 arrests for public drunkenness. At one court hearing he was found to be addicted to "fermented grape."

In his affidavit, Stephens claimed that at about 6:00 p.m. on April 4, 1968—just after he'd heard a gunshot—he'd seen the "profile" of a person running down the flophouse hall. Stephens added that he'd seen this profile earlier in the building and told the British court he'd "looked at" an FBI profile photograph of James Earl Ray and identified it as "looking very much like the man" he'd seen running out of the flophouse after the King shooting.

Stephens, the primary source for an artist's rendering of the shooter that ran in the April 5 *Memphis Commercial Appeal*, concluded his affidavit by stating, "The pointed nose and chin are the principal features that stand out in my identification of the man pictured."

The artist's rendering doesn't resemble me in the least. Moreover, Stephens told the FBI that the man he'd seen running down the hall had "sandy hair." At the time, my hair was dark brown.

The June 23, 1968, date of the Stephens affidavit is significant: in June, the Justice Department hadn't yet learned of my L.A. nose job. Before the surgery, my nose was pointed, but Dr. Hadley's hand—and my own post-operative tinkering—had modified it. FBI agents showed Stephens photos of me from 1955, 1960 and 1966. Stephens said he didn't recognize the man in the photos from '55 and '60. However, he said the 1966 photograph, a profile in an FBI "Wanted" flyer published two weeks after the assassination, resembled me—but that picture had been taken a year before my plastic surgery. Stephen had based his identification on a profile that no longer existed.

> *Grace Stephens, Charles Stephens' common-law wife, was an eyewitness on the scene at the flophouse on the day that Dr. King was murdered. Mrs. Stephens described the shooter to the Memphis Police and stated that Ray was not the man. On July 8, 1969 she was taken to John Gaston Hospital for treatment of an ankle injury. There a psychiatrist appeared and instantly diagnosed her problem as mental, not physical. Declaring her a suicide risk, the doctor committed Mrs. Stephens to the psychiatric ward. She was kept there more than three weeks, then committed to Western State Hospital in Bolivar, Tennessee, and held there until 1978, when she was freed at the demand of attorney Mark Lane. Mrs. Stephens had no history of mental illness and claims she was confined only because of her being a witness in the King case.*

My court-appointed counsel, Michael Eugene, made no effort to impeach the affidavit or the character of Charles Stephens, and the magistrate ordered me sent back to the United States. It was technically possible to appeal the extradition order to a higher tribunal, but the British authorities with power to appoint counsel in appellate matters refused to name a solicitor to appeal the order. This, combined with Arthur Hanes' advice to forgo appeal and return to the United States, led me to waive appellate review of the extradition order.

Before leaving England, I wrote to U.S. Attorney General Ramsey Clark, FBI Director J. Edgar Hoover and Hanes, stating that I would not discuss the King case with the officials accompanying me on my flight.

On July 19, Scotland Yard officers transported me from Wandsworth Prison to a U.S. Air Force base outside London, where a TWA jet waited. Once I was aboard, FBI agents handcuffed me to a seat. During the non-stop flight to Memphis, I said nothing to anyone since I was concerned about authorities later claiming that I made a confession. Later one of the men who'd escorted me said he'd thought I might be suicidal.

The plane landed at Millington Air Force Base at about 4:00 a.m. From there an armored bus took me and my captors to the Shelby County Jail in downtown Memphis.

Part IV

Caught
in the Web

Chapter Twelve

Midnight Sunstroke

At the jail I was confined in the third-floor A tank, a block of six cells, none occupied but mine. It was a standard cellblock setup—each cell 8' x 6'3" inches, with a bunk 6'3" x 2'3" at one side and a toilet and sink in the opposite corner. The block seemed to have been through a recent and thorough refurbishing. The gray paint smelled fresh. Every window had been sealed over with a thick metal plate. For fresh air, a blower blasted me with warm, then cold gusts. For light, I saw no sun—the whole block was flooded with the bright, artificial glare of bulbs that burned 24 hours a day. I soon lost track of time, and all sense of day and night.

I lived under the eyes of two TV cameras. One monitored my every movement, the other scanned the surrounding cellblock. Two guards—a city policeman and a county deputy sheriff—stood watch at all times. And the cellblock was wired—I could see an open microphone aimed into my cell. The sheriff swore the mike was turned off during my meetings with attorneys, but I didn't believe him.

The entire environment was straight out of a police state handbook.

My first day inside, a deputy placed a small table at the far end of the cellblock for Arthur Hanes Sr. to use when he visited. In the unoccupied cell across from the table stood what appeared to be an old X-ray machine bristling with pipes and horns. The apparatus spooked me, so I'd sometimes make deliberately misleading statements to Hanes about the King case for the benefit of any eavesdroppers who might be connected with the machine. While speaking untruths, I wrote down the correct information on paper for Hanes to read.

The machine remained in place a month or so, until one night—or day—I was awakened by the sound of sheriff's deputies lugging the thing away.

A couple of months passed. I slept in fits and starts, never getting a genuine rest. I began to have nosebleeds, which I blamed on the total lack of natural light, fresh air and privacy. My lawyers asked the court to order the Sheriff's Department to lay off on the surveillance and 24-hour lighting. "The presence of said illumination and surveillance has deprived Defendant of the opportunity to rest or sleep and has a tendency to cause Defendant to be nervous and disturbed and constitutes an electronic form of cruel and unusual punishment," Hanes wrote.

Prosecutor Philip M. Canale said the TV cameras were necessary "to protect the defendant Ray as well as to keep the defendant Ray from effecting an escape." At the hearing the prosecution informed Judge Preston Battle that their jailhouse logs showed me to be sleeping eight-and-one-half hours each night. They assumed that a prisoner lying on his bunk motionless—and sleepless—actually was asleep.

On November 22, Judge Battle found the sheriff's treatment of me "reasonable." If the bright lights irritated me, he added, I could sleep with a mask over my eyes. With rare exception, this ruling presaged future decisions by the courts on any issue of importance related to the King murder.

In September 1968 a conflict of interest arose among myself, my attorney and writer William Bradford Huie. The root was the publishing contracts that Hanes had executed on my behalf with Huie. They agreed that Hanes provide Huie with whatever I said or provided pertaining to the King case and related matters. If Hanes failed to do so, there would be "no deal"—and no money from Huie.

I got angry when *Look* magazine published information Hanes had given Huie. Soon after, the prosecution began listing witnesses who would testify against me—lists generally reflecting what Huie had written. As the trial approached the original list of 67 prosecution witnesses lengthened to 377. It looked foolish for a defendant's attorney to be giving away so much before trial, enabling prosecutors to manipulate the information and coach or intimidate potential witnesses.

My anger at Huie focused on his revealing the defense too soon. Hanes and I fell out over his decision to let a representative of the commercial communications industry infiltrate the defense before trial. Then, as now, I thought if the case went to trial, Hanes at worst would have obtained a hung jury—and if he hadn't compromised the defense by selling our ammunition to Huie.

Hanes and I also disagreed about whether I should testify. I felt it essential that I do so. Hanes disagreed. At the time, I didn't know that Huie had used his "no deal" clause to keep me off the witness stand, but through my brother Jerry I found out how and why this came about.

Less than a week before the trial was to begin, Huie heard that I had been insisting on taking the stand. He summoned Jerry from St. Louis to Huie headquarters in Hartselle, Alabama, and explained the finances of the case. Since he and his publishers were underwriting my defense, Huie said, Hanes had to dance to their tune. I wasn't going to be permitted to testify in my own defense because that would put my side of the story into the public domain, destroying Huie's exclusive hold on it.

Huie told Jerry that he'd give us $12,000 up front and amend his contract with me and Hanes to get me more money, if I'd stay off the witness stand.

Jerry came directly to Memphis on November 8, 1968— three days before my trial was to start. After nearly four months of living like a laboratory rat, I had trouble thinking rationally. But I had enough willpower left to reject Huie's terms and his plans, and enough energy to get very angry when Jerry told me Huie and his publishers were committed to a solution of the King case that fit in with their position on all political murders: Martin Luther King Jr. had to have died at the hands of a nutty loner or as the victim of a Ku Klux Klan-oriented conspiracy of the type for which Huie was famous for writing about.

"I think you need a lawyer," Jerry said.

"Who?" I asked. "I don't know of any more."

"I saw this famous Texas lawyer, Percy Foreman, on a TV talk show," Jerry said. "He looked to me like he knew his business."

Enter Percy Foreman

When Jerry left me, I was prepared to stand trial the following Monday, regardless of Arthur Hanes' dependency on Huie for payment. I was even looking forward to it.

Judge Preston Battle and the local press were both hostile toward Hanes and his son, Arthur Jr., also a defense team lawyer. This animosity was a pretty good sign: My attorney was beholden to New York money, but he hadn't crawled into the prosecutor's vest pocket. Which is more than I can say about Percy Foreman.

Nearly 70 years old, a super salesman despite an Alfred Hitchcock physique, Foreman showed up at the Shelby County Jail the day before the trial was to begin. He wasn't listed in the jail record as representing me. I never requested to see him. Yet the sheriff promptly ushered him into my presence. This official deference should have tipped me to Foreman's status with the local political establishment—the prosecution knew him to be a man willing to make a deal.

Like Huie, Foreman seemed to be motivated mainly by money. He'd talked with my brother before coming to see me, telling Jerry, "Don't call me 'Mister Foreman,' call me 'the Texas Tiger.' " He'd also asked Jerry for copies of the Hanes-Huie-Ray contracts, which he brought to the cellblock. We introduced ourselves, and I asked him how he thought those contracts would affect the trial.

"The only thing Hanes and Huie are interested in is how much money they can exploit from this case," Foreman said indignantly. "They're personal friends, and if you stick with them you'll be barbecued."

He derided the idea of keeping me from testifying merely to preserve a writer's scoop. "If you dismiss Arthur Hanes and retain me, there will be no literary contracts entered into until after trial," he said, adding that although he expected a fee for his services, he could finance the defense without going into hock with publishers.

"My fee will be $150,000, which will be realized from literary contracts I'll arrange after the trial," Foreman said.

Foreman mentioned his fame several times, taking care to tell me he'd tried a thousand murder cases. Few of his clients had gone to jail, and only one had been executed. He said my case was the easiest he'd ever seen. I was so impressed with this display of success and integrity that I agreed to have him replace Arthur Hanes Sr. as my attorney. Foreman suggested I write a note announcing the change of defense counsel. He even helped compose it.

About 8:30 that evening Hanes Sr. and Jr. came to see me. The guard told them the sheriff wanted to talk to them. At the Sheriff's offices, someone gave them a photocopy of a note from me saying, "Dear Mr. Hanes, I thank you for all you've done for me, however I've decided to change lawyers and obtain other counsel. Sincerely, Jim."

That Monday was Armistice Day—November 11, 1968. I appeared in court, accompanied by the Haneses and Foreman, for a hearing on my motion to change counsel. Foreman argued for the change. Judge Battle, showing no displeasure at the proposal, since it would take Hanes Sr. out of his hair, granted the motion. However, he warned that he wouldn't permit further changes in counsel, and urged Foreman to prepare quickly, since he wasn't inclined to grant additional delays. The court also obtained Foreman's promise that he wouldn't enter into contracts such as those between Hanes, Huie and me.

The next day, Foreman asked me to sign over title to my Mustang and the rifle allegedly used to kill Dr. King. Both now were being held by the prosecution as evidence. I said the rifle wasn't mine to sign away. He said he was confident prosecutor Philip M. Canale would let him have it and the Mustang after the trial.

Several weeks later, Foreman visited the Hanes offices in Birmingham. My former attorneys offered him my entire file, consisting of thousands of pages of documents, reports, photographs, interview transcripts and trial briefs.

"You can have it all," Hanes Sr. said. "You're the trial lawyer now."

Foreman spent about ten minutes rifling through the file before going out to dinner with the Haneses. "He wasn't interested in the case," Hanes Jr. said. "He wanted to drink some Scotch, eat some dinner and talk about his famous cases. He also told us about how he made speeches all over the country."

Hanes Sr. concurred. "We tried to outline the case for him, to tell him what we knew," he said much later. "He didn't seem to be too interested. We offered him everything we had. He took nothing with him. My judgment is that the man never even considered trying the case. Far as I can ascertain he never prepared and he never investigated. He never considered giving James Earl Ray a trial."

As far as Foreman's investigative technique went, the two main questions in the case were: "Was there a conspiracy to kill Dr. King?" and "Did James Earl Ray fire the weapon?"

He never asked me either question. I would have answered that I did not shoot Dr. King but that I was unwittingly part of a conspiracy since I was hired to purchase a weapon of the type allegedly used in the killing and did bring it to Memphis.

Public Defenders

Foreman told me he never asked for a client's version of the events that had led to a criminal charge until he'd investigated the state's case. Besides not asking many questions, Foreman wasn't much on giving out information—at least to me. On December 18, deputies whisked me out of my numbing isolation and into Judge Battle's courtroom. There I heard for the first time that Foreman wanted the state to help pay for my defense. The setting was a hearing on that very motion.

Foreman said there were no funds to cover the cost of an investigation. In addition, he said, there were no prospects of obtaining funds through publishing contracts—directly contradictory to what he'd said weeks before.

To a casual listener, the exchanges involving prosecutor, judge and defense attorney might have seemed spontaneous and unrehearsed, but I could sense—and the record reflects—that Foreman's "request" and the courtroom conversation about it had been engineered in advance as a way of insinuating the public defender into my case.

The morning's proceedings seemed to be following a script. First, Judge Battle suggested that a public defender assist Foreman's investigation. Lo and behold—public defender Hugh W. Stanton Sr. just happened to be sitting at the front of the courtroom. The judge mentioned this. When his name was spoken he popped up like a jack-in-the-box and informed the judge of his availability. To spectators, including the press and even me, they seemed to be acting spontaneously, but in reading the official transcript I noted that Foreman said he and Stanton had discussed the appointment *before* the hearing. At the time no one picked up on this important nuance, which suggested that the fix was in well before the hearing opened.

At the next hearing, on January 17, 1969, the defense was to describe its progress in preparing a case. When I was led into the courtroom, I found only Stanton Sr. and his son, an assistant public defender named for his father, on hand to represent me.

Foreman had called in sick. His absence enabled Judge Battle to get the public defenders further into my case, by declaring that, should illness prevent Foreman from defending me, Stanton Sr. would assume control of my defense. To underscore this ruling, Battle upgraded Stanton's status in the case to co-counsel with all the responsibilities of lead counsel.

I knew a few things about public defenders. The public defender too often sees his job as plea bargaining. He assumes that if the state could convince a grand jury to hand down an indictment, his client probably is guilty. On my way back to the midnight sunshine, I passed chief jailer Billy Smith and told him not to permit the Stantons to come into my presence.

On January 20, Stanton Sr. appeared in the cellblock, saying he wanted to discuss my case. I refused to see him. I wasn't going to risk playing what might turn out to be a variation on the Confession Game.

Stanton already seemed to be living up to the standard model of a public defender. In the January 3 *Memphis Commercial Appeal*, pro-prosecutor reporter Charles Edmondson wrote that "unnamed defense sources" had said I might plead guilty to Dr. King's murder. At the time, Foreman was in Texas. Who could have spoken to the press except his cohort in the public defender's office?

I got permission to telephone Foreman in Houston, and when he came on the line I asked if he still intended to defend me. If his health was going to be a problem, I said, I'd look for another lawyer. I also told him I thought Judge Battle was trying to maneuver Stanton into the role of chief defense counsel. Foreman said he'd be in Memphis soon. He claimed he'd be physically fit to represent me. When I got back to the cellblock, I wrote to Stanton and told him I didn't want him representing me.

Foreman got to Memphis on January 21. He took up residence at the Peabody Hotel, one of the city's luxury landmarks. He didn't come to see me for a week. When he did show up at the jail, I was surprised by his appearance. Illness seemed to have left him in better health—he actually appeared somewhat chipper.

I couldn't say the same for myself. Neither could my former British solicitor, Michael Eugene. He'd been in town two months earlier to testify in the case. While in court, we spoke briefly. He later said I looked sick, weak and nervous. That was how I felt, thanks to the unsettling environment in which I was confined.

Foreman's first visit after his illness was a replay of our initial conversation in November except that he brought a new set of publishing contracts from Huie. The only difference between these documents and the contracts involving Arthur Hanes Sr. was that Foreman's name had replaced Hanes' in all the appropriate blanks.

The new contracts puzzled me. Not only had Foreman condemned Hanes and Huie for financially exploiting my case, he'd promised Judge Battle there'd be no more pre-trial publishing contracts. Yet here he was, holding out exactly that for me to sign. Worse, the contracts were backdated— evidence that Foreman had spent some time negotiating with Huie over transferring the monetary rights from Hanes to Foreman. (Later, Huie said the first time he spoke with Foreman, in November 1968, Foreman made clear his intent. "Now, you know of course that I'm depending on you for my fee," he told Huie. "So, tote that bale, boy! Get to work!")

Foreman also had with him a check from Huie for $5,000— perhaps that was the source of his chipperness. He had me endorse the check over to him so he'd have cash to hire John Jay Hooker Sr., a prominent Nashville attorney, as co-counsel. I protested that Foreman already had enlisted the public defender in that capacity. But Percy said he needed Hooker— and his son, too—and that I'd soon see why. On that note, he pocketed the five grand and left. Afterward he forged my signature on another $5,000 check from Huie. This happened after he had starting touting a guilty plea—he apparently assumed I wouldn't endorse the check to him.

(I learned later that Hooker's ties to Foreman went back 25 years. He was a big shot among Tennessee Democrats. His son, John Jr., was close with John and Robert Kennedy and ran for governor in 1966 and then in 1970.)

The prosecutors seemed increasingly desperate. One day they sent a barber to cut my hair. They were trying to link me to a July 1967 bank robbery in Alton, Illinois. Investigators had found hair at the bank, and the prosecution wanted to see if mine matched. Nothing came of the ploy, although it did serve to add to the state of emotional siege under which I was operating.

Foreman didn't show up again until February 3, this time with another contract for me to sign. He chatted about how well the investigation was progressing and how he expected the jury to acquit me. As he talked, I went through the motions of reading the contract, which said that, in return for his service as my defense lawyer "in trial or trials" pending in Memphis, Tennessee, I authorized all past and future funds accruing from publishing contracts be paid directly to Percy Foreman at his office in Houston, Texas.

After nearly seven months of debilitating confinement, I was exhausted. My resistance was flagging. I signed the contract. The next day, February 4, Foreman went before Judge Battle without my knowledge to present two propositions that could only be termed despicable. He asked the court to let a *LIFE* magazine photographer take pictures of me in jail. In exchange for exclusive rights to publish the photographs, *LIFE* would contribute $5,000 to my defense fund, better known as Percy Foreman's pocket. Foreman also asked the court to let William Bradford Huie interview me in jail. Judge Battle denied both requests.

Knowing my attitude toward Huie, why would Foreman try to do this? Years later, I learned that Foreman had persuaded Huie that there had been no conspiracy in the King murder, that I alone was responsible and implied that there'd be no trial. Foreman's remarks led Huie to change the title of his proposed book from *They Slew The Dreamer* to *He Slew The Dreamer*. My guess is that at the time Huie was hoping I'd play his version of the Confession Game, enabling him to write that during our conversations I'd confessed to the King murder.

Selling Me Out, Part I

Soon after I'd signed the latest round of contracts, Foreman showed me several photographs of white males. The photos, which he said he'd gotten from the FBI, were supposed to have been made in Dallas on November 22, 1963, near the scene of President Kennedy's assassination. Foreman described the men in the photos as either anti-Communist Cubans or persons associated with anti-Communist Cubans. He said the government wanted them off the streets, and asked if I could identify one of the men, an individual referred to as "Frenchy." To those familiar with the conspiracy theories growing out of John F. Kennedy's murder, he's also known as one of the "tramps" said to have been part of the plot to kill the president.

If I'd identify "Frenchy" as someone I knew during 1967-68 in an association that led to my arrest in the King homicide, the prosecution would have "Frenchy" arrested and transported to Memphis, Foreman said, making it clear that he, with the prosecution's approval, intended to sell the information on "Frenchy" to *LIFE* magazine.

I looked at the pictures. "Frenchy" bore a striking similarity to Raoul, and I said so, but added that I couldn't say for sure that they were the same man.

"Is this your final word on the subject?" Foreman asked when he got up to leave.

"Yes," I said. Later, I learned that this was part of Foreman's continuing liaison with *LIFE*. When he wasn't trying to sell that magazine the right to photograph me, he was trying to get me to corroborate some outlandish statement the press wanted to publish.

Finally, Foreman showed up and asked for my side of the story. Confident that this meant he'd thoroughly investigated the state's case, I began to talk, with him taking notes on a yellow legal pad.

After a few paragraphs, he said his hand was cramping up, and asked me to write out the rest of my narrative.

"I'll pick up the paper next time," he told me.

Foreman was asking for the same information I'd given Hanes Sr.—a written account of my life from April 23, 1967, the day I escaped from JeffCity until my June 8, 1968, arrest at Heathrow Airport.

In going through this exercise for Hanes, I hadn't described my movements on April 4, 1968—I knew anything I told Hanes would show up in *Look* magazine before the trial, courtesy of Huie, who kept nagging Hanes to nag me for details. In such circumstances, I tend to become sarcastic. Remembering Huie's obsession with the KKK, I told Hanes that in the minutes after the shooting I was sitting idly in the Mustang, which was parked out front of the flophouse.

Suddenly, I said, Raoul raced to the car, jumped into the back seat, and pulled a bedsheet over his head, saying "Get the hell out of here fast!" Bedsheet, Klan—the joke seemed obvious to me, but I guess not everyone got it.

I misled Huie one other time, telling him I'd escaped over the wall at JeffCity. If I'd come clean about the breadbox, he might have written about it and brought on reprisals against the prisoners who helped me escape. Unfortunately, these deliberate misstatements gave prosecutors and the press grounds for promoting the notion that "the only truth Ray ever told was when he pleaded guilty as charged."

Not knowing Foreman had neglected to look at my former counsel's files on me, I figured he wanted me to write out my account because the earlier version was somehow inadequate. I was in far worse mental and physical shape than when I'd constructed the account for Hanes, but I applied myself, and included more detail than before.

However, Foreman didn't use this statement to defend me. He handed it over to another writer, Gerold Frank, who previously had written about the Boston Strangler and who was mentioned in a clandestine FBI memo as a "friendly

1. Lorraine Motel balcony where Dr. King was shot.

2. The entrance to Bessie Brewer's rooming house.

3. Ewing School-1938, Ray,10, last boy on right in third row

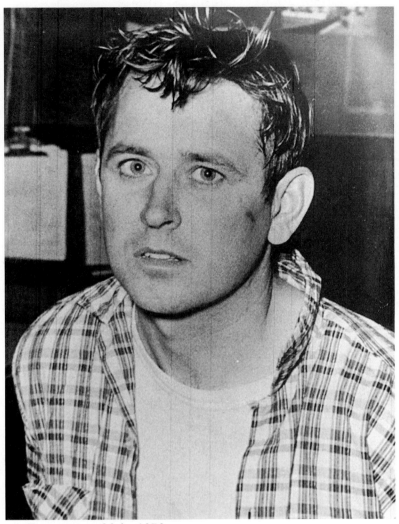

4. Ray at age 30 in 1959 .

WANTED BY THE FBI

CIVIL RIGHTS - CONSPIRACY
INTERSTATE FLIGHT - ROBBERY
JAMES EARL RAY

FBI No. 405,942 G

Photographs taken 1960   Photograph taken 1968
(eyes drawn by artist)

Aliases: Eric Starvo Galt, W. C. Herron, Harvey Lowmyer, James McBride, James O'Conner, James Walton, James Walyon, John Willard, "Jim."

DESCRIPTION

Age:	40, born March 10, 1928, at Quincy or Alton, Illinois (not supported by birth records)		
Height:	5' 10"	**Eyes:**	Blue
Weight:	163 to 174 pounds	**Complexion:**	Medium
Build:	Medium	**Race:**	White
Hair:	Brown, possibly cut short	**Nationality:**	American

Occupations: Baker, color matcher, laborer

Scars and Marks: Small scar on center of forehead and small scar on palm of right hand

Remarks: Noticeably protruding left ear; reportedly is a lone wolf; allegedly attended dance instruction school; has reportedly completed course in bartending.

Fingerprint Classification: 16 M 9 U OOO 12

M 4 W IOI

CRIMINAL RECORD

Ray has been convicted of burglary, robbery, forging U. S. Postal Money Orders, armed robbery, and operating motor vehicle without owner's consent.

CAUTION

RAY IS SOUGHT IN CONNECTION WITH A MURDER WHEREIN THE VICTIM WAS SHOT. CONSIDER ARMED AND EXTREMELY DANGEROUS.

A Federal warrant was issued on April 17, 1968, at Birmingham, Alabama, charging Ray as Eric Starvo Galt with conspiring to interfere with a Constitutional Right of a citizen (Title 18, U. S. Code, Section 241). A Federal warrant was also issued on July 20, 1967, at Jefferson City, Missouri, charging Ray with Interstate Flight to Avoid Confinement for the crime of Robbery (Title 18, U. S. Code, Section 1073).

IF YOU HAVE ANY INFORMATION CONCERNING THIS PERSON, PLEASE NOTIFY ME OR CONTACT YOUR LOCAL FBI OFFICE. TELEPHONE NUMBERS AND ADDRESSES OF ALL FBI OFFICES LISTED ON BACK.

J. Edgar Hoover

DIRECTOR
FEDERAL BUREAU OF INVESTIGATION
UNITED STATES DEPARTMENT OF JUSTICE
WASHINGTON, D. C. 20
TELEPHONE, NATIONA

Wanted Flyer 442-A
April 19, 1968

5. FBI wanted poster for James Earl Ray dated April 19, 1968

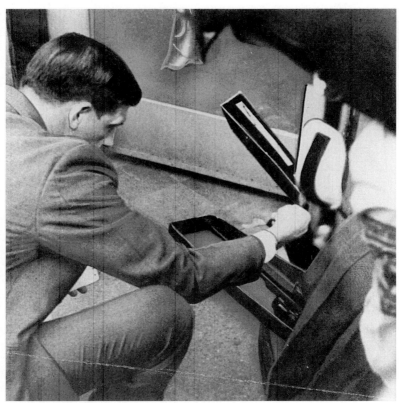

6. *Minutes after Dr. King was shot Memphis police detective examines weapon abandoned outside of Bessie Brewer's rooming house. Notice that the rifle is packed neatly in a box, not something that a killer is likely to do with a murder weapon when fleeing the scene.*

7. *Charles Quitman Stephens, the only eyewitness to identify Ray, later recanted his story in full.*

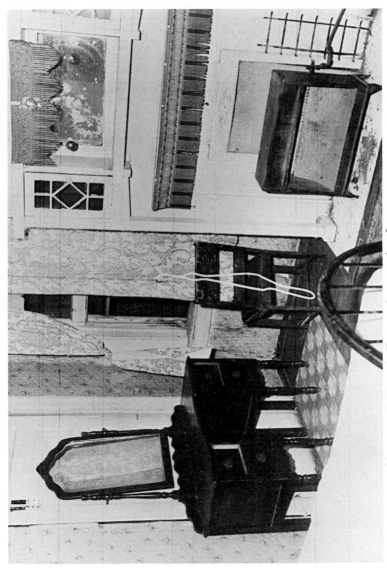

8. Room rented by Ray in Bessie Brewer's rooming house.

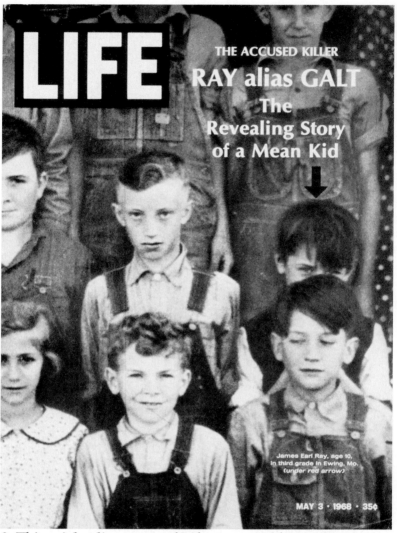

LIFE

THE ACCUSED KILLER

RAY alias GALT

The Revealing Story of a Mean Kid

James Earl Ray, age 10, in third grade in Ewing, Mo. (under red arrow)

MAY 3 · 1968 · 35¢

9. This misleading cover of Life magazine focused attention on the "mean-looking kid," who is not Ray. Ten year old Ray is in the second row, right-hand side.The same issue of Life contained numerous lies about Ray's family, building a false case that he was a "lone nut."

10. *Cartha DeLoach, a close aide to J. Edgar Hoover, directed the FBI's harassment of Dr. King, and then was assigned to investigate his assassination.*

11. *Percy Foreman was paid $165,000 to defend Ray and conduct his trial. Instead of defending him, Foreman coerced Ray into pleading guilty, avoiding the necessity of a months-long trial.*

12. *Judge Preston W. Battle died of a mysteriously-timed heart attack at his office while considering Ray's request for a new trial.*

13. *Federal Judge William E. Miller also died of a mysterious heart attack at the courthouse when considering Ray's request for a trial.*

14. Ray at Memphis federal court after testifying in 1974.

Attorney Mark Lane with Ray before the Select Committee in 1978.

16. *Anna Sandhu Ray with Rev. James Lawson just after Anna's marriage to James Earl Ray. Rev. Lawson, who was a close associate of Dr. King, performed the wedding ceremony.*

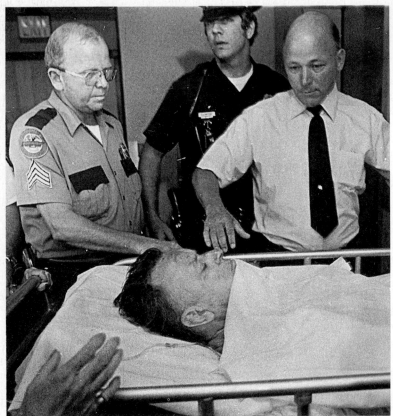

Ray was stabbed 22 times in the law library at Brushy Mountain prison in a 1981 murder attempt. He is shown at the hospital where 78 stitches were needed to close the near-ly-fatal wounds.

Photo Credits

Photos 1-3 are courtesy of the Ray family. Photo 9 is courtesy of *Life* magazine. Photos 4-8, 10-12, 14-17 are reprinted with permission of AP/Wide World Photos.

journalist" who could be counted on to support the official line in the King murder story.

On February 13, a very agitated Percy Foreman showed up at the jail. He presented a paper for me to sign, claiming he needed "evidence" that he had advised me to let him negotiate a guilty plea on my behalf.

The document stated that I knew a guilty plea couldn't be entered after March 3, 1969, but didn't explain why. I knew of no court order to this effect. In my experience judges are amenable to cop-outs any time. (Foreman's strange document was another in a series of curious improprieties rendered understandable by time. In 1974, I sought a habeas corpus—literally, "you have the body," a Latin phrase for the doctrine of law under which the authorities can be forced to release a prisoner—hearing. That hearing revealed the existence in early 1969 of a secret contract between Huie, Cowles Communication, Inc. and Foreman. Drafted fully except for a blank by the date, the contract says, "Ray is expected to plead guilty on or about March 10, 1969, to the charge of murdering Dr. Martin Luther King . . ." and provides for Foreman to be paid $1,000 to write a post-plea article appearing among three *Look* magazine stories by Huie.)

Full Court Press

I signed the plea document but told Foreman I didn't intend to plead guilty. He went to work trying to persuade me to do so. He said I should cop a plea because the media had convicted me already. Besides *LIFE* and *Reader's Digest*, Foreman pointed to local reporting—such as Charles Edmondson's extremely prejudicial November 10 *Commercial Appeal* article. He also said the court clerk would manipulate the juror pool so I'd be up against a panel of angry blacks intent on revenge and chamber-of-commerce types who only wanted to lock me up and get back to business. And star prosecution witness Charles Quitman Stephens was to get $100,000 in reward money for his testimony, Foreman reminded me. Lastly, Foreman told me why he'd brought

John Jay Hooker Sr. in on the case: Hooker Jr. was destined to be Tennessee's next governor. Given his ties to the Hooker family, Foreman said, a pardon would be arranged after I'd served two or three years.

In response, I listed my reasons for taking the case to a jury.

Media exposure was a problem, but the jury was supposed to assess the facts as presented in court, not as twisted on TV and in the press. A thorough cross-examination of state witnesses, coupled with convincing defense evidence of the sort that we could produce, surely would counteract the poisoned atmosphere generated by the press.

And so what if many members of the jury wound up being black? The black community's interest in discovering the truth about Dr. King's murder would outweigh any resentment it might feel toward me personally.

The argument that the "chamber-of-commerce types" would vote their pocketbooks—find me guilty to avoid an acquittal and possible riot—simply didn't hold water. Tennessee didn't have enough fat cats to pack a jury with them.

I didn't address the issue of prosecution witness Stephens, but Foreman was bamboozling me. He didn't tell me the prosecution would never put Stephens on the stand. Foreman himself had found a credible witness to impeach Stephens' testimony—a cab driver named James McCraw— as well as Stephens' own common-law wife, Grace Walden Stephens, who was standing firm against state offers of bribes to adjust her testimony to convict me.

I tried to get Foreman to talk about a defense. I'd given him the last four digits of the New Orleans phone number Raoul had given me in Mexico. Had he checked it out? I'd also given him the Baton Rouge number listed under the name "Herman A. Thompson." When Jerry had checked it in July, it had been working—had Foreman looked into it?

Professional digging into these numbers might shed considerable light on the case, I said. My enthusiasm only offended Foreman, who told me if any phone numbers were introduced as evidence, he'd supply them—and he'd obtain them through his contacts with mobster Meyer Lansky.

Statement of James M. McCraw

On April 4, 1968 I was driving for Yellow Cab Co. and was dispatched to 422½ So. Main St. to pick up a fare. When I arrived at this address, I double parked as there were cars and trucks parked at the curb. I observed a Cadillac owned by Mr. Jones, owner of Jim's Grill on So. Main, 526-9910. I also observed two white Mustangs parked at the curb and several delivery trucks. All of this traffic was parked on the East side of So. Main St. facing North. A woman who ran the rooming house directed Mr. McCraw to a certain room, stating that the occupant of that room directed that a cab be called. The door of the room was open and McCraw went in the room and found Charles Stephens lying on the bed fully clothed, he was in a very drunked condition. Stephens was well-known to Mc-Craw, as he had picked him up many times before. Mr. McCraw refused to transport Stephens as a fare because of his drunken condition. McCraw stated that Stephens could not get off the bed. Mr. McCraw left the rooming house, got back into his cab, made a U-turn, went South on South Main St. When Mr. McCraw got to the corner of So. Main and Calhoun Sts. the dispatcher said that Mr. M.L. King had been shot and for all cabs to stay out of the So. Main area. . . . McCraw estimates that he was in the rooming house about three minutes and that from the time he left the rooming house until the time the dispatcher called about King being shot was about two minutes.

During this period my family was my sole source of emotional support. February 18, Foreman traveled to St. Louis in an attempt to get my father, sister and two brothers to back a guilty plea. They refused. When he visited me in jail afterwards, however, he lied and said they agreed that I should plead guilty.

Huie had come up with another $5,000 check, this time made out to me and Foreman. Normally, a two-party check must be endorsed by both parties to be negotiable, but Foreman apparently didn't want to ask me to sign. He forged my signature and deposited the check in Union Planters Bank of Memphis, where he'd put the first check.

In between attempts to get me to cop a plea, Foreman would gossip to me about the characters he was dealing with in handling my case. Some of his stories clashed with his arguments for a guilty plea. For instance, Foreman said chief prosecutor Canale had no real interest in whether I had killed Dr. King. Rather, Canale was preoccupied with identifying those who had crucified Jesus Christ.

Foreman also described frictions within the prosecution team. Second-in-command Robert Dwyer wanted to take the case to trial no matter what. He figured the resulting publicity would set him up to run for office. According to Foreman, Canale had doubts about Dwyer, claiming the chief prosecutor had told him, "If Dwyer ever detached from the state payroll, he'd expire of malnutrition."

Foreman said Judge Battle would go for a guilty plea owing to business community pressure to avoid a trial. Merchants and judge alike feared a black riot. Foreman even said Judge Battle was neglecting his husbandly obligations out of concern about the impact of an acquittal on the city's image. This concern led him to dispatch a courthouse lawyer, Lucius Burch, to ask the Southern Christian Leadership Conference, Dr. King's organization, to accept a guilty plea, Foreman said.

As February was ending, Foreman had no assurances that I'd plead guilty, so he resorted to terror tactics usually attributed to dictators. He said if I didn't plead guilty, my brother Jerry might be arrested for conspiracy to kill Dr. King. And, he added, my failure to cop a plea could bring federal authorities after my 77-year-old father. Already killed erroneously in print by *LIFE*, Daddy would be run down by government agents and sent back to the Iowa prison he'd escaped from 40-odd years before. Finally, Foreman said, if I insisted on a trial he couldn't swear that he'd do his utmost to defend me.

Foreman had begun promoting still another attorney as possible co-counsel. Well connected with the Republican and Democratic machines in Memphis, Benjamin Hooks had served as a criminal court judge there before resigning to accept a position with the SCLC. I didn't want Hooks as co-counsel—a defense assisted by a former criminal judge was tainted with conflict-of-interest, I said. Foreman never mentioned Hooks again, except to testify years later that I had vetoed him because he was black, which is untrue.

Copping A Plea

I was succumbing to the grind—the cage, the glare, the stale air, Foreman's incessant demands that I plead guilty. In late February, I tentatively agreed to enter a plea of guilty. Although I continued to press Foreman to take the case to trial, on reflection I suspect it was almost a feeling of relief to enter the plea and regroup.

Once I compromised my position by signing a paper saying Foreman had advised me to plead guilty, he began wearing a path between the jail and the attorney general's office with stipulations for me to sign. In all, there were 55. "Stips," as they're known in court lingo, describe the case against the defendant, step by step. My job was to ratify the state's case down to the last comma. The drill involved Foreman bringing me a list of allegations and asking me to certify their accuracy. Every time I objected to a stip, he marked it in pencil. Once we'd gone through a page of stips, he'd have me initial it, indicating my concurrence with all but the checked stipulations. Sheet in hand, Foreman would scuttle to the attorney general's office, where prosecutors would revise their version of the stips to conform to my objections.

This went on for days, until the stips were down to a few, leaving only those Judge Battle would read at the hearing where I'd officially plead guilty. This wasn't the last I saw of the stip sheets, however. Foreman later used them to defend himself in a suit I brought against him. My signature of approval appeared on each page, but Foreman had erased the penciled check marks where I had objected to the stipulation. With this kind of defense counsel, who needs a prosecutor?

The date for entering my guilty plea was set for March 10, 1969 (my 41st birthday). The package was wrapped up by March 7 in negotiations attended by Foreman, prosecutor Canale, Judge Battle and public defender Hugh W. Stanton Sr. Curiously, Stanton Jr., who was investigating the case for the defense, wasn't told I was copping a plea. He only learned about the deal by accident. On March 7, he telephoned Sheriff Morris on another matter and later said he was "amazed, surprised and astounded" when the sheriff told him I'd be pleading guilty on March 10.

During the final days before my plea, my brother John visited the jail. I said I was thinking of asking Foreman to withdraw from the case and defending myself. News of this promptly reached the media, probably via the cellblock microphone. Other reports had it that I was going to plead guilty. Alerted by these news stories, Foreman, who was at the Memphis airport about to board a plane for Houston, called Canale and said he'd received "a note from Ray" indicating I might discharge him. He was lying—prisoners weren't allowed to send "notes" out of the Memphis jail.

The next day Foreman phoned Huie from Houston, musing about whether I was still a client, then returned to Memphis and visited me in jail. He was upset, again implying that if I forced him to try the King case before a jury he wouldn't put forth his best effort, and again raising the specter of my brother and father going to jail. During this

March 9 meeting, I finally agreed not to stand trial for the assassination of Dr. Martin Luther King Jr.

Believing Foreman's desire for a plea to be solely financial, I suggested we contract with Huie and his publishers to have them pay Foreman $150,000. This was what we'd agreed would happen when Foreman first entered the case. Out of that sum, Foreman would give my brother Jerry $500 and would ask to withdraw from the case. Once the court approved this move, I'd use the $500 to retain another lawyer and take the case to trial.

Foreman refused. He said existing contracts entitled him to all proceeds anyway. And he reminded me that when he entered the case, Judge Battle in effect had said I wouldn't be able to change counsel again. But Foreman had a counter-offer: I'd plead guilty, he'd take a $165,000 fee generated by the contract with Huie and his publishers, and Jerry and I would get $500 to use in retaining another lawyer.

Short on options, I accepted. Foreman had two contracts drawn up. One covered the big payment, the other that $500 "donation." The second contract stated, "this advance [$500.00 for another attorney] also is contingent upon the plea of guilty."

The following morning I appeared in court to play my part in the scene scripted three days earlier by Foreman, Canale and Judge Battle. The stage directions called for the judge to ask me a battery of questions based on the stipulations and for me to answer yes or no as appropriate.

The only variation occurred when, after I formally entered my plea, and after explaining that he'd helped engineer my guilty plea to avoid seeing me sentenced to death, Foreman ad-libbed a speech praising those associated with the prosecution, including government agencies that had handled the investigation and their conclusions. He closed by endorsing the prosecution's no-conspiracy interpretation of the events of April 4, 1968.

I'd already pleaded guilty, but I stood up and objected to my attorney's underwriting of the prosecution's case. Foreman cut me off, saying I wasn't required to agree to anything. Judge Battle jumped in, rereading several questions he'd put to me during my guilty plea. When he finished the rereading, he directed me to sit down.

The sham squeaked to an end with Judge Battle registering some complaints of his own. He complained about having sentenced several convicted defendants to death only to see the perpetrators receive gubernatorial commutations, implying the futility of sentencing me to die. He also was exercised about a *Time* magazine article casually deriding Memphis as a hick town, and in response recited one of Winston Churchill's WWII exhortations to the embattled people of London, redirecting its message to his townsmen.

The day after I pleaded guilty, Foreman invited my brothers for drinks in his suite at the Peabody. When he'd first met them, he'd described himself as the "Texas Tiger." Now he seemed to feel he owed them an explanation for his meek performance in court. He told John and Jerry that commitments elsewhere would have kept him from devoting the necessary time to my case, especially since the trial would have run on a long time. After a couple of drinks, Foreman asked my brothers to appear with him at a news conference and back his story that the guilty plea was the wise thing to do.

Before they could answer, the telephone rang. It was Stanton Jr., with some news: Renfro Hays, the private eye Hanes had hired to investigate the case, hadn't been paid and was about to file a lien against the $10,000 Foreman had received from Huie.

Foreman broke for the door, complaining about "some bastard" being after his money. The last my brothers saw of him was his backside gathering speed down the hotel hallway. The Texas Tiger still had enough in his tank to beat his opponent to the teller's window and withdraw the cash before it could be frozen by a court order.

Chapter Thirteen

Music City Prisoner

After nearly eight months of midnight sun, on March 11, 1969, I was moved from Shelby County Jail to the state prison at Nashville, that sits beside the Cumberland River in west Nashville. Reporters had besieged the jail, waiting to tail the convoy, so deputies outfitted me with a disguise—a deputy's jacket over my prison uniform and a police riot helmet on my head. Taking me out just before dawn in a squad car, they fooled the newshounds for a while, gaining enough time to rendezvous with the state Highway Patrol on the outskirts of Memphis.

The Highway Patrol took me to Nashville, where my mid-morning arrival involved considerably more press attention than my departure from Memphis. My Highway Patrol escorts wanted to be in any news photos showing me in chains being led into jail, so they let the press know I was coming, and when. The first thing I saw at the prison entrance was a mob of reporters, photographers and TV cameramen.

It's been noted that the Nashville prison is a perfect outbuilding for a city known as an entertainment capital. I'd have to agree. From the outside, its turrets and bastions suggest Disneyland. But inside, there are far fewer laughs.

Once I'd run the gantlet of lenses and microphones, I was taken to Unit Six, a pillbox-like building inside the prison compound. Unit Six was Nashville's segregation section, but it was a far cry from my straw mattress days at JeffCity. Two small administrative rooms sat on either side of a lobby containing a guard desk where the keys were kept. The building's rear consisted of four narrow halls—"walks," in local slang—each 13 cells long, except for Walk Four. That hall had only eight cells. The rest of it was given over to the prison's electric chair.

Before locking me into cell two of Walk Three, the guard took the personal property I'd brought with me from Memphis. One piece of paper, a receipt from Shelby County for $10 my sister had sent me, also contained odd bits of information: backward phone numbers, partial phone numbers, fragmented addresses—all of which I'd obtained while in jail. Phone numbers from my 1967-68 association with Raoul also appeared on it. After confiscating my property, my jailers put me in the cell. Only a few minutes had passed when an inmate several cells down threw me a bar of soap with a note tied to it, warning me that the prisoner beside me in cell one was an informant. It looked as if the Confession Game was going into extra innings, this time with the prison administration trying to set up a revelation by a stool pigeon that I'd "confessed" to Dr. King's murder and whatever else the state wanted people to hear.

My cell in segregation was like any I'd ever occupied: drab and tight-fitting, about nine feet deep by six feet wide by ten feet high, with bars at the front, concrete at the back and a light at the center of the ceiling.

That afternoon, I got to stretch my legs when guards took me to one of the small rooms off the lobby for an interview with Harry Avery, the commissioner of corrections and one of Governor Buford Ellington's political appointees. He was accompanied by Warden Lake Russell. I was sure they had in mind to see if they could get me to make some self-incriminating statement about Dr. King's murder.

Avery began by returning the property confiscated from me, then set off on a meandering recital of his exploits as an insurance investigator before going on the state payroll. After expounding on several cases he'd solved, he said he thought the prosecution explanation of the King assassination was "silly," mocking the official story's "lone nut on the run" theme.

For a moment, Avery had me thinking I might have an ally in officialdom. It was nice to feel, however briefly, that someone in authority might think I'd been wronged.

But Avery quickly brought me to my senses, saying he thought I'd been properly tried and convicted, although he believed I'd committed the crime on behalf of clients. These "clients" had paid me large sums of money that I'd stashed away, he said, claiming he "knew" I'd buried the loot. He even offered to "dig it up" and place it in a bank for my exclusive use if I'd tell him where to find it. If I did this and didn't appeal my conviction, Avery said, I'd be treated like any other prisoner—that is, I'd be released from segregation. Commissioner Avery said he'd been authorized to make this offer by the "highest authority"—presumably Governor Buford Ellington.

Afterward, I wondered whether Avery had been serious. I'd never met a lawman who offered to dig up a prisoner's ill-got gains and deposit them in a bank for the culprit's personal use. Nor have I heard of any such offer since.

My second day at the Nashville prison, I was summoned for another audience. I was expecting Avery again, but my visitor was a man identifying himself as Robert G. Jensen, special agent in charge of the FBI field office in Memphis. He mainly wanted to hear what I knew about the conspiracy to murder Dr. King. Though Foreman no longer represented me, he had okayed the interview, apparently thinking the FBI would bolster his position by quoting me as incriminating myself.

Trying to get me to cooperate, Jensen offered the usual encouragement—if I refused, the authorities might jail one or another of my relatives. After a few minutes of nonproductive conversation, we returned to the lobby. There, Jensen introduced two other FBI agents; he said they'd visit in a day or so. I suggested they not bother, and they didn't.

The day after Jensen's visit, Commissioner Avery came calling again, bearing mail addressed to me. He said he'd had the mailroom intercept it, asked a few questions about the letters before giving them to me. He later told a congressional committee he had some of my letters but he had lost them.

The Death of Preston Battle

Commissioner Avery wasn't alone in his efforts to reinforce the prosecution's analysis. Now Foreman was talking it up in interviews and articles of his own, such as one in the April 15, 1969, *Look* magazine, in which he claimed I shot Dr. King because I wanted to become famous. He said I'd deliberately left my suitcase where it would be found after the shooting so that I'd be sure to get credit for what I'd done!

I'd intended to retain another lawyer, mount a serious investigation and then file for a new trial based on the resulting new evidence. Foreman's actions torpedoed that. I responded with a letter to Judge Battle stating that "famous Houston Atty. Percy Fourflusher [Foreman] is no longer representing me in any capacity." I added that I'd be asking the judge to set aside my guilty plea and said Foreman's comments about the King case didn't represent my view, but those of prosecutor Canale.

Around this time, my brother Jerry, who was searching high and low for any assistance he could muster, came up with another attorney, Richard J. Ryan of Memphis, as well as another lawyer recommended by Raulston Schoolfield, the former Tennessee judge who'd run afoul of a 1954 congressional inquiry into Teamsters Union corruption—an inquiry headed by Robert F. Kennedy and assisted by the then-young Memphis lawyer John Jay Hooker Jr. and the then-reporter John Siegenthaler, who later ran the *Nashville Tennessean*. Although Schoolfield had to get off the bench as a result of allegations that he was bent, he remained a player in Tennessee politics, and his Teamster connections had attracted Jerry's and my interest.

Ryan said he'd help. He also enlisted Chattanooga attorney Robert Hill and J.B. Stoner of the Georgia bar. In late March, Ryan drove the 200 miles from Memphis to Nashville to visit me in his status as my defense attorney. Commissioner Avery refused to let him into the prison, offering no explanation for that action.

I was increasingly apprehensive about Avery's informant in the next cell. As politely as I could, I told Avery in a note that I didn't intend to 'fess up to any murders. Soon after, he announced that as long as he was commissioner of corrections I'd never get out of segregation.

Denied the assistance of an attorney in seeking a new trial, I wrote out in longhand a formal petition dated March 26, 1969, and mailed it to Judge Battle. I asked the court to grant me a hearing before the expiration of the 30-day time limit on moving for a new trial. As grounds, I cited Foreman's reneging on his promise not to enter into publishing contracts before the trial. I knew Judge Battle was aware that Foreman had violated the court's order. I thought by formally raising the issue in my motion, I'd force him to rule officially on the misrepresentation.

But Judge Battle had rendered his last opinion, in my case or any other. After my guilty plea, he'd taken a vacation, then returned to his official duties on March 31. Sometime that afternoon, while perusing the papers I'd mailed him, he asked assistant prosecutor James Beasley to call River Bend and see whom I intended to have represent me in my petition for a new trial. A prison official relayed the judge's inquiry, and I gave him Ryan's name. The word got back to Beasley that afternoon. When he entered Judge Battle's office to give him the report, he found the judge slumped over my papers on his desk, dead of what would be described as a cardiac arrest.

I can't help but think Judge Battle's indirect query to me about representation indicated he was giving serious consideration to my petition. Even his death caused headaches for the no-trial crowd over speculation about the applicability of a Tennessee law, Statute 17-117, that states in part:

> *Whenever a vacancy in the office of trial judge* shall exist *by reason of death* . . . after the verdict but prior to the hearing of the motion for a new trial, *a new trial shall be granted* the losing party if motion thereof shall have been filed.

Briefly, it seemed that the King murder might go before a jury after all. But the day after Judge Battle died, Hamilton Burnett, chief justice of the Tennessee Supreme Court, informally stated that I wasn't entitled to a trial under Statute 17-117. The Tennessee court's ethics code deems it inappropriate for a jurist to go public with an opinion about a legal issue on which he might be called to adjudicate, particularly when he hasn't even had an opportunity to review the legal briefs submitted by attorneys for the opposing parties.

But Judge Burnett's extrajudicial pronouncement had its desired effect. When Ryan—by now certified to represent me, along with Hill—petitioned the Tennessee courts for a new trial under Statute 17-117, every lower court judge ruled against him. When my appeal finally reached the Tennessee Supreme Court, Justice Burnett recused himself from the case.

Chapter Fourteen

Brushy Mountain

I didn't have to put up with Commissioner Avery for long. His use of my case as a platform for grandstanding began to rile his patron, Governor Ellington, and on May 29, 1969, Avery got his walking papers—although he resurfaced later that year at a hearing on a petition I'd filed seeking to get out of segregation.

Judge William E. Miller put Avery on the stand, where he was asked why he'd confined me to segregation when I hadn't violated any prison rules—usually the reason inmates wind up in such a punitive setting.

Avery responded by pulling a letter from his pocket and beginning to read it, but the judge interrupted, asking to see the document. After scanning it, Judge Miller told Avery to put the document away. The contents of the letter, which from Avery's introductory remarks seemed to have come from Governor Ellington or William L. Barry, the governor's assistant, never entered the public record. However, I think it ordered Avery to keep me in segregation no matter what.

Judge Miller, a compassionate man who was dedicated to justice, ended the hearing by suggesting that my lawyers and the prison authorities enter into a consent decree keeping me in segregation, but not cellbound. I had to stay in that little pillbox—but at least I could walk around inside it.

The compromise robbed the politicians of the big stick they'd tried to use on me: embrace the official version of the King murder or you'll rot in segregation.

Of course, the prison administration soon was subverting the terms of the decree, imposing Mickey Mouse rules on my work schedule. For example, if someone else entered the building I often found myself suddenly hustled into my cell and locked up, ostensibly for "security" reasons. And if I did break a rule, I'd be back in 24-hour lock-up.

But the prison managers could see that this situation rendered them vulnerable to a court reprimand, and one morning in April 1970 I was given ten minutes to get ready for a transfer to Brushy Mountain state penitentiary outside Petros, Tennessee.

Located 40 miles west of Knoxville off a gravel road leading from Highway 116, Brushy Mountain became a maximum security prison in 1968, thanks mainly to topography. "Brushy," as it's called, sits in a narrow valley with the Appalachian Mountains at its sides and back. A small stream passes beneath the prison through a fortified conduit and empties out at the front of the enclosure. Trees grow as close as 35 feet to the walls. Towers manned by armed guards look down on either side of those walls, which are strung with high-voltage wire. About 40 feet out in front of the entrance stands a separate tower equipped with a machine gun and other weapons. Seeing the layout at Brushy, it's no surprise to hear that no one's ever escaped successfully from the place.

I did a few days in segregation, then was called into the office of Warden Lewis Tollett. Like most of his guards, Warden Tollett came from the mountains of East Tennessee. He was an old-school jailer who carried a pistol shoved down below his belt. Some prisoners said he packed a piece as much for protection from the guards as from the inmates.

"Judge Miller let it be known that you ought to be released from segregation," the warden said. "He's from East Tennessee, too, you know. He suggested your transfer here to Brushy."

I was soon moved to C-Block, whose occupants numbered about 20. We were somewhat segregated; we went to the recreation yard as a group, rather than with the two larger blocks, A and B. No doubt to make it easier for guards to check on me, I was assigned to a clean-up detail, which restricted me to C-Block.

The inevitable routine set in. I had heard from other convicts that an escape might be possible by entering a steam-pipe tunnel through a manhole behind C-Block. Between work and exercise periods I spent a lot of time checking my cell for flaws in its construction. Two sides were solid mortar, nearly impossible to penetrate. Bars covered the front of the cell. I figured at least one of my neighbors was an informant, so it wouldn't have been prudent to start sawing on the bars.

This left only the back of the cell from which to attempt an exit. Except for two ventilation grills near the ceiling, the rear cell wall was cinderblock, each block about eight by 16 inches. One night, after all the prisoners had been locked up, I began punching at the seams between the blocks with a piece of welding rod I'd gotten from another convict. I was looking for a weak spot at which to start a hole.

Nothing gave until I tested the seam holding one of the ventilation grills in place. On my first stab, my tool went in several inches—an indication that convict labor had laid the blocks and, having run low on concrete, had used any mixture at hand to seal the grill into place. I planned my next moves: assemble material to replace the mortar I'd be pulverizing, and schedule a little wrecking party.

Several nights later, having mixed a paste of soap, cigarette ashes and clothing lint to replace the mortar. I removed the grill. The guard had just passed my cell—he wouldn't be back for an hour or so. I crawled through the opening and set the grill back into place, then emerged into a narrow space separating two of the cell-block walkways. It was a pipe at the back of the chase—a hollow chamber containing plumbing and an exhaust fan big enough to crawl through, as I'd done so many years before at the Chinese restaurant in L.A. Of course, that time I was breaking in; this time, I'd be breaking out.

But someone had thought of that possibility. There were bars over the fan opening on the far side. However, if the fan could be turned off, one could reach in and saw out the bars. All I'd need to escape from C-Block would be a tool capable of bending the fan blades enough so I could squeeze through, and a couple of hacksaw blades to use on the bars at the front of the fan. Hacksaw blades are always available in a penitentiary if you have the price; it would be harder to find the crowbar or big wrench needed to bend the fan blades.

I needed help. Another C-Block resident, Jake Morelock, was the prison's plumber, which gave him access to pipe wrenches and the like. Jake was a big guy, with a belly to match. After deciding he wasn't an informant, I sounded him out about an escape attempt and outlined my plan. He said he was in. Since we weren't in strict segregation, we could talk in the yard or as we walked around. Cells usually aren't locked during the day, because inmates have to get to meals, work, classes and other activities.

I collected some saw blades. Jake had the other tools we needed. Then began my nightly trips into the chase to saw at the bars blocking the fan. During these ventures, I'd leave a dummy in my bunk so the guard would count me as present. I was satisfied that my work site was too far away for a stool pigeon to hear the scraping and sawing.

I worked carefully, sawing each bar nearly through but leaving a strand of steel to hold the bar in place. Then I'd take a variation on the soap-ashes-lint paste and smooth it over the gap left by my saw blade. All Jake had to do was wait for me to finish. Then we'd work together to stop the fan and slip outside. I'd figured a route that would take us to a manhole leading to a steam tunnel beneath the prison wall emptying 200 feet away in the woods. Unless we got careless, there seemed to be nothing that would expose us.

But early one morning, after a long stint of sawing, I lay sleeping in my bunk, so exhausted that I didn't hear the captain of security come up to my cell, watch me for several minutes, then begin tugging at the cell bars until he'd yanked on them all. When I woke up later and heard this story from a fellow who lived nearby, I realized we'd been turned in and could expect a shakedown at nightfall. I anticipated the guards locking us into our cells, then searching the building with a fine-toothed comb. That afternoon, Jake and I put extra effort into camouflaging the seams holding the ventilator in my cell in place.

Our work wasn't wasted. Around midnight, a dozen or so guards landed on C-Block in a surprise raid, herding us out of our cells into the walkways. They examined the bars of every cell for indentations, not bothering with walls or passageways, but found nothing incriminating.

Even so, Jake and I laid low for two weeks. After things cooled down, I started back on the night shift in the chase, working two nights a week while relief guards were on duty. Unlike the regulars, the night relief crew never conducted routine security checks near the point in C-Block where the passageway exited into the back area of the building. I also worried about informants hearing prolonged sawing noises, so I only worked for five minutes at a time, breaking for ten minutes before starting up again.

By April 1971, everything was ready. Each day, Jake left a pipe wrench in the passageway when he knocked off. I'd need it to bend the fan blades. The crowbar was in place. The bars had been sawn. We'd gotten some hair from the barber shop and made toupees for a couple of dummies—sets of clothing stuffed with shirts and other filler. We were going to make our break after the midnight count, but since it was April, we didn't need a lot of extra clothing. But we did need to get Jake into my cell at the appropriate time.

The Escape

The key was the log book in the guard office at the front of the block. Each night, the prisoners were counted in their cells. Some had cellmates, some didn't, but all cells had two bunks, so if a guard coming onto a shift saw two inmates in one cell, it wouldn't arouse his suspicion.

We'd noticed that about ten minutes before the C-Block guard shift changed at 2:00 p.m., the departing guard would move to a spot near the front door and wait for his replacement to arrive, leaving the office out of his line of sight. The day Jake and I were going to leave, I waited for the guard to move to the front door to await his replacement, slipped into the office and altered the log book. I erased Jake's name from his assigned cell and added it below mine in the space for my cell number.

Jake, whose plumbing chores gave him more mobility, joined me in my cell before the second-shift guard got around to making a head count. He took the upper bunk, I took the lower—both of us feigning sleep until the guard passed.

Midnight approached. We heard the guard jingling his keys as he ambled down the walk. The beam of his flashlight nosed around my cell for a moment, then the jingling noise receded. We waited 15 minutes, got the dummies out from under my bunk and removed the ventilator grill. Standing on a locker, we each squeezed into the passageway. Jake's girth made it a tight fit. As he was replacing the grill I was crawling to the switch that controlled the exhaust fan. I shut off the fan, picked up Jake's wrench and returned undetected. We were ready for business.

First we snapped the nearly severed bars on the far side of the fan housing—that was easy. Bending the fan blades apart took longer than we'd expected. I could feel the adrenaline beginning to pump as we struggled to shove the heavy blades to the side.

Jake tried first. His paunch kept hanging him up. He scraped himself up as he tried to force his way through the space, but finally had to give up and head back for the cell.

I made it through with no trouble. My main concern was the tower guard observing the ground outside C-Block, but I was able to crawl unseen the 20 feet or so to the manhole leading down to the tunnel. My information on that passage proved correct—up to a point. Once inside I found that the insulation on the steam pipes had deteriorated, leaving the tunnel far too hot to linger at an obstruction sawing bars. The heat drove me out of the tunnel where I crawled to the rear of nearby D-Block.

Suddenly, guards were everywhere around me, brandishing shotguns and sidearms. They hustled me to the segregation building, with nothing to show for my efforts but burns on my legs and arms.

Jake and I spent two months in segregation—not much time for an offense like ours, but perhaps a result of politics. The Tennessee governorship had gone to a Republican, Winfield Dunn, who replaced Warden Tollett with Robert Moore, who assigned Jake and me to A-Block.

I also changed jobs, moving into the laundry—a familiar place, since I'd worked in the laundry at other prisons. Things quieted down for me until February 1972, when guards found a sledgehammer, chisels and other tools obviously stashed for an escape attempt in a loft behind the movie screen in the auditorium where movies were shown on weekends. This was someone else's work, but because I'd been seen in the area—as had any prisoner who'd attended a movie—I was charged again with attempted escape and sent back to segregation for a couple of months. When I got out, I was assigned to B-Block. The state might have been able to stifle my attempts to get a trial, but it couldn't keep me from looking for a crack in the wall.

Chapter Fifteen

Shifting Around

At most prisons, few inmates are interested in trying to break out. The usual advice from a jailhouse honcho is to sit tight, keep quiet, and do your time. If you need sex, get yourself a punk. Whatever you do, don't start talking escape—that only brings down the heat.

But Brushy Mountain was different. A lot of guys were serious about breaking out, especially in the summer of 1972. Things were tense. The guards were pushing the administration for more money and better working conditions. And the administration wouldn't budge.

Things got so threatening that, like his predecessor, Warden Moore took to packing a pistol—not to defend himself from inmates, but from guards, who correctly saw him as the governor's man and therefore an adversary.

In July, the entire guard force went on strike, replaced immediately by Highway Patrolmen. Rather than give in to the union, Governor Dunn did what observers had been saying he'd wanted to do anyway. He closed Brushy Mountain and dispersed its inmates to facilities around the state.

On July 22, I was among the first group of Brushy Mountain prisoners sent to the main prison at Nashville. Not surprisingly, I was taken to segregation. Everyone else joined the regular prison population. On July 27, I asked for a release from segregation. Within two days, Warden Jim Rose granted my request. But on August 1, Warden Rose reneged. At a meeting in his office, he handed me a document claiming that as an escape risk, I'd be confined to segregation.

Rose said Governor Dunn had ordered the resegregation but might reconsider if I'd call off my lawyers. I declined.

Meanwhile, I was tangling with the Texas Tiger over the publishing contracts he'd had me sign. He wanted to keep the proceeds, which were supposed to finance a trial, not line his pockets. Since he'd crowbarred me into a guilty plea instead of fighting to get my case before a jury, I'd sued in civil court, asking Judge Miller to void the contracts. My attorney this time was Bernard Fensterwald Jr. of Washington, D.C. He was assisted by James Lesar and Robert Livingston.

In Foreman's corner was his old pal John J. Hooker Sr. His first move was to use a technicality to move my suit from Judge Miller's court in Nashville to a Memphis federal court presided over by Judge Robert McRae, a political ally of Hooker's. Judge McRae dismissed my complaint and ruled for Foreman straight down the line.

But the case didn't end there. When Hooker tried to collect his fee from Foreman, he got stiffed! Hooker had to sue to get his money.

After five months in one segregation unit, I was moved to another. Unit One was crammed to capacity, housing more than 350 prisoners, each of whom seemed to have a radio or stereo playing at full blast all the time. Unit One also had the usual extra tenants found in segregation—rats and insects flourished there.

Normally prisoners spent five or six months in segregation. I stayed in Unit One for three years. For the first 18 months, I was let out of my cell only once a day to take a four-minute shower. But I wasn't doing badly. One young prisoner was thrown into a cell with a known rape artist, who brutally worked him over. Within weeks the youth had set himself afire and burned to death. That was it—no administrative inquiry, no victim's rights protests, just a kid's corpse charred to a crisp.

Periodically, bad conditions or anger at being kept in segregation drove the inmates in Unit One to stage disturbances. The warden would send in the goons to drag a few honchos out for beatings—once enough heads had been whacked, things would settle down. But some protests were individual. To demonstrate against the depravity of living conditions in segregation, prisoner Charles Goins set fire to himself, burning 70 percent of his body.

All the time I was in segregation at Nashville, I never heard of any serious criticism about prison conditions by local politicians, including those with humanitarian reputations. Representative William R. Anderson (D., Tn.), in whose district the prison lies, once visited South Vietnam. Trailed by an army of reporters, he toured an island where prisoners were detained in "tiger cages." Anderson got a lot of ink for denouncing the "inhumanity" of Vietnamese-style detention, but he never opened his mouth about Nashville's rat-infested rape cages.

I was still trying to get a trial. In 1973 a ruling was pending concering the habeas corpus petition that I'd filed earlier. My petition sought an evidentiary hearing concerning the propriety of my guilty plea. This hearing would include live testimony and documentary evidence from both sides, after which the court would decide whether my guilty plea had been obtained by constitutional means.

I felt I had a sympathetic listener in Judge William E. Miller, now elevated to the U.S. Court of Appeals. However, Judge Miller's replacement in the Nashville U.S. District Court—to which I had to direct my request for a hearing— was a greying, cantankerous politician named L. Clure Morton, who'd managed campaigns for Senator Howard Baker (R., Tn.) and who didn't hesitate to deny me a hearing. He'd already gained control over the Tennessee prison system through a suit by informants and others in protective custody. They used federal funds from Legal Services Corporation to charge that the Tennessee prisons were operating unconstitutionally. When the state lost, Judge Morton ordered the prison to hire consultants who "suggested" ways to "improve" the system—to put an end to prisoner access to cash or tokens to spend in the commissary, for example, and handcuff prisoners being taken to and from segregation cells.

To understand Judge Morton's rulings in general and against me in specific, you need to take into account the motives of his patrons—Senator Baker and the Nixon administration, as well as former New York Governor Nelson Rockefeller, whose wing of the Republican party outlived its founder. The Rockefeller wing's big bucks and national influence flow to local allies who carry out the organization's wishes and reinforce its line of logic.

Regarding political murders and excesses by intelligence agencies, the Rockefeller thesis follows a pattern: form a commission to investigate the matter; publicize selected information from that inquiry that generally clears any government agency of any suspicion; classify material that doesn't support the commission's position.

This was how it worked when a Rockefeller commission investigated the CIA in 1975, following the model established by the media and legal system after Dr. King's murder.

In 1973, I was naïve about Tennessee politics—and national politics, for that matter—but I soon began to learn that the clannish nature of Mountain State political life had its echoes in the greater political process, where the Democrats and Republicans differ only in the width of their pinstripes, cooking up phony "issues" on which to take opposing stances when they have to go through the charade of an election.

Shifting Alliances

In December 1973, 16 months into my stay at Nashville, my health was again deteriorating. This, and my lawyers' efforts to get me a trial, led Governor Dunn to ask the Federal Bureau of Prisons to take custody of me—no surprise to me. The governor seemed to think his job was to continue my prosecution, not oversee my incarceration. Asked once how long he intended to keep me in segregation, he told a reporter he had no interest in furnishing me with comforts.

Now Dunn seemed intent on shifting me to the federal bughouse at Springfield, Missouri. One of his deputies came by my cell and told me to pack. Instead, I typed up a petition asking for a federal restraining order barring Tennessee from transferring me into federal custody, on grounds that Tennessee law makes no provision for the forcible interstate transfer of state prisoners.

My petition went to Judge Morton, who quickly ruled that his court had no authority to interfere. But while he was deliberating, news of the state's move reached the press. One report quoted state Attorney General David Pack as saying the legislature might have to pass a bill authorizing my transfer. Another article noted Pack's concern about potential legal difficulties that Tennessee authorities might encounter if the latest ruckus should cause the courts to order a trial in the King case.

The crew at the Federal Bureau of Prisons was panting at the prospect of locking me up at Springfield, where the United States was running a mind control program for "problem" prisoners.

But I never found out what the feds had in store for me. As federal interest in a transfer grew more voracious, Tennessee politicians began cooling to the idea. Following Pack's lead, other pols worried that if they let me out of Tennessee custody they might have trouble re-establishing custody should a trial materialize and the state have to prosecute, and the momentum behind a transfer vanished. I was still in segregation at Nashville, but I missed out on the mind control sessions.

I took heart from the state's abandonment of its proposal to transfer me. And I soon had more good news: my first favorable court ruling.

On January 29, 1974, Judge Miller's three-member appeals panel reversed Judge Morton's denial of a hearing on my habeas corpus petition, ordering a "full judicial inquiry" to see if the prosecution had acted unconstitutionally in procuring my guilty plea.

Judge Miller himself wrote the opinion in the 2-1 decision. The dissenting vote, by Judge Anthony Celebrezze, puzzled many. An old Great Society liberal whose appeals court votes usually were consistent with his long-time advocacy of individual rights, especially those of the poor, Judge Celebrezze did a complete about-face on my request to get to the heart of the King murder.

The appeals court ruling quickly drew fire in Tennessee media and political circles. *Nashville Tennessean* publisher John Siegenthaler and William Bradford Huie shared the stage on a TV talk show. Siegenthaler said I should never be released from prison. Huie questioned Judge Miller's integrity, suggesting he had ulterior motives in backing an inquiry.

There were official reactions as well. Judge Morton responded by refusing to take refuge in judicial discretion and ordering the inquiry transferred to the Memphis U.S. Court. There it was assigned to Judge Robert McRae, who had refused to dissolve my publishing contracts with Foreman. Like Judge Celebrezze, Judge McRae was a Democrat. He also liked to portray himself as a civil libertarian. He ordered attorneys for both sides to meet with him, and scheduled the inquiry to begin in October 1974.

My brother Jerry had been helping me all along. Now he and I had several months to amass every bit of information we could on the King case. It was a hard job, made harder by the dispersal of data and the aging—and sometimes the dying—of those involved in the case.

Back in 1969, I'd had Jerry get hold of Lawrence "Larry" Callahan, the steamfitters union president I'd met in 1956-57 while in Leavenworth. I wanted Callahan to use his connections to check into the phone numbers Raoul had given me prior to the King murder. Jerry had taken my list of numbers from Baton Rouge and New Orleans to the union man and asked Callahan for this favor.

Callahan took the lists. Three weeks later he called Jerry. Callahan was being careful. He had Jerry meet him in his car, where he handed over a slip of paper bearing the name "Z.T. Osborn" and a telephone number. He said Osborn wouldn't meet with Jerry personally for fear of government surveillance, but he would arrange to provide Jerry with information on the Louisiana telephone numbers. Callahan told Jerry to use the name "Larry" when calling Osborn.

Jerry did so, and got this message: "The male resident listed under the Baton Rouge phone number is a parish law enforcement officer named Herman A. Thompson. Thompson is under the influence of an official of the Teamsters Union named Edward Grady Parton, who is engaged in questionable activities, including connections with organized crime."

Jerry also had given Callahan a partial phone number somewhere in New Orleans, about which the report wasn't as conclusive. Callahan's connections had run down two possibilities with the same last four digits: "Laventhal Marine Supply" at 866-3757 and "Town & Country Motel" at 833-3757. The motel was run by Carlos Marcello, characterized in the press as a leading Southern mobster. Osborn, by the way, died on February 1, 1970, allegedly by his own hand.

Dusting off all these five-year-old nuggets, Jerry and I thought of trying to contact former Teamsters Union president James Hoffa, who might know things we could use in the hearing.

I'd had indirect contacts with Hoffa in the small world of prisonerdom. In 1971, at Brushy Mountain, a convict named Junior Grooms had approached me on the prison yard. He'd served time in the federal penitentiary at Lewisburg, Pennsylvania. During the same period Hoffa was at Lewisburg as a result of his conviction in a 1964 jury-tampering trial in Chattanooga, Tennessee. Grooms said he and Hoffa had become friendly. Hoffa was interested in the King murder, so much so that he asked Grooms to watch for and pass along any published material on it.

However, in 1971, Hoffa was attempting to gain a new trial and also maneuvering for a parole. Any involvement with the King case might have hurt those efforts and in the process foreclose our chances of learning what, if anything, the former Teamsters boss knew about the murder. So Jerry and I decided to put off contacting him.

But now it was 1974. Hoffa had been paroled, and it seemed like a better time to get in touch with him. Jerry telephoned his son, Michael, at the younger Hoffa's Detroit law office. The son seemed evasive and non-committal. Jerry sensed that another party, possibly even Hoffa Sr., was listening in. After this dead-end, Jerry contacted another source with Teamster connections: Raulston Schoolfield, the ousted criminal judge who had interceded on my behalf by asking attorney Robert Hill to represent me.

True, Schoolfield had credibility problems, but we weren't looking for a lecture on ethics. We were looking for hard information. Instead, we got riddles and enigmas.

Schoolfield told Jerry that Parton, once business agent for Teamsters Local 5 in Baton Rouge, had been a confidant of Hoffa's—until he testified against Hoffa in the Chattanooga trial. That case had grown out of an earlier one in Nashville, presided over by Judge Miller. In the Nashville case, federal prosecutors—using the powerfully persuasive tool of a 1962 indictment for embezzling funds from the Baton Rouge local—had gotten Parton to inform on Hoffa, sending him undercover to hear the Teamster leader's remarks about bribing jurors to block a conviction.

All this was a preface for Schoolfield telling Jerry that he couldn't talk about Hoffa or Parton in relation to the King case, although he did mention "shifting alliances" within the Teamsters Union. He implied that Parton was considering recanting his testimony so Hoffa could be exonerated for the jury-tampering conviction. This would erase a clause in Hoffa's parole barring him from holding office in the Teamsters Union.

The phrase "shifting alliances" recurs often in my case. Perhaps someday we'll learn why Jimmy Hoffa asked Junior

Grooms to clip all the stories he could find on the King assassination.

Chapter Sixteen

The 100-Mile Farce

While Jerry was talking to Raulston Schoolfield, Judge McRae was meeting with my attorneys and prosecutors. One participant was assistant state's attorney Henry Haile. The other was Bernard Fensterwald, my attorney and founder of the Committee to Investigate Assassinations, an outfit that inquires into politically oriented murders in the United States.

The appeals court had ordered a "full-scale inquiry," but Judge McRae sabotaged that possibility by ruling that no subpoenas would be issued for individuals or records located more than 100 miles from his court. Percy Foreman, a probably hostile but important witness, lived 500 miles away, in Houston. Worse, the 100-mile limit killed chances for subpoenaing the mounds of FBI records on the King murder, which were sealed and stored in Washington, D.C. Judge McRae and the powers he was protecting had less to lose by violating due process than by risking exposure of the FBI file on King.

We probably could have challenged and overturned the 100-mile limit, but Judge McRae had another gambit to use in the pre-hearing conferences. At these sessions, conducted in a judge's chambers, the threats and promises, the dealing and double-dealing, the bluffs and folds all take place. At one meeting the judge was talking with Haile and Fensterwald when Fensterwald voiced disappointment at the 100-mile limit. Judge McRae indicated that if Fensterwald would stop griping about that rule, he'd see to it that there'd be a public trial of the King murder once the inquiry was over.

Haile seemed to like the deal—which would have tipped me to think something wasn't straight. Haile had a reputation for being abrasive and aggressive. The only way he'd sit still for a judge's promise of a public trial in the King case would be if the judge had told him beforehand that he had no intention of delivering on that promise.

But Fensterwald took the judge's word, letting the limit go without an appeal. It was a great victory for the cover-up forces.

When the inquiry convened in October 1974, I was moved back to Shelby County Jail in Memphis. My lawyers—Fensterwald, Lesar and Livingston—visited me in jail.

"Judge McRae is offended if anyone laughs in his courtroom before he does," Fensterwald warned. "We should let the court decide what's funny."

Thanks to the incestuous nature of Tennessee politics, Haile took the lead for the state instead of the new state's attorney for Shelby County, who was none other than Hugh Stanton Jr.—a party to my guilty plea, which tainted him in the eyes of the law.

We had collected a lot of material to support our contention that my guilty plea had been the product of fraud and deception. We showed how Stanton Sr. had hot-footed it to the prosecutor's office the same day he was appointed to represent me, seeking to arrange a guilty plea. We showed the secret contracts between William Bradford Huie and his publishers, including a clause specifying that none of the proceeds was to go toward my trial, suggesting that they expected a guilty plea.

And besides the documentary evidence, we had live witnesses. Cab driver James McCraw already had testified that the state's eyewitness, Charles Q. Stephens, had been too drunk to walk when McCraw appeared at the Stephens room to pick him up a few minutes before Dr. King was shot. In a sworn February 3, 1969 statement, McCraw also had said when double-parking to fetch Stephens, he saw *two* white Mustangs parked at the curb in front of the building from which Dr. King allegedly was shot, casting great doubt on the official story. (McCraw's statement appears on page 129)

We also produced records proving that Shelby County Sheriff William N. Morris had intercepted my letters to my first lawyer, Arthur Hanes Sr. and forwarded them to prosecutor Canale. Copies were also made for the FBI, where they were scrutinized by Cartha DeLoach, the Bureau's number three man and head of its Counter-Intelligence Program, better known as COINTELPRO.

These documents were significant in that they showed why the state of Tennessee wanted a guilty plea and revealed what the state had done to obtain that plea. But the best evidence in favor of a trial in the King case were the actions of Percy Foreman, Phil M. Canale and William Bradford Huie.

Although he was outside the 100-mile subpoena zone, we asked Foreman to testify voluntarily in defense of his role in obtaining my plea. He refused. Huie, who also lived too far away to be subpoenaed, said he had to look after his sick mother. Memphis resident Canale did testify, but without producing certain papers demanded by the subpoena served on him. These were memoranda chronicling Canale's negotiations with Foreman and others trying to engineer a guilty plea.

At the beginning, Judge McRae seemed solicitous of my attorneys. But as the inquiry wound down, his attitude hardened.

The defense rested. The prosecution offered little of substance. Without his principal mouthpieces, Huie and the Texas Tiger, Haile had to rely mainly on disruptive tactics, objecting to questions and challenging subpoenas.

Haile's sole witness had a vested interest in the official line on the King murder. He was Victor Timkin, general counsel for Bantam Books, which had published two books echoing the state's version of the case and would publish another.

Timkin testified that my guilty plea hurt sales of his firm's King assassination books. His appearance permitted Judge McRae to decide that my plea also hurt Huie and Foreman by diminishing cash flow from their publishing ventures on the subject.

After Haile's presentation, Judge McRae took the case under advisement. In February 1975 he ruled on my request: there would be no trial in the King murder.

Beneath a photograph of the judge a United Press International article in the February 28 *Knoxville News-Sentinel* described the state's reaction:

> Members of the State's Attorney General's staff cheered exultantly and pounded each other on the back when the news came that a federal judge in Memphis had ruled in favor of the State following an evidentiary hearing for Ray last year.

Judge McRae's decision reflected the nature of power. Rather than look for judicial precedent to rationalize his denial, he took refuge in judicial discretion, as Judge Morton had in moving the inquiry to Memphis. Instead of addressing my arguments on their merit, Judge McRae simply deflected them. Again and again throughout his opinion, he referred to the points my attorneys had raised, and one by one discarded them without refuting them. On the issue of the sheriff violating client-attorney privilege by intercepting and copying my letters to Hanes Sr., Judge McRae said these actions hadn't contributed to my guilty plea—without answering the question of whether fear of being caught in this practice had spurred the prosecution to push even harder for a guilty plea. And anyway, the judge said, my guilty plea automatically absolved the prosecution of any "deprivations of constitutional rights that occurred prior to the entry of the guilty plea."

The only constitutional issue before the court, the judge said, was whether I had pleaded guilty "voluntarily," as if the events that followed my arrest in London were some dream, ending when I awoke in that courtroom in Memphis and said, "Guilty, your honor."

Judge McRae capped his opinion by again invoking attorney-client privilege, saying this limited any judge's inquiry into that relationship, financial or otherwise. Any such inquiry should necessarily have limitations, he said—obviously a reasonable finding, but one from which he extrapolated that the late Judge Battle should not have been expected to inquire into contracts between me and Percy Foreman. Judge McRae's invocations of attorney-client privilege offer strange counterpoint. In his court, a sheriff can steal, read and circulate copies of privileged mail from a client to his attorney, but a trial judge can't ask about a potentially corrupting influence—such as the Ray-Foreman contracts—involving attorney and client.

Upon obtaining a transcript of the hearing, my lawyers appealed to the U.S. Court of Appeals in Memphis, where Judge William Miller had been part of the panel that had provided my lone success with the judicial system since the King murder. We felt chances for a reversal of Judge McRae's decision were good, which would pave the way for a trial.

The Appeal

After both sides had filed briefs, the appeals court ordered oral arguments before a three-judge panel, to take place February 3, 1976. Immediately after such a presentation, the judges retire to chambers and vote on their decision. Then a member of the majority writes the opinion, which is published months later, with copies furnished to the parties involved—and, if the case is sensational, to the media.

The appeals court's ruling would be crucial. For practical purposes, such decisions are final—only about three percent of appeals court decisions are granted a hearing by the U.S. Supreme Court. The rest are summarily affirmed. If the Sixth Circuit ordered a trial, all the humbug strewn by state and national politicians and collaborators in the press would go up in smoke, especially if, during the trial, government agencies had to declassify their records on the King murder.

Those opposing a public trial reacted predictably, led by *Time* magazine. Continuing in the tradition of the "Mean Kid" story by sister publication *LIFE*, *Time* now went on the offensive. Its January 26, 1976 issue included an article about me that swerved between hysteria and malice. Timed perfectly to influence the appellate judges, the article took the form of a feature story cum book review. As yet unpublished, the book—*The Making of an Assassin*—was by so-called "Southern writer" George McMillan, who'd once unsuccessfully offered me $5,000 to do an interview. *Time's* write-up occupied four pages at the front of the issue—a lot of space and some very prominent placement for a story about an unpublished book. It should be noted, McMillan's publisher was Little, Brown—a Time, Inc. subsidiary.

Time clearly had two goals: to let the judges on the Sixth Circuit Court of Appeals know the media would support them if they let stand Judge McRae's decision not to allow a trial, and to intimidate the panel into affirming.

In May 1976, the appeals court ruled unanimously against a trial in the King assassination.

The Death of Judge Miller

But was the panel truly unanimous in its decision? On April 12, after the vote in chambers on the oral arguments, but before publication of the decision, Judge Miller suddenly died—in circumstances closely resembling those in which Judge Preston Battle had succumbed. Just like Judge Battle, Judge Miller died of cardiac arrest in his chambers, while studying papers on the King murder case.

The powers opposing a jury trial had reason to be concerned about Judge Miller's disposition. He was of East

Tennessee mountain stock, a breed not known for relying on the guidance of Manhattan media moguls. And he'd been appointed to the bench in 1955, before the Tennessee courts came under the influence of Nashville publisher John Siegenthaler and the Rockefeller organization. No one can say how Judge Miller would have come down on my appeal, but his earlier opinions had reflected an independent and analytical mind, one unlikely to be railroaded into opposing a trial. (In 1971, Judge Miller had condemned Foreman's dabbling in publishing while my trial was pending, describing them as "strongly suggestive of an inherent conflict of interest on the part of defendant attorney.") In a footnote to their ruling, his colleagues, Anthony Celebrezze and Harry Phillips, claimed Judge Miller had been on their side. We have only their word for it.

Chapter Seventeen

Media Madness

Time's "lone nut" solution to the King assassination is part of a pattern. Whether writing of politically oriented killings in the United States or abroad, the magazine tends to argue against investigations and to ridicule the results of such inquiries. Rather than admit to the possibility of conspiracy or encourage readers to wonder what really goes on in the world, *Time* promotes the more comfortable notion that such murders are the work of madmen on the run. *Playboy*, for different reasons, supported the government line on the King case.

Consider the 1981 shooting of Pope John Paul II, of which *Time* lamented, "Somewhere in the tangled skein of Mehmet Ali Agca's life lay answers. As his history unravels in the weeks to come, the best news, after all, might be that *he did indeed act alone* [emphasis added]."

When that article appeared, Italian authorities were investigating leads suggesting that agents of the Bulgarian government, acting in complicity with the Soviets, had been behind the shooting in St. Peter's Square. Findings to that effect would have rocked *Time's* cozy worldview, as noted by NBC correspondent Marvin Kalb on January 25, 1983.

"The CIA has been attempting to suppress the investigation into the shooting by discouraging newsmen and the Italian Magistrate's investigation of the shooting because of its possible effect on United States/Soviet relations," Kalb said.

Time seems to see its job as regulating readers' anxieties about many matters, but especially political murders—unless the killing happens to involve someone whose viewpoint doesn't fit its cookie-cutter. *Time's* reporting on the 1978 assassination of newspaperman Pedro Joachin Chamorro in Managua, Nicaragua, blamed a conspiracy within the Nicaraguan government, whose agenda didn't match up closely enough with *Time's*.

A certain type of person writes on political murders for the American media establishment. One such writer is George McMillan.

McMillan, who came up in Knoxville, has roots below the Mason-Dixon line but debts on the eastern seaboard. He began writing professionally in 1938, at the federal Office of War Information, which churned out propaganda and managed the news of World War II. He left that job in 1943 but continued writing, over the years gaining admission to the fraternity of "Southern writers."

McMillan was clear about his agenda regarding the King assassination right from the start. "I have always believed James Earl Ray did it alone," he told the *New York Times* in 1969. "And I have never investigated any aspects of a conspiracy, which has left me free to work on his biography."

McMillan spent six years on his manuscript, often contacting my sister Carol and brother Jerry. He won their cooperation by pretending that his writings on the King case would help me gain a trial.

In the early days, he considered shelving his book, first because of a severe case of hemorrhoids, then due to depression. In the early 1970s he wrote Carol that he'd become despondent, implying he might not finish the book. He probably was down because my guilty plea precluded the need for any more propaganda about the King assassination.

McMillan's fortunes improved dramatically when the specter of a trial rose again, and he continued to gain credence during efforts by the House Select Committee to investigate the assassinations of both Dr. King and President John F. Kennedy. *The Making of an Assassin* hewed to the "lone nut" line, receiving rave reviews throughout the literary establishment and earning its author a gratuity from the Rockefeller Foundation—a scholar-in-residence position in Bellagio, Italy.

In 1976 another McMillan got into the assassination publishing business: Priscilla Johnson McMillan, George's second wife and herself an author writing on JFK's murder.

A 1953 Bryn Mawr graduate who majored in Russian, she got an M.A. in Russian studies at Harvard and eventually wrote several books about Soviet personalities, demonstrating a link with her husband by showing an interest in individuals somehow entangled in the workings of American intelligence agencies. Like the husband's work, the wife's tends to reflect the official opinion of whatever is under discussion.

After Harvard, Priscilla Johnson worked as a researcher for then Senator John F. Kennedy (D., Ma.). She left his staff in 1955 and moved to Russia, where she found work as a translator for a Moscow press service operated by the embassies of several Western nations.

In 1959 she became a reporter for the leftist newspaper *The Progressive,* covering Moscow. American consul John McVickar suggested she do a story on an American defector, Lee H. Oswald, giving her Oswald's address on November 16, 1959. That evening, at the Metropol Hotel, she interviewed the former Marine. The next day, McVickar debriefed her on the Oswald interview. After Kennedy and Oswald were shot, Priscilla McMillan's early contacts with the alleged assassin made her an authority of sorts. She was among those promoting the "lone gunman" theory, and later wrote a book about Kennedy's murder.

Her acquaintance with Lee Harvey Oswald wasn't the only example of Priscilla McMillan's impeccable timing. In

1967, Svetlana Alliluyeva, Joseph Stalin's daughter, came to the United States, winding up as a guest of Priscilla's parents. Priscilla soon established a relationship with Svetlana, translating her memoir, *Twenty Letters to a Friend,* into English. The finished product was a best seller.

With her insider's credentials and her tacit acceptance of official explanations, Priscilla McMillan was tailor-made for a book on the Kennedy murder. Not only had she been laboring over her book about the Kennedy assassination for 13 years, she'd been maintaining a lock on access to the main witness in the Kennedy case, Marina Oswald. At times the two shared a residence, perhaps as a way for Priscilla to fend off the competition.

The House Select Committee inquiry into Kennedy's assassination coincided with the publication of Priscilla's book, in which the lone nut line was a bit juicier. Priscilla wrote that Marina had a crush on JFK. When Marina informed her jealous husband, he set out to eliminate his "rival," Priscilla wrote.

Both McMillans' books advanced the analysis embraced by the establishment and the media princes. George McMillan even claimed—to my brother John—that the FBI had given him access to its otherwise sealed files on the King murder.

The McMillans were only two of the newsgathering herd thundering around the King case. Once the Select Committee on Assassinations began its work, the panel was covered by a succession of writers selected by their various employers for their ability to integrate new information into the official version of the case without changing its essential conclusions, and without lending credence to any perspectives challenging the official line.

The tone and content of *Time's* article are clear from one caption: "I'M GONNA KILL THAT NIGGER KING!"—a vow McMillan claimed I'd made in Memphis the day before Dr. King was shot. He said his source was my brother Jerry. The article went on to characterize me as a drug user and deviate, and incorporated demeaning sketches, such as one of me aiming a rifle.

McMillan said I'd often watched Dr. King on television in my cell at JeffCity during 1963-64. According to him, each time I saw the civil rights leader's image on the screen, I'd fly into a rage, clench my fists and shout, "Somebody's gotta get him! Somebody's gotta get him!"

This is an extremely effective and dramatic scene, whether in a book or a magazine. But there's one problem: it never happened. In 1963-64, there were no television sets in the cells or on the cellblocks. Prisoners didn't have such access to TV until 1970, three years after my escape.

In fact, during my abbreviated stay at Missouri State Prison, there was only one TV set to which prisoners had any access. On weekends, guards would put a set on the roof of the recreation shack and tune in ballgames. A lot of money rides on sports events watched in prison, and the tension in the audience at JeffCity during a game was always so high that if someone had wigged out in the manner described by McMillan, he'd have been knocked out—not for slurring Martin Luther King, but *for interrupting the show.*

Libel Proof

I answered *Time's* falsehoods by suing the magazine—and McMillan—for libel, also naming Henry Haile, who'd run the state's side of things in the habeas corpus hearing and had given McMillan access to the attorney general's file in the King case. I also charged the defendants with obstructing justice, by publishing the article with the intent of getting the Sixth Circuit to rule against the habeas corpus appeal.

My suit was assigned to Memphis U.S. District Court Judge Harry Wellford, who carried his use of the court's discretionary power beyond the brink of absurdity. After my attorneys filed the initial papers, the suit inched along, with McMillan's attorneys vehemently resisting discovery. In this process either party to a suit submits pre-trial questions to be answered under oath by the opposing party. After

McMillan's and *Time's* lawyers said it would be burdensome for their clients to have to undergo discovery, Judge Wellford ruled that neither defendant would have to go through the process. If a plaintiff in a libel case cannot compel a defendant to answer questions under oath, it is difficult, if not impossible, to show the court that there is sufficient evidence to justify a trial. This sets up the court to dismiss the suit in summary judgment.

Once the court had insulated *Time* and McMillan from our interrogatories, their lawyers asked Judge Wellford to find me "libel-proof." Due to past criminal convictions I had no standing to sue under the laws governing defamation, they claimed. Removing my standing would let *Time* print known fabrications about me. Judge Wellford accepted this argument and dismissed my suit. On appeal, the Sixth Circuit upheld his decision.

But the "libel-proof" label had been rejected in similar circumstances. In a suit originating in Detroit, the same Sixth Circuit previously had permitted a plaintiff with a felony conviction to sue under defamation laws. And the U.S. Supreme Court rejected the "libel-proof" defense before and after *Time* and McMillan used it on me. But Judge Wellford's acceptance of that argument again forestalled a trial in the King murder.

Playboy

Nashville attorney Jack Kershaw was representing me to handle an interview with *Playboy* magazine, which wanted to talk with me about the King case. I had Kershaw set some ground rules: no funds would be paid to any party for the interview, and Kershaw would have power of attorney to review galleys before publication and delete any answers I hadn't given, as well as any questionable innuendos that might crop up. At *Playboy's* request, the arrangement was expanded to include my undergoing a polygraph examination.

But when the interview hit the newsstands in September 1977, it read like a prosecutor's brief, buttressed with incriminating conclusions drawn from the polygraph results. The article went so far as to challenge my statement about finding a business card bearing the initials "L.E.A.A." stuck down between the seats of the Mustang just before I came from Mexico into the United States in November 1967. *Playboy* claimed the Law Enforcement Assistance Administration hadn't been created until August 1968. But if the editors had bothered to contact the Justice Department, they'd have learned that in 1967 two L.E.A.A. pilot projects were under way—one was in Newark, New Jersey, and another in New Orleans.

Playboy vigorously promoted the issue in the Atlanta area, home of Rev. King's Southern Christian Leadership Conference, suggesting that all along the magazine's editors intended to convince influential blacks to accept the government's story on the King killing.

Only after the interview ran did I learn of what seemed to be a squeeze plan run on *Playboy* by the authorities. The magazine and its editor, Hugh Hefner, had legal problems so great they easily could have persuaded Hefner to help manage public opinion in the King case.

In 1975, the U.S. Attorney in Chicago obtained a conviction and 15-year prison term for Bobbie Arnstein, a very close Hefner aide. The charge: conspiracy to distribute cocaine. Arnstein supposedly committed suicide after being pressured by the government to implicate Hefner in the drug scene.

Had *Playboy* made a deal with Uncle Sam? Consider the fruits of the interview. The government won invaluable publicity backing its version of the King assassination just as Congress was investigating the case. Hefner escaped indictment on drug charges. My attorney, Jack Kershaw, received $11,000 in "consultation fees" from *Playboy*—even though the contract he'd supervised specified that no participants would be paid for the interview. The Tennessee Supreme Court's Board of Professional Responsibility, which oversees

ethics in the Tennessee legal community, saw nothing un-
ethical in Kershaw's receiving money when he'd agreed not
to, but I wasn't quite so comfortable, so I contacted Mark
Lane.

Chapter Eighteen

The Select Committee

In August 1975, after three years in segregation at Nashville, I was finally released into the general prison population. For the next year I worked in the laundry.

One night in September, 1976, guards awoke me at 3:00 a.m. with the news that I was being transferred again, with no hint of my destination. I hastily packed my legal papers and personal items and was on my way, arriving five hours later at Brushy Mountain, recently reopened pursuant to a 1974 campaign promise by Governor Ray Blanton.

Except for some new equipment, Brushy was the same old place. I spent a few days in lock-up, then went back to laundry maintenance, the job I'd had when the strike closed the prison. The laundry was one area that had gotten a renovation. The contractors had put in new washing machines without picking up after themselves, so those of us on the laundry crew had to give the building a good cleaning.

During that task, I came across several sections of pipe three or four feet long. Thinking that they might come in handy, I stashed them temporarily. Later, when I was alone in the laundry, I hid the pipes more permanently inside the motor cover of one of the new washers.

After considerable wrangling, the U.S. House of Repre-
sentatives voted on September 17, 1976, to form a Select
Committee to investigate the murders of President Kennedy
and Dr. King. The main advocates for such a panel had been
Reps. Henry B. Gonzalez (D., Tx) and Thomas H. Dowling
(D. Va.), along with the Citizen's Committee on Inquiry, a
private group founded in February 1975 by attorney/author
Mark Lane.

Representative Gonzalez chaired the committee, whose
staff director and chief counsel was Richard A. Sprague.
Sprague brought impressive credentials as an investigator
and prosecutor. He'd served as an assistant district attorney
in Philadelphia, and numbered among his accomplishments
the conviction of W.A. "Tony" Boyle and others in the 1970
murders of dissident United Mine Workers leader Joseph A.
Yablonski, his wife, and their daughter.

Once installed as chief counsel, Sprague promised a
thorough investigation into the Kennedy and King murders.
He told the *Washington Star* he would subpoena sealed
government files to do so—a signal that he didn't intend to
rubberstamp the results of prior Justice Department.
reviews.

Predictably, Sprague's irreverence shocked the King case
prosecutors and their allies, not to mention the media parrots
accustomed to echoing the prosecution's line. These camps
reacted in character.

The prosecutors began destroying or hiding records related to the King murder. In Memphis, officials did away
with—or said they had done away with—a mass of pertinent
material collected by the "intelligence" unit of that city's
police department. Mayor Wyeth Chandler ordered the
destruction just before the American Civil Liberties Union
filed suit on September 14. It was an odd suit since all parties
wanted the surveillance files destroyed.

The ACLU's goal had been to end extra-constitutional
snooping, not delve into the results of it. Without determining conclusively that the files actually had been destroyed—
Mayor Chandler was quite public in announcing their

elimination, but more than one politician has claimed to have done something while doing nothing—the civil libertarians entered into a consent decree with the city that supposedly guaranteed no more police department snooping. As part of the decree, all parties waived any hearings or fact-finding proceedings—which might have revealed exactly what Mayor Chandler allegedly had destroyed, and whether he in fact did destroy it.

The resolution of the ACLU suit echoed a recommendation by an earlier Senate investigative committee that 1960s-vintage FBI files on the activities of Dr. King and others be destroyed. That suggestion wasn't followed—under a federal court order, these records, including audio tapes, occupy 58 cubic feet of storage space in the National Archives, sealed from public examination until the year 2027.

To many, the abbreviated action in Memphis seemed more cover-up than conflict. Were prosecutors afraid the Select Committee would subpoena the King records assembled in Memphis? Rather than risk charges of contempt of Congress or obstruction of justice by destroying records under a congressional subpoena, did Mayor Chandler use the ACLU suit as a pretext for destroying the records?

The media was silent on the reported file destruction, but Sprague's vow to unseal classified files became an obsession with the scribes. Leading the attack against Sprague were the *New York Times* and *Washington Post*.

The Select Committee's authorization to investigate expired January 3, 1977, requiring Congress to reauthorize the panel if it was to remain in business. On the eve of a vote to do so, a *New York Times* editorial attacked both Richard Sprague and the validity of reauthorization. And on the actual day of the reauthorization vote, the Justice Department leaked a report on the King case.

Task force director Michael Shaheen was an old, if indirect, acquaintance of mine. His first job at Justice had been in the Office of Profession Responsibility, where he routinely rebuffed my requests for files on the King killing. And while in law school, he'd clerked for Judge McRae in Memphis.

Considering these credentials, it was no shock to me that the Shaheen report generally reaffirmed the prosecution's position in the King case, to much media applause.

But editorials and leaked reports don't always prevail completely. The House voted to reauthorize the Select Committee—until March 31, 1977, at which time another reauthorization vote would take place.

This gave the media 60 days to hammer the committee and chief counsel Sprague. Familiar voices rose up to defend the status quo. For example, a February 27 *Washington Star* op-ed article praised the Shaheen report. Its author: George McMillan.

During this period, Sprague and deputy Robert Lehner visited me at Brushy Mountain. In the interview, which was tape-recorded, Sprague reiterated to me and my lawyer his intent to run a thorough inquiry into Dr. King's murder and to uncover and prosecute all those who'd had a hand in it. I said I'd tell what I knew, but emphasized that my cooperation wouldn't include acting as a state witness in any prosecution. We came to terms: I would testify fully and the committee would not hold anything back that might help my case.

His conversation with me was Sprague's last substantive act as Select Committee chief counsel. He'd promised to be thorough in his inquiries, but the real thoroughness on display was that of the media, which worked overtime to discredit him. This campaign succeeded so well that Sprague's continued presence on the staff seemed likely to doom reauthorization. In late March, he resigned, followed soon after by panel chairman Gonzalez.

With Sprague and Gonzalez gone, the House authorized the committee to complete its work; however, the resignations of its main players reduced the panel's bang to a whimper.

Chairman Stokes

When Representative Gonzalez gave up the Select Committee chairmanship, House Speaker Thomas O'Neill replaced him with Representative Louis Stokes (D., Oh). Stokes, a black, represented Ohio's 21st Congressional District, which includes a large section of Cleveland. To fill out the panel's Republican side Minority Leader John Rhodes (R., Ca.) recommended four members of his party.

Chairman Stokes replaced departed chief counsel Sprague with G. Robert Blakey. Like Sprague, Blakey had strong credentials as a lawyer and criminologist. Unlike his predecessor, Blakey was more fluid in his stand on organized crime. In 1965 a presidential crime commission chose Blakey, then a law professor at Notre Dame University, to prepare a special report on organized crime bosses in Chicago who had been able to corrupt law enforcement officials, including judges.

Blakey may have talked tough about the Chicago mob in 1965, but in a 1976 Los Angeles libel suit, he provided what amounted to a character reference for Morris "Moe" Dalitz, a mobster with roots in Cleveland. Dalitz, a close associate of the late mob banker Meyer Lansky, had joined several other plaintiffs suing *Penthouse* magazine over an article referring to Dalitz's underworld ties. *Penthouse* eventually prevailed, but Blakey stood up for Dalitz.

However, Blakey's mob stains interested me less than his media connections; in an earlier life, he'd consulted with *Time* magazine. I didn't need a crystal ball to see which conclusions this edition of the Select Committee would reach.

During the panel's inquiry, Select Committee staff members periodically interviewed me. In answering their questions I usually relied on memory. Relying on recollection alone, instead of going to notes and records, is an effective way to recall incidents from years before in detail. (Few of us have perfect memories, so the process can be flawed, but overall this method, if subjected to challenge and refinement, eventually produces as factual a reconstruction of events as possible.)

A factual resolution of the King murder was the Select Committee staff's stated aim. However, when the committee reports appeared, they suggested or outright stated that all my initial misstatements were deliberate fabrications rather than first-stage attempts to remember what had happened.

The distortions worried me. Mark Lane was suspicious, too. Committee lawyers were interrogating me without putting me under oath but assured me that an unintentional misstatement didn't really matter. Lane demanded that I be sworn in so that if I perjured myself, the committee would have to turn to the courts to get at the truth. When the committee began putting me under oath, Lane and I could see my inquisitors were trying to maneuver me into making misstatements. After my December 2, 1977 session with them, I stopped testifying altogether.

Radio Silence, Secret Transmissions

As of 1978, the Select Committee curtailed its official contacts with the media. Members eschewed press conferences and interviews—although members often leaked tantalizing bits of information as the panel was asking the House for more money. These well-timed clandestine releases tended to cause a ruckus on the House floor, instigated by congressmen skeptical of the Select Committee, ostensibly on economic grounds.

The main voice of skepticism was that of Representative Robert Bauman (R., Md.), a strident conservative who said the committee shouldn't get any more money until it shared its preliminary findings with the rest of the House. Bauman interpreted the panel's reluctance in this regard to mean that nothing was being accomplished. He found allies among those who had other reasons to squelch any inquiry into the King case.

By keeping a low media profile, the Select Committee was able to conceal the ways in which its members were operating outside the law in developing hypothetical solutions to the King murder. Indeed, the committee may have deliberately introduced misleading information into the investigation to draw attention away from those responsible for Dr. King's murder.

During the committee's two-year existence, I learned a great deal about people alleged to be connected with the case. Some information came from identifiable sources; other reports were sent anonymously. I suspect some anonymous information was coming from Select Committee staff members trying to get me caught in a public error by accepting one of their secret transmissions as gospel and taking it to the press, permitting the committee to shoot down their straw man once the hearings started.

One of the more intriguing anonymous communications arrived in early 1978. Someone sent a photograph to my brother Jerry, attaching a note asking him to show it to me. The picture was of a Latin male who looked like my old traveling companion Raoul. On the back of the photo was written the name "Carlos Hernandez Rumbaut." I asked Jerry to compare the photo with pictures in publications and elsewhere. He found nothing solid. (In July 1979, after the Select Committee investigation ended, I sent the photo to my brother John in St. Louis, asking him to check it against picture archives at the main library, especially those showing alleged drug dealers. He made a copy of the photo and sent the original back to me, along with other materials. I got the package but not the photo. A few days later, federal marshals arrested John at his residence, booking him for violating his parole on an aiding and abetting a bank robbery conviction. This put him behind various bars for six months. Upon his release, John found that his house had been rifled and numerous things taken—including his copy of the "Rumbaut" photo.)

I finally did find out about the Raoul lookalike in the mysterious picture. Tom Jennings, a Mobile, Alabama, reporter, sent me an article he had written for the March 4,

1974 *Mobile Register* about the arrest of Carlos Hernandez Rumbaut, spelled "Rumbant" by some, for possession of 500 pounds of marijuana. Convicted, Rumbaut skipped bail and later turned up in Costa Rica. The article was accompanied by a photograph—which showed not the man depicted in the photo I'd been sent, but someone who strongly resembled one of the fellows I'd seen eyeballing me in Jim's Grill, the bar beneath the flophouse, shortly before Dr. King was shot.

The First Hypothesis

The committee's first hypothesis about the King homicide grew out of the FBI files. In March 1978, agents at the Bureau's St. Louis field office were going through a standard procedure—reviewing an informant's file. The dossier contained a March 19, 1974, memorandum that referred to 1973 remarks by St. Louis mobster Russell G. Byers. The informant quoted Byers as saying that he once was offered big money to kill Martin Luther King Jr.

According to the Select Committee, as soon as the FBI came upon this document, a copy was given to committee investigators, who found Byers at his residence outside St. Louis. Byers denied the story about being offered a bounty to kill Dr. King, or so the investigators said.

But after consulting with an attorney, Byers said he'd testify about the matter in exchange for immunity from prosecution. The panel agreed, and on May 9, 1978, Byers appeared before the committee in executive session. He testified essentially as follows:

In later 1966 or early 1967, a buddy and business associate, John R. Kauffman, asked Byers if he'd like to earn $50,000. Byers asked what he'd have to do. Kauffman invited him to the home of attorney John H. Sutherland in a St. Louis suburb. Sutherland met them at the door wearing a Confederate soldier's hat, complete with crossed sabers on the crown. He led Byers and Kauffman to a den carpeted with a Confederate flag. The walls were adorned with all kinds of

Rebel regalia. After some small talk, Sutherland asked Byers if he'd like to make some money. Byers said he would. Sutherland offered him $50,000 to dispose of Dr. King.

"Where's the money coming from?" Byers asked.

"A secret Southern organization I belong to," Sutherland replied.

But Byers decided he couldn't do the job, and within minutes he and Kauffman left.

Byers told the committee this was the last time he saw John Sutherland. Chief counsel Blakey asked Byers if he'd mentioned Sutherland's offer to anyone. Byers said he'd told his attorney, Murray L. Randall, later named a criminal court judge in St. Louis.

The committee subpoenaed Judge Randall, who played it close to the vest, conceding that Byers had talked to him about the offer but not until 1974.

This was a pretty thin mix, but the "Byers Memorandum" and Byers' testimony enabled the Select Committee to begin forming its first explanation for Dr. King's murder. The scenario:

As Sutherland was dangling his $50,000 offer in front of Byers and Kauffman, Byers' brother-in-law, John Paul Spica, was serving time at JeffCity with me. In 1963, Spica had been convicted for conspiring to murder St. Louis businessman John J. Myszak, allegedly on a contract let by Myszak's own wife. The wife was acquitted. Her lawyer was Murray L. Randall—later Judge Randall—and the only person Russell Byers claimed to have told of Sutherland's offer to murder Dr. King.

Using this foundation the Select Committee built a framework in which Kauffman supplied illegal drugs to the Jefferson City prison doctor, Hugh Maxey, for whom Spica worked as a technician. According to the committee, Kauffman talked up Sutherland's $50,000 bounty on Dr. King to Dr. Maxey or Spica, one of whom relayed the offer to me. The committee reasoned that, with the offer in mind, I escaped from the prison in April 1967 and took Sutherland's $50,000 contract—which, the panel decided, I didn't get in advance.

Rather, I either got the money through Kauffman after I shot Dr. King or was unable to collect due to a double-cross or missing a meeting with the bagman.

This hothouse flower of a theory had several peculiar outcomes. The $50,000 solution to the King assassination was developed behind tightly closed doors, but before the panel had put on the finishing touches the *New York Times* was publishing articles whose hypothesis was nearly identical to what the committee would say. And within a year of being drawn into the Select Committee investigation, John Paul Spica died mysteriously—and violently.

After ten years in JeffCity, Spica had gotten out of prison, paroled in October 1973. He returned to his hometown of St. Louis, where he supposedly was earning his living as owner of a produce stand at the corner of Shaw Boulevard and Vandeventer Avenue. However, his ties to the city's underworld must have remained somewhat intact. One morning, Spica went out to start the engine of his car. When he turned the ignition key, a bomb went off. Spica died almost instantly.

More Hypotheses

Perhaps to be ready if nobody went for their first theory, committee investigators assembled a second. Trying to explain the source of funds I spent while a fugitive in 1967-68, they made me out to be a bank robber.

On July 13, 1967, two robbers held up the Bank of Alton, in my old sometime home of Alton, Illinois. After brandishing a pistol and a shotgun and scooping up $25,000 to $30,000 in cash, the robbers fled on foot, eluding the police.

The FBI investigated. Agents heard from an informant— Catman Gawron, no less—that I and an accomplice had pulled the job. When the FBI checked out the Catman's story, they found that at the time of the robbery, the other man he'd fingered had been in jail. When they tossed this tidbit back to the Catman, he came up with another name. The FBI decided he was unreliable, and turned to other business.

Meanwhile, in approximately 1973, Gawron died. Tales about my hand in the robbery remained forgotten until the Select Committee revived them, this time suggesting that my brothers were in on the heist as well.

This notion of a fraternal conspiracy was the basis for the panel's third scenario. Amid all these hints of cloak-and-dagger activity, the committee hired its own undercover operative, Oliver B. Patterson. A St. Louis native, he'd done undercover work for the FBI during the 1960s. The bureau code-named him "Phil" and gave him the identification number 105-293. His case officer was Stanley F. Jacobson of the FBI's St. Louis field office. Patterson's assignments called for him to join such right-wing groups as the paramilitary Minutemen. Once inside, he provided his handlers at the bureau with less than earth-shattering information—usually gossip about internal squabbles.

After my arrest in London, I had an indirect offer of legal representation from J.B. Stoner, a lawyer whose clients included the right-wing National States Rights Party—another of Patterson's infiltration targets. I declined Stoner's offer, but sent my brother Jerry to ask the Savannah attorney about instituting legal action to halt the prosecution's avalanche of negative publicity. That meeting developed into an acquaintanceship between Jerry and Oliver Patterson.

In the early 1970s, Patterson quit his undercover work, losing touch with the FBI until a January 1978 telephone call from Jim Haggerty, an FBI agent in St. Louis, who asked to meet with Patterson.

Haggerty told Patterson the Select Committee intended to subpoena him to testify about his efforts on behalf of the FBI. Soon after, two Select Committee investigators, Conrad "Pete" Baetz and Mel Waxman, knocked on Patterson's back door. Until he signed on with the committee, Baetz had been a deputy sheriff in Madison County, Illinois. He and Waxman suggested Patterson take up his old line of work, this time in the committee's employ. Patterson reluctantly agreed. He got a code name—"David Rogers"—and an emergency telephone number to use if needed. His first assignment: renew his friendship with Jerry Ray.

Patterson looked up my brother, let time pass and began phoning Jerry regularly at his home, posing questions fed him by Baetz. Patterson followed the same drill with my attorney, Mark Lane. Baetz recorded every conversation for possible use by the committee.

But it wasn't all work and no play. When there were no phone calls to tap, Patterson let Baetz watch porn films on his VCR. One "starlet" so impressed the committee investigator that when he found out she was a local girl, he had Patterson round her up for a private audience.

In April 1978, the committee summoned Jerry to Washington, D.C., to testify in executive session, conveniently timing his appearance to coincide with Patterson's. The two flew to Washington together. At Baetz's direction, Patterson suggested they bunk together at the Capitol Hill Quality Inn. This gave Patterson the chance to follow Baetz's order that he search Jerry's belongings and obtain a sample of his hair, along with any other "clues" that might be of use to the committee.

Jerry and Patterson checked into the hotel on April 15. On April 18, while Jerry was talking to the committee, Patterson conducted his search. Rifling Jerry's shaving kit for a hair sample, he came across a bundle of letters, including several from me. Patterson picked up the phone and called Baetz's emergency number, leaving his code name. Within minutes Baetz was on the line, excited by the news of the letters. He told Patterson to copy them and mail the copies to Box 306, Woodriver, Illinois.

Baetz said Jerry was at that moment testifying before the committee staff. Patterson asked Baetz to keep Jerry tied up for at least 30 minutes more so he'd have time to copy the letters and stick the originals back into the shaving kit. Baetz said he'd do what he could. Patterson left the hotel and ran across New Jersey Avenue to the Hyatt-Regency Hotel, where he ran off three copies of my letters. He kept one set for himself and sent the other two to the Woodriver address.

Activities such as these illustrate the potential for devastating mischief posed by the committee's subversive espionage operation. Thanks to Lane, however, the network collapsed in August 1978. Lane had realized Patterson was a Select Committee mole and said so in a telephone conversation being monitored by someone with ties to the panel. Word of Lane's remarks got back to the committee staff, which immediately changed Patterson's code name to "Carl Drake."

Baetz offered Patterson a couple of options: he could get a new identity through the Justice Department's witness protection program, or he could hold a news conference and give out information damaging to Lane and other allies of mine.

Patterson went for the idea of media manipulation. On August 5, Baetz gave him notes to use during a press conference set up by the Select Committee in St. Louis for the next day. These notes included scurrilous accusations about individuals the committee considered adversaries. One claimed Mark Lane was homosexual.

But Pope Paul VII died on August 5—there was little chance of other topics getting coverage for days, so Patterson agreed to meet on the afternoon of August 7 with *New York Times* reporter Nicholas Horrock. Horrock had promised a cozy affair, but when Patterson arrived, another Timesman, Anthony J. Marro, was on hand instead. So were Mark Lane and several TV reporters he'd invited, including Chuck Neff of KITV-TV and KSD-TV's John Auble.

What had happened? The day before, Patterson had a change of heart. He met secretly with Mark and said he'd decided to defect. He'd still meet with the *Times*, but to give a truthful account of his illegal activities in the committee's service.

Instead of a quiet interview that confirmed the status quo, the *Times* reporter's tête-à-tête turned into a media ambush. Marro and Lane got into a shoving match that ended when Marro left, pursued by Lane, who was shouting, "Don't you want to hear the truth?"

Patterson then revealed his role in the Select Committee's work. He described how, while giving testimony in executive session, he'd responded to staff questions by reading answers those same staffers had given him.

Patterson's allegations were quite serious, involving criminal acts on the part of congressional agents, but Congress handled the charges as might be expected. The Select Committee was permitted to conduct its own investigation of the matter, with predictable result.

After his look in the mirror, Select Committee Chairman Stokes held a news conference to announce the findings: that the material Patterson stole from my brother consisted mainly of an "escape map" I'd drawn as a blueprint for my Brushy Mountain break-out—Stokes said Patterson had forced the committee to accept the "map"—and that if Patterson had stolen the letters, he'd done so without committee authorization. Stokes justified obtaining a hair sample from Jerry by invoking the fraternal conspiracy theory.

"Given the existence of unidentified hairs in the FBI investigation of Dr. King's murder and the necessity of determining Jerry Ray's possible involvement in the assassination, it is most appropriate for the committee to seek the production of this type of evidence," he told reporters.

Surely, if the committee had found any connection between Jerry's hair sample and the King assassination, it would have been shouted from every rooftop in Washington. But Chairman Stokes' September 6, 1978, report to the Committee on House Administration makes no mention of any such connection.

The media accepted Stokes' analysis of the internal investigation on blind faith.

Public Hearings, Part I

As politicians, the captains of the Select Committee were keenly aware of the impact of timing on public opinion. This is why they scheduled me to testify publicly when they did. They were sure that my appearance would be preceded by

Oliver Patterson's disclosure to the *New York Times* that I had admitted to Dr. King's murder and that Mark Lane was gay.

When Patterson went over to the side of truth, though, that expectation was dashed—but not the committee's desire to control me. For example, in the August 10th *Washington Post*, reporter George Lardner quoted Representative Mendel J. Davis (D., S.C.)—who was not on the Select Committee—as saying a panel member had told him they were going to "nail James Earl Ray to the cross." Three days later, in the *Washington Star*, reporter Ron Sarro described chief counsel Blakey as "the Tchaikovsky of congressional hearings" for orchestrating the interrogation technique the Select Committee would employ.

"Witnesses will not be permitted the usual opening statements, but instead, will be allowed only to respond to carefully selected questions by Blakey's staff and congressmen who have become experts in varying aspects of the investigation," Sarro wrote.

Meanwhile, Blakey and four committee members—Robert W. Edgar, Samuel L. Devine, Harold Sawyer and Chairman Louis Stokes—had arranged to meet with Mark Lane and me at Brushy Mountain prison. Their purpose was clear as soon as we'd sat down. They asked for an outline of my testimony. Lane and I handed over a written statement outlining my position. They said my remarks looked to be acceptable. Then, at Representative Sawyer's suggestion, all but he left the room.

The congressman began talking about his experience as a prosecutor before his election to Congress from Michigan's 5th congressional district. Mark and I listened without comment. Then Sawyer made his pitch: if Lane or I could provide him with enough information to obtain a conspiracy indictment in the King killing he'd urge Governor Blanton to reduce my sentence.

We didn't reply, which probably didn't surprise this seasoned prosecutor. His proposal was only a replay of the decade-old routine the Justice Department had run in 1969.

The idea was to dangle the carrot of early release to lure me into telling all I might know—not to expose the truth, but to reveal any cracks in the cover-up. And knowing in advance what I'd be saying would enable committee staff members to control the situation rather than be caught off guard when I testified.

Except for my visitors' informal approval of my proposed statement, nothing was resolved, and they returned to Washington.

Getting to Washington to testify before the Select Committee was half of the fun. On August 15, a helicopter landed just outside the front wall at Brushy Mountain, and a contingent of federal marshals loaded me aboard for the flight to Knoxville, where we boarded a small plane that flew to a seemingly abandoned airport somewhere outside Petersburg, Virginia. At the edge of the strip were several automobiles containing more marshals.

My escorts and I climbed into one of the cars and were driven a short distance to a prison—I didn't see any signs giving the name. The front security fence was topped by a double roll of razor wire, which improves on old-fashioned barbed wire by replacing the barbs with three-inch blades. These rolls rose 25 feet in the air.

The caravan paused at the gate while the marshals identified themselves. Then the gate opened, and we went inside. I was taken to a waiting room. Several guards were there. One of them handed me some forms to fill out and sign. He said I'd have to be fingerprinted and have my picture taken. I objected, attempting to explain that I was not a federal prisoner and would only be around until the Select Committee finished with me.

At this a civilian who looked like a Sumo wrestler entered the room. He said he was Warden Stephen Grzegorek, and that I'd do whatever he ordered. A guard grabbed me, and the row was on.

One guard tried to shove my arms up behind my back. Another came at me from the front. I turned and kicked, trying to dislodge the guard on my back.

But it ended as quickly as it had started, with the only casualty being my shirt. In the brief melee, someone tore it off my back. The marshals stepped in and stopped the tussle, as I expected they would, or I'd have let Grzegorek have his way. The marshals told him the committee didn't want me testifying in public looking banged up.

Guards took me to a basement cell. A bright ceiling-mounted light protected by shatterproof glass shone down all night, kindling memories of Memphis and its midnight sunshine. I figured the little scene in the waiting room was part of a softening-up process intended to render me more inclined to sing the tune called by the Tchaikovsky of congressional hearings.

My sleepless night ended with guards rousing me out of the cell for another helicopter flight, this time to Washington. I came out of the cell carrying my torn shirt. I was going to show the committee my ruined clothing. But a guard snatched it, warning me that I could only take legal papers with me. At the gate the marshals took over again, and we reversed our path to the desolate airport and boarded the helicopter, which landed on a pad inside the D.C. line. We traveled by car to the hearings.

I was allowed to meet briefly with Mark Lane in a conference room before we both were summoned into the Select Committee's hearing chamber. A clerk swore me in, after which I was allowed to read the statement that the committee's Brushy Mountain delegation had approved. In it, I chronicled my itinerary from the day I broke out of prison in Missouri in April 1967 until my June 1968 arrest in London.

That done, I came in for the Blakey interrogation technique: one panel member would discuss a specific area in the King investigation, followed by another questioning me on a different topic. Representative Sawyer, the ex-prosecutor from Michigan, got the job of showing that I could, with sufficient motivation, kill someone. He went at the task with vigor, asking such questions as, "Would you shoot someone in a robbery if the victim resisted?"

Mark Lane objected to this shyster question. In a rare ruling in my favor, acting chairman Richardson Preyer (D., N.C.) upheld the objection, and Sawyer withdrew the question.

But Sawyer's "potential killer" message had reached the media in attendance, who relayed it to newspaper readers and television viewers.

The hearing functioned like an ersatz trial, draped in the trappings of legitimate inquiry but devoid of due process. It was a cover-up artist's dream: black legislator Stokes trying the case and in the process allaying many blacks' doubts and dissatisfactions about the official version of the King assassination.

Chairman Stokes clearly wanted to show that beginning in Los Angeles on March 18, 1968, I started following Dr. King, tailing him to Selma, Alabama, then to Atlanta, and winding up in Memphis on April 4. To illustrate this premise, an easel set up by committee staffers bore a huge blowup of a change-of-address form Stokes claimed I'd filed with the L.A. post office listing Atlanta as my forwarding address. I'd filed the form, all right, but not as part of any effort to shadow Dr. King. I did it in case mail from Raoul or others was en route to Los Angeles.

Chairman Stokes quoted a March 18, 1968, *Los Angeles Herald Examiner* article about a visit by Dr. King to L.A. the previous day, then insinuated that I had King in mind when I filed the change of address form, leaving town the same day to "follow" the civil rights leader.

Neither Mark nor I could see the enlarged postal form. At the next recess, he got a copy of the original, which rebutted Stokes' conclusions: the form was dated March 17, the day before the *Examiner* story appeared.

When the committee resumed, Mark pointed out the discrepancy. The panel responded in typical fashion, abruptly moving on to the next question. Ignoring Mark's efforts to clear up the misrepresentation, Chairman Stokes steamrollered on, stating that I left L.A. and eventually ended up in Memphis in the proximity of Dr. King at the approximate time he was shot on the balcony of the Lorraine Motel.

So what?

I've never denied those facts. But now they'd been tainted by suggestion—a suggestion intentional or erroneous—and my lawyer's objection to the misrepresentation went ignored by both the public officials at whom it was aimed and the press that supposedly struggles to find the truth.

The chairman and I disagreed sharply as to my whereabouts on April 1, 1968. He produced a receipt from the Piedmont Laundry in Atlanta indicating, that I had deposited laundry there on April 1st and therefore must have been in Atlanta on that date. I did leave laundry at the Piedmont, but that was on or before March 29—I'd left Atlanta that day to begin my trip to Memphis. And on April 1 I spent the night in a motel in Corinth, Mississippi—240 miles from Atlanta. But I couldn't document my Mississippi motel stay, or explain the April 1 Piedmont receipt.

This matter of timing was important to the committee because the sequence described by Chairman Stokes suggested that on or after April 1, I learned of Dr. King's intent to return to Memphis and so followed him out of Atlanta.

But if I'd been able to show conclusively that I was in Corinth on April 1, a logical conclusion would have been that Dr. King's killers had an inside line on his travel plans. Knowing before the news became public that Dr. King would be going back to Memphis, they could have had Raoul and associates direct me toward Memphis, making me, in the words of Jim Garrison, "a gift of accommodation from the planners" of the King assassination to their allies, my prosecutors.

The Select Committee knew that the apparatus monitoring Dr. King was a leaky bucket. As Chairman Stokes was questioning me, he and the committee had in their possession classified FBI material documenting that in April 1968 the Bureau had an informant inside the Southern Christian Leadership Conference. The informant, James E. Harrison, an SCLC bookkeeper, had been recruited in 1964 by FBI special agent Alan G. Sentinella of the Atlanta office. Harrison's duties as an informant included obtaining and relaying Dr. King's itinerary to the FBI before that information was made public.

The April 1 Piedmont Laundry receipt turned out to be the committee's only credible evidence that I might have followed Dr. King anywhere. The delicacy of that single piece of evidence is suggested by the fact that the committee avoided documenting my location on April 2, 1968, when I stayed overnight in the DeSoto Motel in Southhaven, Mississippi, just outside the Memphis line on Highway 51.

The committee assigned one of its most blatant fabrications to Representative Samuel L. Devine (R.,Oh.), its ranking minority member and one of its elder and less erudite members. He announced that the panel recently had obtained a statement from a former Scotland Yard inspector named Alexander Eist, who claimed to have obtained incriminating admissions from me following my arrest in London. Eist had kept silent about what I'd said until an American couple touring England convinced him it was his "patriotic duty" to come forward, Devine said. Keeping a straight face as he described a policeman waiting ten years to provide information invaluable to the prosecution, Devine admitted that committee staffers hadn't verified Eist's allegations. With this in mind, Devine said if Mark Lane or I objected to his reading the entire document he'd read only excerpts.

Mark and I saw the ruse: if we objected, Devine would read only the juicy parts and let the press have a field day with headlines such as "Ray Objects To Reading of Murder Confession." So we let him read the whole thing, and sat back to enjoy Eist's "revelations."

The Eist submission was lengthy. Before Devine had reached the halfway mark, a clerk tapped Mark on the shoulder and told him he had an urgent telephone call. The congressman kept reading while Mark left the room, returning in a few minutes. When Representative Devine had completed his reading, Lane told the committee that his urgent caller had informed him that Scotland Yard had cashiered Alexander Eist for his involvement in jewel robberies.

This was no surprise to the committee. They knew that in the world of public opinion, Eist's fabrications—which corroborated nearly every accusation against me since Dr. King's death—didn't need to be true to be effective. Their timing was beautiful: Mark Lane couldn't investigate Eist and come up with any meaningful challenge to his statements before my testimony ended.

Next, the panel attempted to link me to the July 13, 1967, robbery of the Bank of Alton. Representative Floyd J. Fithian (D., In.) handled that assignment, asking questions aimed at establishing my itinerary after I broke out of prison in April 1967. He strongly suggested that my brother Jerry and I had robbed the bank, and that my share of the loot went to finance my "trailing" of Dr. King.

The next day, Jerry and St. Louis television reporter John Auble went to the Bank of Alton. In the presence of bank officials, Jerry denied robbing the establishment. From the bank, Jerry and Auble went to the Alton police station, where my brother denied the robbery accusation in the presence of the chief of police. He even offered to waive the statute of limitations and stand trial. Declining the offer, a department spokesman, Lieutenant Walter Conrad, said Jerry "was not then, nor had he ever been, a suspect in the robbery."

That didn't deter the Select Committee, which simply added another brother as a target, revising its accusations so they entangled my brother John (See Chapter 20).

As my testimony came to an end, my inquisitors still hadn't raised any questions about the conspiracy theories they'd promoted through the media, especially the *New York Times*. At the end of my third day before the panel, the committee said I'd be recalled for further examination in respect to the conspiracy issue.

Then the committee summoned Lance McFall and his son Phillip. In April 1968, they'd owned a Texaco gas station at 2nd and Linden Avenue in Memphis. Their testimony was intended to challenge my claim that as Martin Luther King was being shot, I was trying to get a flat tire repaired at a gas station near that intersection. The McFalls said that at the time of the King shooting neither I nor a white Mustang had been at their station.

Only one thing was out of kilter. I never said I'd been at the McFall station at any time. Nor had I told the committee McFall's was where I'd stopped for service only to learn that the attendant was too busy to help me until later.

So why did the committee solicit testimony from the Mc-Falls? The answer lay with the next witness, Dean Cowden.

Cowden, a close friend of prominent black Memphis politician and Select Committee member Harold Ford (D., Tn.), had gotten involved in the King case in 1973, while a patient in the psychiatric ward at Memphis Veterans Hospital. As is often the case with VA facilities, the psych ward at Memphis also serves alcohol and drug abusers. Cowden, was a drunk in need of a place to dry out.

While on the ward, he struck up a friendship with Renfro Hays, the private investigator who had done some work on my case when I was being represented by Arthur Hanes Sr. and son. According to Cowden, his friendship with Hays grew so tight that Hays asked him to help assemble a bogus story about the King shooting. Done up right, Hays told Cowden, a hoax like this could make them both a lot of money.

Having learned through court records and news stories about my report that I'd been at a gas station during the assault on Dr. King, Hays asked Cowden to claim he'd seen me at McFall's Texaco at that time. Cowden said he'd do it, and they sold their tale to the *National Enquirer,* which ran a story on it October 11, 1977.

Cowden repeated the story to Mark Lane, but without charge. Mark recorded Cowden's statement and played it for me at Brushy Mountain. I responded by explaining that when I stopped at a station to ask about the tire I hadn't behaved in the manner described by Cowden. Cowden claimed I got out of the Mustang and walked around. Nevertheless, Lane incorporated Cowden's story into *Code Name Zorro,* his book about the King case.

The third time Cowden told his story it was to Select Committee investigators, with a difference: he admitted it was a hoax. The committee loved hearing this. A buoyant Cowden boasted about conning Lane, and by the end of his testimony, several panel members were praising his "courage." When it came Ford's turn to offer congratulations, Cowden gushed, "I voted for you, too, Harold!"

The committee chose not to acquaint its television audience with Dean Cowden's less wholesome side, leaving out any mention that the Texaco station story had been cooked up in a VA psycho ward, of which Cowden had been a regular customer for years. Neither did the committee see fit to enter into the record the fact that its investigators had sequestered Cowden to keep him straight for his appearance at the hearings; he got "temporary leave" so he could show up at the hearings and make follow-up TV appearances. Nor did the committee mention that while Cowden was testifying, his collaborator in the hoax, Renfro Hays, was back on the bug ward.

In a jury trial, only the most foolish prosecutor would try to challenge a story that the defendant never offered as an alibi. But the Select Committee wasn't presenting evidence to a jury—it was playing to the media, and succeeding wildly.

For example, after Cowden's testimony, the *Commercial Appeal* dated August 19, 1978, ran a story weaving falsehoods in among facts. "Ray had said" he was at McFall's service station at the time Dr. King was shot, the reporter wrote, ignoring the truth. The McFalls' rebuttal could only mean that "Ray was lying to mask his guilt, which can only mean that the state has been right all along...." the story continued.

The Tiger Returns

No showman can resist the spotlight, and Percy Foreman was a showman. The lights hadn't been bright enough in 1974, when he had an invitation to testify at my habeas corpus hearing—or perhaps the glare of cross-examination seemed a trifle too bright. But when the Select Committee summoned him into a forum where he wouldn't have to risk being questioned aggressively, the Texas Tiger sprang onto a plane and arrived in Washington to preen before the panel.

Basking in the warm smiles of those who wanted his assistance in applying the last dabs of cement to the prosecution's version of the King murder, Foreman performed like a champion.

Having served as my attorney in the months after I was moved to Memphis, Foreman was a prize for the committee. He could quote me as admitting to whatever the panel wanted to hear.

And he did. Had Foreman not been on the record as stating that he'd never asked me if I'd shot Dr. King, he no doubt would have told the committee I spilled my guts to him and said I'd pulled the trigger.

Old Percy played to the questions with maximum cleverness, arranging his answers to suggest that I'd hinted that I'd shot Dr. King. In one rambling answer, he not only intimated that I'd admitted to the shooting, but also advanced another prime committee goal—planting the notion that my brother Jerry was involved in the killing. Asked about my connection to the alleged murder weapon, Foreman told the panel:

> Jerry was with him when he first bought the rifle. . . . Jerry was not with him . . . when he bought the gun that killed Dr. Martin Luther King . . . but he was with him the day before . . . he was alone when he obtained the rifle with which he killed Dr. King. . . . He was very protective of Jerry . . . The only time ever I learned from cross examining him, and from a slip that Jerry helped him.

The committee resolved the ballistics of the King shooting by noting in its final report that neither the FBI nor the Select committee could identify a particular rifle used in the assassination.

The rest of Foreman's testimony, laced with psychiatric jargon, consisted mainly of what he contended the prosecution would have proved if the King case had gone to trial. Asked about the location of a letter he claimed I wrote him "beseeching" him to represent me in the King case, he said his Nashville lawyer, John J. Hooker Sr., had lost the entire file on my case. Hooker's firm denied losing the file.

As Foreman's performance was winding up, Chairman Stokes jumped outside committee business to stroll down Memory Lane, chummily recalled the days, 20 years past, when he and Foreman had founded the National Association of Defense Lawyers in Criminal Cases. This was the committee's sole allusion to Foreman's background, in sharp contrast to its hectoring inquisitions into the beliefs and affiliations of witnesses who didn't support the committee's theories.

If the committee had scratched the surface of Foreman's career, it would have noted his involvement with the billionaire Hunt family of Texas, which is worth examining for its insights into Foreman's behavior in front of the committee.

In 1975, as Chairman Stokes knew but failed to mention, brothers Nelson and William Hunt, sons of company founder H.L. Hunt, were indicted along with Foreman for obstruction of justice. The indictment originated in an illegal wiretap allegedly ordered by the Hunts. In 1970 private investigator Jon Joseph Kelly was arrested in Richardson, Texas with wiretapping equipment, then charged—as were Nelson and William Hunt—with illegally monitoring Hunt Co. employees.

The brothers claimed they were only investigating the embezzlement of $50,000,000 from the family firm and eventually were acquitted. But before that they and five others, including Percy Foreman, were indicted by a Dallas federal grand jury for conspiring to cover up the wiretap case by paying Kelly to take the fall.

Foreman, who was representing Kelly, said if he'd plead guilty and in the process exonerate the Hunt brothers, there'd be a tidy piece of change for him. While out on bond, Kelly managed to pilfer Hunt Co. documents showing that the money Foreman was offering came from the family. Kelly turned over the documents to the Justice Department, bringing down the misdemeanor obstruction charges against the Hunts, Foreman and others.

In 1976, the Hunts and the others were convicted on the conspiracy charges. However, the case against Percy Foreman was held in abeyance—perhaps to assure his cooperation in the future, should the Justice Department need him to lay on a little mortar in, say, the King murder case. That's not for certain—the Justice Department says all of its records on Foreman's obstruction indictment have been "lost."

Chairman Stokes' skirting of Percy's extralegal activities is even more intriguing in light of Stokes' vehemence in attacking anyone with opinions on race akin to those of the Hunts—who are known for holding highly conservative views on the topic. Stokes' silence on Foreman's patrons cast doubt on the chairman's sincerity in regard to race, confirming what others have observed, namely that Stokes plays the race card only when politically expedient. For example, in 1983, while driving in Montgomery County, Maryland, Stokes was stopped by policemen who suspected he'd been drinking. Noting his condition, they ran him through the usual sobriety tests, which Stokes failed, resulting in a drunk driving charge. But Stokes said he was the victim of racist cops, loudly protesting his innocence. Later, he pleaded guilty to a lesser charge.

Had Stokes and his panel not been so eager to buttress their preconceived notions about what happened in Memphis on April 4, 1968, some genuine information could have been uncovered about the actual events of that day. I refer to telephone numbers in New Orleans that Foreman claimed were connected to the case. In a deposition taken for my habeas corpus hearing, he said he'd gone to that city and checked the numbers. However, earlier he'd told me that if my case went to trial he'd get the numbers run down by the

Lansky mob. With Foreman under oath, the committee could have gotten deeply into the questions surrounding these telephone contacts, possibly revealing the scapegoat on whom Lansky and clients wanted to blame the King assassination, and why.

But even though its staff had developed a file on the mobster—accidentally released to the press, it consisted of a transcript of an FBI wiretap on Lansky indicating that he was privy to the personal affairs of U.S. Attorney General Robert F. Kennedy—the panel danced around this matter, seemingly trying to avoid causing anyone on either side of the microphone to pronounce the name "Meyer Lansky."

Phil Canale

Some of the most interesting testimony at the hearings came from Phil M. Canale, who directed the prosecution of the King case. He testified from ten pages of notes that he described during the hearings as memoranda he compiled in advance of my non-trial. He told the panel he'd saved the notes "to try to protect myself."

One of the startling elements of Canale's testimony was his response to questions about Grace Walden Stephens, common-law wife of prosecution witness Charles Q. Stephens. When she refused to corroborate her husband's claim that he'd seen me running out of the washroom at Bessie Brewer's rooming house at the time of the King shooting, Mrs. Stephens was put in a mental hospital and warehoused there until 1978—a confinement supposedly unknown to Canale until he was served habeas corpus papers seeking her release, according to his testimony before the panel. To paper over this matter, the committee included discussion aimed at supporting the claim that Mrs. Stephens had been put in the bin because she was an alcoholic, not because her version of events didn't match up with the official line.

The Canale memoranda also reveal the extent of the maneuvering behind my guilty plea. For instance, one memo shows that immediately after Judge Battle named him co-

counsel with Foreman, public defender Hugh W. Stanton Sr. asked Canale if he'd accept a guilty plea—before Stanton had even begun his investigation of the case! The memo also establishes that Foreman endorsed Stanton's contact with Canale, suggesting that Stanton's inquiry was a test balloon.

Canale said he then discussed the idea of my pleading guilty with Tennessee Governor Buford Ellington. That would be "an excellent disposition of the case," Ellington said, according to Canale's memoranda, which also supposedly described how Canale floated the guilty plea concept to Dr. King's family and associates through King family attorney Harry Wachtel. They, too, approved. The Canale memos verify that all the negotiations and agreements to settle the case through a guilty plea were achieved by December 1968, before I even heard about any proposal to plead guilty.

After December 1968, all that remained was to iron out the details, such as persuading me to surrender my right to a jury trial—an easy job, considering I'd been living in the midnight sunshine for months.

And there was the minor matter of timing. It would look awkward for Foreman to start selling his client (and the public) on a guilty plea within weeks of taking the case. Engineering some sort of delay would avoid making Foreman look bad, and also gave him time to renegotiate with Huie for more money on the publishing contracts.

In fact, the process of entering a guilty plea began before the defense had investigated the case against me. This surprised a few people on my defense team. Hugh Stanton Jr., whose job it was to investigate for my defense, told the committee he'd interviewed only 31 of the state's 360 potential witnesses when he accidentally learned that the case was about to be settled with a guilty plea.

The Canale memoranda illustrate the political logic in favor of a guilty plea. Besides fearing that I'd be acquitted, politicians worried that a trial might lead to the release of FBI files that could embarrass the bureau. Canale himself had talked with the FBI about declassifying those files.

Politicians' aversion to a trial is easy to understand, but the inclination of Dr. King's family and associates to go along with the politicians is less easy to comprehend—unless they were under pressure, such as had been brought to bear on Martin Luther King Jr. and the SCLC right from the start and until well after Dr. King was in the ground.

W.B. Huie and Other Pressing Matters

As the hearings were gaining momentum, a familiar player elbowed his way back into the footlights. William Bradford Huie, Percy Foreman's ally in "resolving" the King case, contacted me at Brushy Mountain through attorney Jack Kershaw.

Huie had a vague proposition. If, during exclusive one-on-one interviews with him, I provided certain "admissions" regarding the King murder, an unspecified amount of money would pass into my account. Huie would be free to use his purchase in any way he deemed appropriate.

I discussed the offer with Mark Lane and my brother Jerry. We decided to have Jerry phone Huie and ask him to be more specific—taping the conversation for safety's sake. Jerry spoke with Huie twice on October 29, 1978. Huie said if I would, in effect, confess to the murder of Martin Luther King Jr., he'd come up with $220,000 for me, plus a parole, which Huie claimed he could "arrange" with Tennessee Governor Ray Blanton.

"I know how to sell him on doing that," Huie told Jerry. "He's got problems." (Blanton did have problems: they eventually landed him in a federal penitentiary for two years, convicted of trading state liquor licenses for political favors and cash.)

As for the source of the $220,000, Huie wouldn't say. He knew better than to name his paymasters.

I never gave his offer serious consideration. Instead, Mark transcribed the recorded phone conversation and mailed a copy to the Select Committee. He also published the transcript in *Code Name Zorro*.

The Huie transcript is eloquent proof that the prosecution had no admissions, confessions or any other statements from me incriminating myself in Dr. King's murder, but you'd never know it from the press coverage as the hearings were coming to a close. No Bernstein rose up to question the Select Committee's unusual investigative techniques, or the conclusions drawn therefrom. No Woodward cut through the pomp to expose the outrageous violations of truth, logic and justice that mottled the testimony of Cowden, Foreman and Eist. Instead, reporters regurgitated the statements of those who parroted the panel's theories, leaving undisturbed the skeletons in Cowden's, Foreman's and Eist's closets.

But things were different when my brothers testified. Newspaper headlines speculated about their "possible involvement" in Dr. King's murder; stories insinuated that they helped finance the assassination via bank robbery. The press seemed to think the Select Committee had given me a proper "trial" and found me guilty:

> James Earl Ray said yesterday many of his past statements on the Martin Luther King assassination were deliberate lies, but insisted he is now telling the whole truth. —*Nashville Tennessean*, August 17, 1978

> James Earl Ray proved he is still what he always has been—a wily crime-wise, penny-ante crook for whom aliases and lies are instinctive. Indeed, if the hearings did one useful thing it was to reveal Ray's mentality in an unfiltered state. —*Memphis Commercial Appeal*, August 21, 1978

> For all intents and purposes Ray received the trial he had been asking for for years. . . . If it had been a real trial instead of a congressional hearing, the jury would quickly have brought in a verdict of guilty. . . The star prosecuting attorney, Rep. Louis Stokes (D.Ohio), who calmly and repeatedly blew Ray's flimsy alibis to smithereens, is a

veteran criminal lawyer. It is also important to note that
Stokes is black.—*Knoxville News-Sentinel*, August 22, 1978

The primary purpose for the committee being formed in
1976 was to allay the rampant suspicions about the deaths
[of King and Kennedy]. . . . —*Memphis Commercial Appeal*,
September 6, 1978

Another chorus of endorsement came from the television
networks. During and after the hearings, panel members and
witnesses embracing a particular committee position often
were interviewed on or had their press conferences covered
by the networks. For example, Dean Cowden appeared on
CBS-TV's *Face the Nation* on August 27, 1978. Panel member
Richardson Preyer was on the same program on September
24; Chairman Stokes, on December 31.

A joint appearance by Stokes and Rep. Harold Sawyer on
the July 18, 1979 *MacNeil/Lehrer Report*, summed up the
committee's work, purporting to air those two members'
"contrasting views" on the King assassination. The only
dispute seemed to be over whether there'd been a conspiracy, and who'd paid for it. Stokes said the plot to kill Dr.
King involved several conspirators. Sawyer disagreed. But
Stokes spoke for both when he said, "We think James Earl
Ray did it for money" and then revived the old story about
St. Louis businessman John Sutherland and his supposed
$50,000 bounty on Dr. King's head.

After Stokes and Sawyer, MacNeil and Lehrer interviewed
New York Times reporter Nicholas Horrock, chief of that
paper's investigative unit and a party to Mark Lane's media
blitz in St. Louis. Horrock solemnly endorsed Stokes' performance as panel chairman, slightly qualifying his praise by
noting that it might not be in the public interest for the
committee to have gone with the "lone nut" analysis in the
Kennedy and King murders. Horrock finished with the cant
of those opposing public trials in political murders: due to
the passing of time, the deaths of witnesses and faded
memories, a trial would not really be worthwhile.

What was worthwhile about the Select Committee hearings? For one thing, they enabled chief counsel G. Robert Blakey to pick up some spare change. Bantam Books paid Blakey a $10,000 "consultant fee" for helping out with its 1979 book, *The Final Assassinations Report*, a collection of excerpts from the Select Committee's report to Congress. In 1980, Times Books, a subsidiary of the *New York Times*, published Blakey's own book, *The Plot To Kill the President*.

Blakey had done what he could to eliminate competition. One of his first acts after becoming chief counsel was to require staff members to sign an agreement precluding them from publishing any information about the King case if the information was obtained as a result of their employment by the Select Committee—unless the House of Representatives or the CIA approved it beforehand.

Chapter Nineteen

Another Escape

In early 1977, I could see the handwriting on the prison wall. The fix was in at the Select Committee, and an interview with *Playboy* to which I'd agreed was turning out to be more aggravation that it seemed to be worth. It was time to find a use for those pipes I'd hidden in the washing machine.

Spring was coming, and the area around me was greening. They don't call it Brushy Mountain for nothing. The thick foliage would offer concealment. I approached another convict, Doug Shelton, about breaking out.

Doug was about 35 and worked on the maintenance crew. I'd known him for several years and was satisfied that he wasn't a snitch. He was open to my proposal. His enthusiasm rose when I described my idea for making a ladder out of the pipes and using it to go over the wall at a spot where the mountain serves as part of the wall. There, instead of electrified barbed wire, the only barriers were a series of big stone steps. I planned to construct a ladder that could grab onto the top of the chiseled mountain. Over several months we assembled pipe and connections, and by June we had the makings of a fine ladder, including a pair of curved pipes to act as hooks at the top of the wall.

On June 10, I worked later than usual in the laundry, using the excuse that I had to oil the washing machine motors. One last laundry worker was in the room, pressing his punk's clothing. To stall, I removed the back plates from all the machines but the one with the pipes stashed inside. The guy at the ironing board shut up shop and left, but I still had to watch for a roving guard. I removed the back plate from the machine with the pipes inside and laid two sheets nearby. Pretending to service the machine, I slipped the pipes between the sheets, then stuffed the sheets into a laundry bag. I got the bag back to the cellblock without a hitch.

Doug and I had decided to make our break just before the end of the evening yard period—around 6:00 p.m., leaving the guards less daylight in which to look for us.

After the evening meal, I returned to the cellblock and taped a couple of pipes to my legs, sticking other sections down my shirt and holding them in place with my belt. When the 4:30 p.m. whistle signaled evening yard period, I hid my bulges by going outside in the company of one of the few fat prisoners, keeping him between me and the guard at the door.

Out in the yard, some prisoners were playing baseball. I got with Doug. At six, we eased over in the direction of our exit point, the northwest corner of the yard. We had to cross under a guard tower. As we did I could hear Tammy Wynette singing "Stand By Your Man" on the guard's radio. I looked up and saw his feet sticking out of the tower window.

A small drainage ditch runs along the base of the carved-out mountainside. Here, about 30 feet from the wall, Doug and I had a bit of cover in which to assemble our ladder. After spreading out the pipes and connections in the ditch, I screwed them together into a ladder. Doug kept watch for guards.

As I finished assembling the pieces, a fight broke out on the baseball field. A runner had punched the umpire for calling him out at the plate. The benches had emptied—prison isn't that different from real life. Guards were swarming around trying to separate the combatants. Up in the observation tower, however, the Tammy Wynette fan remained oblivious.

I moved our new ladder to the wall. It was too short. I had to hook it onto the lowest step. There the hook touched the insulator for the electric wire. As the ladder touched the insulator I felt a slight jolt, but the contact must have tripped the circuit breakers. When I touched the ladder again, all I felt was a slight humming. In seconds, I was up the ladder and running along the wall, then jumping into a shallow ravine leading to the rear corner of the prison. From there it was only a 12 to 15 foot crawl up an embankment to level ground, where I could find concealment among the trees.

Doug Shelton was close behind, followed by four or five others who'd seen the ladder and couldn't resist its call. When a guard spotted the last climber, Jerry Ward, he began firing his weapon.

By then I'd found a dry creek bed leading in the direction of Kentucky, and was running along it, with Doug and my cellmate, Earl Hill, coming up fast. Suddenly we all heard what sounded like an elephant stampeding past in the woods. How the hell had the guards gotten onto our trail so quickly, I thought. The noise faced and the elephant, or whatever it was, continued up the mountain.

Doug, Earl and I kept running. Around midnight we reached the crest of the mountain and paused in the solitude peculiar to such places. In the distance towns showed up as clusters of lights. Near one cluster, a red beacon flashed. The three of us decided to split up. I headed for the flashing beacon, but it quickly went out of sight as the terrain became rougher.

I moved on through the night in a northerly direction. At daybreak I crawled beneath a ledge to hide and sleep. Later in the morning I was awakened by leaves rustling. I opened one eye; a big groundhog was staring at the intruder encamped on his turf. When he saw I wasn't going to move, he meditated a few moments, then turned and walked off.

Now and then a plane whined overhead. I spent the day under the ledge. I stayed under the ledge in case a plane had a heat-seeking device that can detect the presence of humans or animals below.

At sundown, I began scrounging around the area, finding a plastic gallon jug, such as moonshiners use. I found a stream and filled the jug. My travels might take me to an elevation where water was scarce. Spotter planes don't fly at night, and search parties weren't likely to be tracking around the mountains in the dark. I walked all night, trying to keep to a northeasterly course. Just before dawn, I bedded down in some underbrush near a small settlement that seemed to have a population of about 100 mountaineers. All day long I heard rifle and shotgun fire. I was initially concerned about the shooting but I later assumed it was someone target practicing.

At nightfall, it was raining. I began moving again and crossed Highway 116, turning east to follow the New River— actually, little more than a creek. After about a mile, I heard shooting and hollering behind me. Thinking I could have been seen, I hopped to the far bank and then over the railroad tracks that paralleled it. I began zigzagging up the mountainside. When I stopped to rest, I listened intently for pursuers but could hear only the tiny popping sounds made by water droplets shaken loose from leaves by the wind. I decided the shooting didn't concern me.

I was wrong, and 15 or 20 minutes later I discovered how wrong. Lights suddenly flashed on in a semi-circle around me. I lay back and covered myself with leaves.

"Don't move!" someone hollered. I didn't, but I could see that I was surrounded by dogs, and behind them, prison guards.

The dogs were pointers, trained to track silently. When they get within 100 feet or so of their quarry, they snap into a pose, snouts aimed at the object of the search. These pointers had gotten closer; I had a lot of noses in my face.

The dogs were exhausted. Pointers have stubby legs, a drawback in the mountains. I heard a guard announce into his walkie-talkie that the dogs couldn't keep after the original trail they'd been following.

The original trail was Doug Shelton's. The shooting and hollering I'd heard had been directed at him. Around midnight, he'd tried to cross the highway near the town of New River but had run into an ambush laid for someone else. A local resident whose house had been burned down that evening was lying by the roadside waiting for the culprit. When Doug ran up, this man jumped up brandishing a rifle and a flashlight and shouting for Doug to halt.

An automobile approached. Taking advantage of the oncoming headlights, Doug broke across the highway, dodging several shots. He ran in the direction I'd taken shortly before, winding up in the same river I'd crossed at the sound of the gunshots. Doug made his way downstream. Meanwhile, the hoopla in New River had alerted the guards and their pointers, which picked up Doug's trail but lost it on the river bank. Assuming he knew he was being chased with dogs and had jumped the river to hide his scent, the guards took the dogs across the river and ran them up and down the bank. Soon the pointers picked up a trail—mine.

Doug waded some distance before getting back on land and stealing a panel truck. He was captured soon after when the truck turned over as he was being chased by the police.

As for the mystery beast just outside the prison, that was no elephant—it was Larry Hacker, the second-to-last man in the escape. The final convict up the ladder, Jerry Ward, had to give up when he was winged by one of the guard's shots. Hacker was a couple of steps ahead of Ward. When he passed us he was running on pure adrenaline, and he kept on for 20 miles, finally collapsing in exhaustion in an abandoned church, where sheriff's deputies and FBI agents caught up with him.

The FBI men asked Hacker where I was. He couldn't tell them. He didn't even know who'd put up the ladder. One of the agents hit him on the head with a pistol, after which he and his colleagues tried to take Hacker away. The deputies insisted he stay with them, otherwise Hack might well have become one of those "shot while attempting to escape" statistics.

The escape failed, but it provided much grist for the media mills, especially the newsweeklies, which once again trotted out the official story on the King killing. *Time* even exhumed George McMillan's worn pronouncements. I went into segregation.

All of us who'd escaped were indicted by a grand jury in Morgan County, Tennessee. Judge Lee Asbury scheduled my trial for October.

The Escape Trial

My trial in Wartburg, Tennessee, for breaking out of Brushy Mountain reminded me of the King case. Prosecutor Arzo Carson contacted Mark Lane four times trying to solicit a guilty plea. Rebuffed, he issued a veiled but curious threat: if I didn't plead guilty to escape, the state might drop the charge.

Carson wasn't playing the clown. He had two good reasons to fear a jury trial: the King killing might become an issue again—and worse, the jury might vote to acquit me as a gesture of support for my efforts to gain a trial in the King case.

Judge Lee Asbury, in whose court the escape case had landed, shared these concerns. At a pre-trail conference in his chambers, Judge Asbury implied that he'd jail Mark Lane for contempt if, during the trial, Lane raised questions pertaining to the King case.

The judge wasn't worried about what his mountaineer constituents might think, nor about the media—he was playing politics. If he allowed touchy questions about the King case to be posed at trial, his waltz with Tennessee's power brokers would be over.

At the same time, Governor Blanton was pushing to get me out of the state prison system. In June, 1977, he petitioned President Jimmy Carter to let me be given over to federal custody, citing "security" as the reason. The petition was denied.

The Morgan County courthouse was being renovated. Owing to the disorder of construction, my trial on the escape charges took place in a school building near Brushy Mountain. Despite the limits on his invoking the King murder, Mark Lane skillfully managed to convey to the jury that I'd been sentenced for killing Dr. King without ever being tried. The jury took three hours to return a jury verdict—assessing the minimum penalty required by law. After the verdict was announced, several jurors told the press they wanted to see the King case tried publicly.

Anna

It may seem odd that a confirmed and confined bachelor like me could find out he had a romantic streak, but that was exactly what happened to me in 1977 while I was on trial for escaping from Brushy Mountain.

One of the Knoxville television stations regularly sent a correspondent and a crew to cover the proceedings. The entourage included courtroom artist Anna Sandhu, a pretty blonde in her 30s. (Tennessee law bars cameras in the courtroom.)

On the days that I was in court, and during a few interviews at the prison, we exchanged small talk and got to know one another. After those sessions ended Anna starting visiting me, and we became close. We enjoyed talking about a variety of topics, such as her career as a painter. I looked forward to her visits and she obviously did too, as they became more frequent.

In mid-1978 Anna and I decided to get married. We both knew that it would be a hard road. My release was certainly not a sure thing. But we thought the congressional committee then investigating the King case would unseal all the documents the government had classified, leading to a trial and an acquittal. Unfortunately, we both overestimated the committee's sense of justice. The committee did not declassify any records. Instead it classified 185 cubic feet of its own records.

In October, 1978 we were married in the prison chapel by Rev. James Lawson, a black minister from Memphis who had been a close friend of Martin Luther King. Mark Lane was my best man. Lane had called Rev. Lawson and asked him to perform the ceremony. Lawson was very skeptical of the government case against me and supported a trial. Right after the ceremony I was returned to the prison compound.

I suppose that in marrying Anna I was getting us both into something that was destined to be rocky, but at the time we felt it was the right thing to do. For a few years things went as well as could be expected. Anna joined my other allies in fighting for an open hearing of the case against me, and along with our affection for each other we began to feel the close kinship that comes with a shared cause.

But due to the actions of the congressional committee and the media, the courts declined to grant me a trial. As time passed Anna claimed that she was harassed by people who followed her from the prison. Then, in an incident described in Chapter Twenty-Two, she and I were attacked by an inmate who broke her arm in the melee.

Between June 1981 and September 1987 I was segregated from the general prison population. This forced me to stay alone in my cell most of the time without exercise. This prolonged isolation affected my health, caused my blood pressure to rise and didn't improve my disposition.

Anna felt a great deal of pressure as well. Her visits became less frequent. Finally, she stopped coming to the prison. Years later she retained famed Hollywood divorce lawyer Marvin Mitchelson to file for a divorce. During our divorce battles Anna appeared on talk shows, falsely claiming that I was involved in the assassination of Martin Luther King.

Chapter Twenty

The Ray Brothers

Unlike most of those who talked with the committee, my brothers Jerry and John weren't "committee witnesses," expected to say what panel members wanted to hear. My brothers hadn't been pliable during executive session questioning—when investigators threatened them with perjury unless they incriminated me—so when the TV lights went on, the panel tried new tactics.

Instead of the strong-arm routine, they produced an array of statements and notes from informants claiming to have heard my brothers confess crimes they'd denied in executive session. Most such informants remained behind the veil of official secrecy; instead, committee staff members read their accusations in the course of "questioning" my brothers. Aware of most Americans' repugnance for stool pigeons, the Committee went to great lengths to enhance their informants' appeal, supercharging this secondhand testimony with a racial bias that ennobled the often anonymous informant while debasing my brothers as unsympathetic toward blacks.

During Jerry's appearance before the panel, his interrogators leaned heavily on George McMillan's "reporter's notes," delivered up to the committee without a whimper by that champion of the little man. These scribblings range across a wide band of topics: Communism, Nazism, illicit drugs, alternate lifestyles. Under these headings appear passages attributed to me by McMillan via Jerry.

For instance, McMillan had me calling Jerry from a public phone in Memphis on April 3, 1968, saying, "Big Nigger has had it"—a lie vivid enough to overcome anyone's aversion to stool pigeons. Is it any wonder the committee was falling all over itself to publicize McMillan's "notes"?

Jerry denies this story, but even if it were true, McMillan had grounds for not trusting everything my brother told me. Jerry had pulled a prank on the writer that should have left McMillan suspicious of anything he said subsequently. Early in his research, McMillan began badgering Jerry to sell him Ray family pictures. In a mischievous mood, Jerry obliged by picking up several old photographs at a rummage sale and palming them off as family photos, for which McMillan paid $250. One picture included a black woman, inspiring McMillan to believe he'd stumbled on a big scoop—until Jerry came clean about his hoax.

The photo prank didn't rate any attention from the committee, but McMillan's notes did, as members used those documents to charge that Jerry's position—or non-position, since he didn't care much about a person's color—on race didn't measure up to committee standards.

To these insinuations, Jerry's counsel, a black attorney named Florence R. Kennedy, responded quite effectively, noting the often-seen hypocrisy of those who adopt a goody-twoshoes stance on race. Her rejoinder didn't sit well with Chairman Stokes. He and Kennedy had several caustic exchanges before he finally backed off.

Not content to malign my brothers from the racial angle, the committee resurrected the Bank of Alton robbery story, vaguely mentioning that the inquiry had information to support the charge that Jerry had been in on that heist. This allowed the investigator to reiterate the old suggestion that Jerry, John and I had collaborated on the robbery and that I'd spent my share of the take following Dr. King around the country—ignoring the Alton police force statement that Jerry had never been a suspect in that case. The investigator knew he could do so because he wasn't addressing his remarks to the panel, or to Jerry, but to the press. Like clockwork, the next day's newspapers carried headlines like the one run on November 30, 1978, by the *Atlanta Journal*: "Ray's Brother Linked to King Assassination."

Next, John got his turn on the wheel. He came in with a contingent of federal marshals. The week before, he'd gotten into a barroom brawl in St. Louis and was picked up as a suspected parole violator. Besides the marshals, he was accompanied by James H. Lesar, who'd assisted Bernard Fensterwald in his representation of me for about six years. (He died in 1991.)

The committee queried John on a broad range of subjects, including politics and, predictably, various solved and unsolved bank robberies. All these robberies, except for the Bank of Alton heist, had followed the King murder. None had any connection with it, at least for purposes of a criminal trial. But under its own rules, designed to enhance the official hypotheses for the killing, the committee could choose subject matter at will, and rely on hearsay as well as secret accusations. Should a witness or his lawyer balk at this approach, the panel could threaten instant sanctions. For example, during John's appearance, Chairman Stokes threatened to eject Jim Lesar from the hearing for objecting too strenuously to the panel's acceptance of hearsay alleging that in 1969 John had robbed a bank in Liberty, Illinois—a robbery in no way connected to the murder of Martin Luther King Jr.

In interrogating John, the committee sought mainly to incriminate me. Along with John's alleged participation in the now legendary bank robberies, another subject getting heavy scrutiny was racially biased statements by him. According to an FBI document dating to the days after I was identified as a suspect in the murder, an agent questioned an uncooperative John in a tavern.

"What's all the excitement about?" John asked the FBI man. "He only killed a nigger. If he killed a white man, you wouldn't be here."

While offensive and imprudent, this remark and the attitude behind it were hardly unique to my brother, especially in the weeks after Dr. King's murder, when the same sentiment was being expressed in neighborhood bars across white America. But to the Justice Department, the Select Committee and the press, John's comment was pure gold. The panel and its allies exploited it relentlessly, piling on other similar remarks ascribed to John by George McMillan.

In repetitious questioning, committee members tried to establish that my brother's remarks expressed my attitudes on race. John's lawyer regularly objected to this tack as guilt by association, the McCarthy-era ploy so hated by the liberals of that day. But the liberals of the Select Committee knew a useful method when they saw it, and Chairman Stokes overruled Lesar's objections.

My racist character firmly if falsely established, the committee returned to the bank robbery theme, wandering even further from standard judicial procedure. This time the "evidence" amounted to a graphic display: an enlarged map of Alton, highlighting addresses where, over the years, the Ray family had lived. Other enlargements showed the locations of banks within a 121-mile radius of the town.

The Alton map at least represented facts. My relatives had lived where it said they lived. The bank robbery display was pure invention, but the committee bandwagon was gaining speed and couldn't pause to let its occupants separate fiction from fact.

Charts in place, the committee lawyer began blending fact with theory, trying to implicate John and another Ray family member in the Bank of Alton heist. Warming to his task, he explained that I'd once lived in Alton. On the day of the robbery, he continued, I'd been in East St. Louis, 20 miles away. This set up the assumption that John and I were together the day of the robbery.

The committee lawyer was about to extend his shaky logic to claim we'd robbed the bank, but Jim Lesar interrupted, asking if he could introduce a piece of evidence. He was referring to an FBI document proving that John hadn't been involved in the robbery. Lesar had obtained the material—a statement by my old pal and FBI informant Catman Gawron—via an FOIA request.

The panel had had access to this document since the executive session at which they'd accused John of the robbery. Chairman Stokes said there was no need to reintroduce it. Lesar expressed skepticism.

"Read it!" Stokes snapped. "Go ahead and read it!"

Lesar read the document, a memo written by an FBI agent after a follow-up interview with Catman, who earlier had told the bureau another individual and I had held up the bank. Subsequently, the FBI learned that the other man Gawron had named was in prison at the time of the robbery. The agent went back to double check Catman's story, asking more about the other fellow. According to the document, during the second interview Gawron

> positively identified same as being a person who visited him July 1967, and told him he and [James] Ray had robbed Alton, Illinois, bank and gave $250. Identified positively as person who visited him May 13-14 last with [censored], [Gawron] was then advised that person was in jail at time of robbery and alleged visits in 1967. Gawron hesitated, then said had realized past eight days he had given FBI bum-steer and bum-beef on Alton bank robbery and whose name he then recalled, stated had been thinking about it and decided it was another [censored] whose identity would be known only to [James] Ray, who had visited and told him of Ray participation in Alton robbery. [Gawron] was reminded that if he lied about [censored] he might also be lying about Ray participation.

Despite the censorship of the memo, the panel knew the other unidentified robber wasn't John or Jerry Ray. Neither of my brothers had been incarcerated at the time of the Bank of Alton robbery. The only reason for reviving this old charge was to keep from having to admit that I was in jail for political reasons.

After Lesar read the FBI document, his exchanges with Stokes became increasingly acrimonious, climaxing with Stokes blowing his cool and calling Lesar "a disgrace."

"Make that statement outside!" Lesar barked, referring to the shield of congressional immunity behind which Stokes was hiding as he hurled his insult. Realizing he'd gone too far, Stokes temporarily relinquished the gavel to D.C. Delegate Walter Fauntroy (D), a panel member. Fauntroy ordered a brief recess, after which a staff lawyer resumed the line of questioning about the bank robberies. Chairman Stokes returned, picking up where he'd left off, with a mixture of map graphics and racial politics aimed more at the press than at learning anything from my brother.

First, he had John view several photos of conservative St. Louis area politicians, claiming they had ties to the American Independent Party, the conservative outfit that had run Alabama Governor George Wallace for president in 1968. Stokes asked John if he knew any of these politicians, or if any of them patronized The Grape Vine, a tavern he co-owned.

John recognized few of the faces. This ended his public interrogation, but before leaving the witness stand my brother had a couple of parting shots for the panel. He accused the Justice Department of covering up its investigation of the King murder by classifying FBI files and suggested that the Select Committee had conspired with Justice in the coverup by not examining the classified files.

Jim Lesar had pointed the way for this observation. His own inquiries had turned up damaging information about the upcoming witness, former Scotland Yard inspector Alexander Eist. He read these documents during John's appearance, forcing the panel and its staff to change course abruptly.

John Ray's Trials

Like the prison system and Tennessee politics, the area adjoining St. Louis is a pretty small place, and eventually everybody runs into everybody else. In February 1980 my brother John was paroled, ending his imprisonment for aiding and abetting a bank robbery. His parole stipulated that he live in a halfway house in St. Louis, a city where the U.S. Marshals had told him they'd appreciate his permanent absence, suggesting in the strongest possible language that he stay out of town. Which he did, electing not to sign in at the halfway house.

In May, a lone gunman held up Farmers Bank of Liberty, Illinois, allegedly getting away with $15,000. A warrant was issued for my brother's arrest. On June 23 John was arrested near Alton. He was wearing an orange leisure suit and cowboy boots and carrying a shopping bag that contained a pistol, according to the arresting officer, who turned out to be Conrad Baetz, the erstwhile House Select Committee investigator, now back on the job as a Madison County deputy sheriff.

Baetz claimed he was "returning from a shopping trip" when he recognized John from their encounters at the Marion, Illinois, federal prison, where Baetz said he'd interviewed my brother while investigating the King case.

But John said Baetz never interviewed him at Marion and claimed the arrest was a set-up. The next day, this apparent conflict was lost amid news reports that the FBI was saying it wanted to question John about the shooting of Urban League director Vernon Jordan, who'd been wounded May 29 outside a Fort Wayne, Indiana, motel. Jordan was in the company of a white woman, suggesting the ambush might have been racially motivated.

The initial FBI statement linking John to Jordan's shooting came from the top man, William H. Webster, who as a judge had sentenced John to 18 years in prison for the bank job. Now Webster was on my brother's case again.

"At least two similarities existed between the shooting of the Rev. Dr. King and Jordan," Webster told a reporter. "One was the fact that both men were 'stalked' by their assailants. The other was that the King assassination was apparently financed by bank robberies."

Soon after Webster's remarks, the party line was in place. Special agent Wayne Davis, head of the bureau's Indianapolis office, told the press, "James Earl Ray financed his activities surrounding the shooting of Martin Luther King with the proceeds of a bank robbery. John Larry Ray allegedly has been involved in a bank robbery in Liberty, Illinois."

At a follow-up news conference, Davis explained the reasoning behind this allegation.

"It's kind of a coincidence that [John Ray] was wanted on a federal warrant at [the] time [Jordan was shot]," Davis told reporters. "His family's name and activities led people to make the somewhat logical connection."

The usual media response to efforts at establishing guilt by association is a scribbling frenzy, as editorialists preach about the evils of McCarthyism. Not this time. The John Ray/Vernon Jordan story petered out after a few days, but not without further tainting the Ray name with suggestions of murderous racist conspiracy.

FBI man Wayne Davis was black and part of the new government practice of using blacks to promote the official line in the King case and related matters. This meant any challenges to these mouthpieces risked the charge of racism.

Eventually, the Jordan shooting was blamed on Joseph Paul Franklin, previously accused of shooting at interracial couples but acquitted of the assault on Jordan. Similarly, the state bank robbery charges against John were dropped—although in December a federal grand jury hauled him in on charges of participating in another bank robbery. He went on trial in Springfield, Illinois. After a mistrial, he was acquitted. Unfortunately, during that sequence he'd refused to provide a sample of his handwriting, incurring a contempt of court charge, drawing three years in prison. And the pistol in the shopping bag he'd been carrying when Conrad Baetz arrested him brought down an indictment for being a convicted felon in illegal possession of a firearm.

The usual sentence for this crime is two years. However, the prosecutor said he might try John as a "dangerous offender," opening up my brother to the threat of unlimited sentencing. John copped a plea, drawing the two years. The United States government benefited from the plea bargain, since avoiding a trial meant Conrad Baetz's knowledge of the machinations that went into John's arrest with the pistol remained sealed in his mind.

Chapter Twenty-One

Alexander Eist

Alexander Eist, whose written statement had been read a few months before by Representative Devine, was the real centerpiece of the committee's trumped-up show. The Devine reading apparently had been a bit of test marketing. When the press made the right noises, the Englishman was invited to fly across the pond and repeat his tales in person.

Eist's earlier written statement and live testimony read like a digest of previously published material promoting the government's case.

Eist told the panel that after my arrest in London in June 1968 he guarded me almost constantly, seldom leaving my side during my six weeks in British custody. He said he gained my confidence by supplying me with reading material and candy bars. I responded by making "incriminating admissions," he claimed. He never said I confessed to the King murder—only that I made these supposed admissions, on a range of topics. During his committee testimony, he picked out those portions most favorable to the government's case, saying I'd told him I hated blacks, saying I'd voiced concern about being convicted of the King murder, saying I'd talked about my worry over being indicted for conspiracy. Eist said I'd told him I had no accomplices and wasn't paid for the shooting, but expected to become a national hero and rake in thousands of dollars by appearing on television and other media outlets. And, he said gravely, I never showed any remorse for Dr. King's murder.

The Committee couldn't have written a more compelling story—although members probably would have added a few bank robberies for good measure.

Displaying the usual American awe for anything uttered with a British accent, Committee members haphazardly questioned Eist, who had a ready answer corroborating every prearranged conclusion. In one such exchange, he quoted me as saying I'd discarded the rifle near the scene because I saw a policeman or police car. This was an old story, leaked by the prosecution and attributed to "unnamed sources." The committee took it to heart, without seeming to note that Eist hadn't said I discarded the rifle after shooting Dr. King.

Eist may have starred in the hearing, but in a real court he'd have wilted like a weed under cross-examination. Between Devine's reading of Eist's statement and Eist's appearance, Mark Lane had delved into the Englishman's past. Evan Williams, an investigator in Clwyd, North Wales, found that Eist had been indicted for several jewel robberies and for falsely claiming to have obtained confessions. British authorities refused to release documents from Eist's trials confirming this.

Like the unsavory backgrounds of other committee witnesses, Eist's tainted history was known to committee investigators, who initially concealed that knowledge. They'd found that in 1976 Eist had been charged with "conspiracy to commit corruption and conspiracy to prevent the course of justice." In a directed verdict—one delivered not by a jury but by a judge, and a familiar pattern when a defendant turns state's evidence—Eist was found not guilty on all counts.

Did Eist's memory of my "admissions" suddenly improve after he was charged with corruption? The committee found that Eist had talked up our time together to three other persons before the panel. Only one of those three instances preceded his indictment. That contact involved Owen Summers, a London newspaper reporter who told the committee in a November 2, 1978, written statement that Eist told him in 1968 about my "admissions." One wonders why a policeman would tell a reporter and not his superiors about something so seemingly important, and why that reporter wouldn't rush the story into print.

But again the hearings machine was running at full speed. The Select Committee knew Eist was fabricating—it had copies of an FBI document to prove it. The document, a memorandum reporting on agency undercover surveillance of me while in British prisons, contains statements considerably at variance with Eist's tale:

> July 17, 1968. Subject (James Earl Ray) refused to see two Scotland Yard officers June 14 last and said he would also refuse to see FBI if they asked to see him. Yard officers made request to see him in an effort to ascertain his activities in London from May 17 to June 8. Subject not saying anything significant to Warders [guards], as he now believes they are trying to extract information for the police.

Scotland Yard doesn't supply guards for the British prison systems. When inspectors come calling, a prisoner needed to consent to see them. Eist had guarded me only during my first days in British custody.

Another Scotland Yard communication to J. Edgar Hoover—available to the Select Committee but ignored by panel members and the press—bluntly characterizes Eist's desire to testify against me as a "financial move," and declares that Eist was "never alone with Ray."

After Congressman Devine had interrupted my testimony to read the Eist statement, Chairman Stokes assured Mark Lane that I'd be called back to testify, but on November 9, when Eist began his appearance, the panel announced that it had "reconsidered" and wouldn't bring me back to testify. The only protest besides my attorney's came from a member of the committee staff: assistant deputy chief counsel Michael C. Eberhardt resigned in protest, declaring that the committee feared my return might enable Mark Lane to muddle "some of the gains" the committee had achieved at my first appearance.

The impact of Eist's appearance can be seen in views expressed once the hearings ended. Panel members Devine and Robert Edgar (D., Pa.) both cited Eist's statements as the primary factor leading them to conclude that I was solely responsible for the murder of Martin Luther King Jr.

Chapter Twenty-Two

Knives in the Library

All along I was at Brushy Mountain, working in the laundry and spending my off-time lifting weights or—especially on Thursday, when I didn't have to work in the laundry—in the prison's law library, located in a remote section of the recreation building. At the time, the library had just been renovated in a way that made it more dangerous. The old layout was more open. The new design was constricted and resulted in what prisoners call "death traps," slang for spaces in which someone who's attacked is unable to get into the open, whether to defend himself or to flee.

In May 1981, I was deeply immersed in the subject of clemency. It was two months after I'd answered the Board of Parole's questions on the King case. A fight erupted in the recreation building between a white gang and a black gang. Guards broke up the battle, but as punishment, the recreation building was shut down. At the same time, inflammatory material about the King assassination—including an *Ebony* article by ex-Select Committee Chairman Louis Stokes repeating the lie that I'd done the job, and done it all by myself—began to circulate around Brushy Mountain.

A week passed and still no law library. I complained to Warden Herman Davis. He said the library would reopen the next day, June 4.

That morning, I ran around the jogging path several times, then went to the law library. The building was empty of guards. The only official presence was an elderly counselor sitting in an office near the recreation building. There was a lot of window light, but few lights in the hallway, so it was sort of dim. I turned right, then left, heading for the chicken-wire partition around the library. You enter through a small door at one end of the partition. I half-noticed one white convict sitting at a desk. He waved me inside.

I passed through the corridors leading to the main library. I sat down at a table, spread out my papers and began studying. A few minutes passed. I was glad to be back at my review of clemency law. I went to the shelves to look for a book.

Suddenly, someone grabbed me from behind, pinning my arms. At first I thought it was a pal, someone like Doug Shelton or Earl Hill. If either saw me going into the law library, he usually stopped by to chat.

But the man pinning me was black, and he had a sidekick coming at me with a shank. I stood up and attempted to shake off the man on my back, moving around and hollering for help. I was aiming to break loose and get to the billiard room, where I might be able to lay my hands on a cue or do some serious defensive jogging. We fell to the floor several times. After about five minutes of stabbing and slashing, the knife wielder dropped the blade and fled, his cohort hot on his heels.

Thinking they might be back for a second round, I crawled over and picked up the knife. It was a classic shank—a foot long, made of some kind of metal and ground to a point.

I heard voices. Several guards came in, followed by Warden Davis, looking not at all surprised by what he saw. But then, he'd been working in prisons since 1948, so he was slightly jaded. Soon stretcher bearers arrived and moved me to the prison infirmary. From there I was hauled by ambulance 15 miles to a hospital in Oak Ridge.

I'd bled enough to need a transfusion, but I wasn't hemorrhaging, which meant my attackers had missed my main blood vessels. On the way to Oak Ridge the prison doctor and medical attendant did what they could to patch the slices. At the hospital, Dr. Ernest L. Hendrix put me under and then counted 22 punctures requiring 77 stitches to close. I'd been stabbed in the left cheek, the side of my neck, my left hand, wrist and arm, and in the chest.

When I came out of anesthesia later in the day, I found my legs chained to the bed, on orders from the warden. That evening, Mark Lane flew in from New Orleans. He and I were concerned that the propaganda machine would be floating stories that the wounds had been self-inflicted, or were superficial. So Mark asked Warden Davis to let us have a photographer record my injuries. Davis said no. Lane took the request to Commissioner of Corrections Harold Bradley in Nashville; he too refused.

Bradley did say he'd let a state photographer handle the job. We knew what that meant: lots of flash work, hold that pose, I think I've got it, gee, the film must have gotten ruined in the processor. We declined.

Right after I was stabbed the state's game became obvious. Bradley began speculating at a news conference about how he might keep me in segregation indefinitely to protect me, or perhaps transfer me to a federal prison. Federal prisons also exert more control over media access to prisoners.

During my second day in the hospital, a doctor told me if no complications developed I'd be back in the prison in two or three days, a schedule that speeded up significantly when word got out that the state was having to fork over $94 a day to keep me in the hospital. That evening guards arrived to haul me down the back stairs and into a panel truck, then back to Brushy Mountain. I was grateful the cost of my hospital care didn't become public while the doctors were stitching me up.

The next day, I had a visit from my wife, Anna, and brother Jerry. Having worked as a courtroom artist in Knoxville until our marriage—after which the TV station for which she'd been free-lancing blackballed her—she's a fast hand with the watercolors. She suggested that with no other way to document my wounds, she could sketch them. I removed the bandages, she roughed out a torso on her sketchpad, then carefully drew in the lacerations, cut for cut.

Anna, Jerry and I also discussed possible concern in official circles about efforts by her and others to get a jury trial for me. Anna had been in touch with Rev. Hosea Williams, a member of the Georgia state House of Representatives from Atlanta and a black leader in his own right who had been urging a trial in the King case. (In October 1986, he and Anna appeared on the *Sally Jessy Raphael Show* to push for a trial.)

We agreed that the state would do little about the stabbing, except stage a "trial" for the defendants or leak more misleading information to the media. News reports said I'd been attacked by members of the Alke-Bulan Society, a supposed self-help group for black convicts. In many ways, outfits like the Alke-Bulans have come to compete with the old-style prison gangs, offering not only muscle, protection and companionship—while I was at Brushy Mountain the blacks in the group kept a couple of white molls around for fun, games and snooping on the white gangs—but a philosophy and a veneer of legitimacy. For example, the Alke-Bulan Society—a black studies organization that takes its name from the oldest known name for the African continent—is chartered by the State of Tennessee. The group even had an office at Brushy Mountain.

I stayed a couple of weeks in the infirmary, during which time a couple of Tennessee Bureau of Investigation agents stopped by trying to interrogate me. They wanted to know who'd attacked me. I said that I didn't know.

The follow-up to the stabbing was a rude awakening in the middle of the night. At 2 a.m on June 14, I was sleeping in the infirmary, still recovering from my wounds, when Warden Davis and several guards shook me awake.

"Get up," Davis announced. "You're traveling."

My nose and his diction told me old Herman had been drinking the shine again. I asked where I was being taken. He told the guards to handcuff and leg-iron me. I objected, starting a brief scuffle that opened up two of my stab wounds and ended with me in the back seat of a Tennessee Department of Corrections car.

Four hours later we pulled into the main prison compound at Nashville and parked behind cell block six, the segregation building and my first roost in the Tennessee prison system. Davis and company escorted me to an empty cell near the back of cell block six—a creepy little neighborhood. That's where Tennessee keeps its Death Row inmates, conveniently located near the electric chair.

But six weeks later I was back on the road to East Tennessee, summoned to testify before a grand jury in Wartburg about the stabbing. I appeared, answered the questions asked of me and got up to leave. The next witness was Brushy Mountain Warden Davis. I figured I was getting the usual tapdance until I got outside and saw Nashville TV reporter Larry Brinton and crew. He was the only media type present, meaning that somebody had tipped him to the grand jury's inquiry.

In the early 1970s, Brinton had covered a lot of crime stories for the *Nashville Banner*, including my case, in which he always bought the state's line. In fact, in any controversy Brinton could be depended on to side with the highest party on the totem pole. If it was prisoners against guards, he was always for the guards. If it was guards against administrators, he'd tilt for the administration. I wondered what Brinton had up his sleeve.

I found out that evening, after a long ride back to cell block six. After a blaring introduction letting viewers know they were about to hear a "Larry Brinton EXCLUSIVE," footage of me being led from the Wartburg courthouse unreeled, as Brinton reported that Brushy Mountain inmate—and Alke-Bulan moll—William Wynn was swearing he'd overheard me trying to get somebody to stab me for $50. Brinton claimed Wynn had passed a polygraph examination, after which ever-smiling Channel 5 anchorman Chris Clark chimed in.

"The stab wounds Ray received were merely superficial," Clark said. It's a good thing some people go into journalism and not medicine.

More Violence

After my transfer to Nashville, Anna moved to that city from Knoxville so she could visit, although we were allowed only two one-hour meetings a week.

The old, endless routine set in, at least for a while. But no routine lasts long, especially in segregation. If the prisoners aren't raising hell, the administration worries that something may be up, and on its own stirs the pot, if only to disrupt any subterfuge that might be going on.

My routine went south when Anna and I were attacked during one of her visits by a prisoner connected with the Alke-Bulan gang. Someone had left the padlock on the visitor's room unlatched, and the guy charged into the room. I tried to move Anna out of harm's way, but he slugged her on the arm. I shoved a table between him and us, which was how the guards found us when they showed up—too late, as usual.

Anna wasn't able to drive home, so she asked a prison official if he'd call an ambulance. At first he refused. She didn't have the $50 cash it would take to pay the driver. But finally he relented and made the call. The ambulance company agreed to take delayed payment. At the hospital, Anna's arm was found to be broken.

There were other byproducts of the attack. The *Nashville Tennessean* complained about the lack of security in cell block six, but in tones that suggested I shouldn't have defended myself and my wife from our attacker—who, by the way, got the transfer he wanted.

This was bad enough, but then Anna had to go through the indignity of seeing the state refuse to pay for its negligence. Tennessee has a claims board that rules on requests for compensation after an injury on state property through the negligence of state workers. This clearly was the case in Anna's broken arm, which could have been prevented if the guards had been doing their jobs. She filed to be reimbursed for her $50 ambulance ride. Her claim wasn't denied; it wasn't even acted on.

The convicts who'd attacked me, as well as a third man who'd acted as lookout, were tried in June 1982 in Knoxville, where the air was fragrant with rumors that I'd paid to be stabbed.

On June 17, I was driven to town and brought to the chambers of Judge John J. Duncan Jr. When prosecutor Robert Jolly showed up to inform me officially that I'd be called as a witness, I asked if it was necessary to march me through the courtroom in handcuffs and leg-irons. Jolly said that wouldn't be necessary. Once he got me on the stand, he had only one question.

"Were you assaulted on June 4, 1981, in the Brushy Mountain Prison law library?" Jolly asked.

"Yes," I said.

Defense attorney Isaiah Gant asked one question as well, but he asked it three times. He had the defendants stand one at a time. As each rose, he asked if I could identify the man as the one who'd stabbed me.

"No," I said three times. Some things you just have to let go by. That ended the questioning.

But as the victim I felt entitled to comment on the difficulty I had in the Tennessee courts establishing facts in any matter related directly or indirectly to the King murder. I felt—and feel—that this is due to the prevailing winds that blow from the *Tennessean*, the state's political establishment and the Rockefeller contingent. I said so that day in court from the witness stand. Having made that observation, I intended to ask a few questions, such as why William Wynn, the informant claiming to have overheard me trying to hire someone to stab me, hadn't been called to testify at this "trial?"

But no sooner had I taken the name "Rockefeller" in vain than a dozen or so sheriff's deputies rushed me, rousted me out of the witness stand, and, aided by prison officials, hustled me down the back way into a squad car. They were so busy jerking me out of the spotlight they forgot the legirons and handcuffs. My feet didn't touch down until I landed in the back seat.

The three defendants were convicted and sentenced to long prison terms—a superfluous gesture, since all were in on extended sentences anyway. Their lawyers didn't even bother to appeal. Given my situation, the state couldn't lose. If I were killed, so what? If I survived, I could be kept in informal but permanent segregation, supposedly for my own good.

Part V

Conspirators

Chapter Twenty-Three

Randy Rosen

One team of Select Committee agents was trying to knit together a plausible conspiracy case against me in St. Louis. Over in eastern Tennessee, another team was working overtime to conceal evidence of a genuine conspiracy to assassinate Dr. King. The Tennessee effort centered on Randolph Erwin Rosenson.

Back in November 1967, as I was about to cross the Mexican border into California, I cleaned the car and found a business card between the seats of the Mustang. Written on the back was the name "Randy Rosen" and a Miami address. Later I did some checking, but couldn't get a line on anyone with that name until 1974. That year, in the course of filing a libel suit in Memphis, I had my brother Jerry ask Raulston Schoolfield to recommend a lawyer. Schoolfield suggested Clyde Watts, who had offices in Oklahoma City, Oklahoma. Watts' schedule precluded him from helping us, but he did provide other assistance. Jerry mentioned the mysterious "Rosen," adding that he might have a police record in Miami or New Orleans. Watts said he had contacts in those cities and would see what he could do.

When Jerry checked in again, Watts told him "Randy Rosen" actually was "Randolph Erwin Rosenson," a sometime carnival worker who'd been convicted in New Orleans U.S. District Court on a narcotics-related charge. Jerry relayed this information to my attorney, Richard Ryan. In February 1975, Ryan obtained a transcript of Rosenson's New Orleans trial, which revealed that Rosenson had been a government informant.

Nothing much was done about this information until 1977 when I mentioned it to the Select Committee, triggering a series of deceptive maneuvers, apparently designed to keep Rosenson under wraps. And, for reasons not clear to me at the time, the Tennessee legal hierarchy was snooping on both the committee and Rosenson. In brief, this is what happened:

In June 1977, as I was escaping from Brushy Mountain, the committee found Rosenson and stashed him in the Andrew Johnson Hotel in Knoxville under the alias Ben Rubin. There, committee investigators interrogated him in his room, unaware that their conversations were being bugged on orders from the Tennessee attorney general.

Apparently both Rosenson and the committee were putting out a cover story that he'd come to Knoxville with a carnival and gotten into an auto accident. When the insurance company's check arrived, local banks wouldn't cash it, so he was staying at the Andrew Johnson for a while until the checks cleared—or so Rosenson told the local media.

The truth isn't so tangled.

The chairman of a congressional investigating committee usually appoints political partisans to key staff positions. These staffers show their appreciation by steering panel expenditures toward deserving party adherents, especially at the local level. It was no coincidence that Boyd Cloud, who owned the Andrew Johnson Hotel, served on Tennessee Governor Ray Blanton's patronage committee and chaired the Knox County Democratic Party. Putting up Rosenson and a couple of staffers at the hotel for an extended stretch was a way of saying thank you to an old Democratic supporter.

Rosenson's curious stay in Knoxville ended when he "hired" a prominent local Democrat, attorney Gene A. Stanley, to "represent" him in the accident case. With Stanley on the job the alleged insurance problem dissolved in short order and Rosenson left Knoxville, resurfacing in September 1977, calling Stanley from the county jail in Richmond, Virginia. News reports had Rosenson detained there in connection with a 1973 drug charge, but when Stanley made inquiries, the sheriff refused to discuss Rosenson's detention.

Stanley inferred that Select Committee staff members had engineered Rosenson's arrest, but he learned nothing concrete. Some reports have him changing identities under the Justice Department witness protection program, but since the telephone call from Richmond, Rosenson hasn't been heard of.

However, Rosenson casts a long shadow. David Allen Bowman, the Andrew Johnson Hotel desk clerk who'd let the state bug the room where the Select Committee staff interviewed Rosenson, was an acquaintance of my wife Anna. Bowman told her that for a price, he could get her a set of the Rosenson tapes.

Anna sought Mark Lane's advice. He endorsed the purchase. But when Anna went back to Bowman, he seemed nervous. He'd given the extra set of tapes to Rosenson's lawyer, Gene Stanley, he told her.

That night, an anonymous telephone caller told Anna to forget about Rosenson and the tapes if she wanted to stay healthy. When she told me about the call, I advised her to drop the matter.

But a few months later I sued Stanley in Knoxville U.S. District Court, seeking release of the Rosenson tapes, which could have shed some light on his involvement in the King killing, or at least proved that he had nothing to do with it. But Judge Robert Taylor dismissed the suit without even requiring Stanley to acknowledge my complaint.

Next, Anna heard from another Knoxville lawyer. Howard M. Ellis told her he had a tape she might enjoy hearing. At his office, he played a cassette of a brief conversation he'd had with Stanley.

"What did you do with the tapes James Earl Ray sued you for?" Ellis asked.

"I did what Richard Nixon should have done," Stanley replied. "I didn't burn them, I recorded over them."

I have a copy of the Ellis tape, as do friends.

Rosenson's testimony to the Select Committee about the King case probably will remain hidden from the public, thanks not only to Stanley's handling of the hotel tapes but to the committee's own rules. When the panel's mandate expired, Chairman Stokes and chief counsel Blakey had the Clerk of the House classify certain parts of testimony recorded in executive session. This keeps the public from hearing the tapes for 50 years. Also classified were documents the committee specifically didn't approve for publication. Between these two immense categories, all but a few scraps of Rosenson's executive session testimony has been suppressed. And Tennessee law forbid release of materials in the attorney general's files—where another copy of the Rosenson hotel tape resides.

Bits of Rosenson's committee testimony appear in a Bantam Books edition of excerpts from the Select Committee investigation. Passages reveal that during 1967-68, while I was a fugitive under Raoul's influence, Rosenson's path was paralleling mine. He was in several cities at the same time that I was. *For example, he was in the Birmingham, Alabama, area while I was buying the rifle allegedly used to kill Dr. King.* Documents under the control of the executive branch of the federal government might reveal the reason for Rosenson's shadow dance, but these are classified.

Perhaps someday, when the 50-year limit is reached, someone will be able to see if the Select Committee files do contain documents indicating whether those who killed—or financed the killing of—Dr. King had a hand in maintaining Rosenson's proximity to me. Perhaps his carnival wanderings, a ploy commonly used by drug dealers, also helped arrange temporary support of some kind for whoever killed Dr. King.

But material in the public domain, such as criminal records, does tell us a good deal more about Rosenson than the committee wanted revealed. The transcript of his 1966 drug conviction shows that Rosenson smuggled drugs into the United States in the cages of exotic birds he'd purchased in Mexico ostensibly to be exhibited at carnivals.

His criminal record also illuminates Rosenson's financial status. Drug smuggling is a lucrative business. Rosenson seldom had the cash to retain lawyers when he was arrested—but attorneys and bail bondsmen always materialized. In the New Orleans bust, Rosenson pleaded poverty, but he made bond, and was able to engage the services of G. Wray Gill, a top New Orleans criminal lawyer. Gill's pre-trial maneuvering was complex and protracted, greatly increasing his fee. Eventually, Gill called in Camille F. Gravel, another expensive lawyer, as a consultant. Between them, they delayed action on Rosenson's conviction for nearly two years—and never complained publicly that they weren't getting paid.

Rosenson wasn't the only Gill client with extraordinary ties to a political assassination. In 1962, Gill needed an investigator. He hired David Ferrie, a former Eastern Airlines pilot who came to figure in the inquiries into President Kennedy's murder. Ferrie's work for Gill included investigations involving Kennedy administration deportation proceedings against Carlos Marcello.

Long reputed to be the kingpin of Louisiana's mob, Marcello owned the motel whose telephone number partially matched one of the numbers I'd gotten during my travels with Raoul. He and the Kennedys had a lot of bad blood between them. In 1961, Marcello had shown up at the New Orleans immigration office for an early stage of the proceedings that eventually involved Gill and Ferrie. When Marcello arrived, he was seized by CIA agents working on orders from U.S. Attorney General Robert Kennedy. The CIA men flew Marcello to Guatemala and left him there in informal exile.

It took Marcello a couple of months to slip the CIA's grip and return to the United States. He flew back in a private plane captained by David Ferrie. Indicted for falsely claiming to be a U.S. citizen, Marcello was tried in New Orleans. He was acquitted on November 22, 1963, the day John Kennedy was killed.

The next day, Jack S. Martin, a stool pigeon for the New Orleans police department and an associate of David Ferrie, told the New Orleans district attorney's office Ferrie may have aided in the Kennedy murder. That evening, Ferrie was driving back to New Orleans from Houston. In route, he telephoned Gill, who alerted him to Martin's statements. Instead of proceeding to New Orleans, Ferrie drove to Hammond, Louisiana, and stayed with friends. He sent two male companions as decoys to his residence, where they were arrested by policemen under the direction of New Orleans District Attorney Jim Garrison. Two days later, Ferrie turned himself in at Garrison's office and was arrested on suspicion of involvement in the Kennedy assassination. Ferrie claimed that immediately before the killing in Dallas he'd been helping Gill prepare a defense for Marcello's citizenship falsification case. Later, the FBI and the Secret Service absolved Ferrie of any complicity in Kennedy's murder.

In 1967, Jim Garrison reopened his investigation of the Kennedy assassination, again placing Ferrie under suspicion. During this inquiry, Ferrie died, allegedly of a brain hemorrhage—however, two typed suicide notes reportedly were found near his body, both with what appeared to be Ferrie's signature.

Chapter Twenty-Four

The FBI Connection

At a December 18, 1968 court hearing in Memphis, Percy Foreman alluded to a "secret file" developed by the FBI on Martin Luther King and associates with authorization from U.S. Attorney General Robert Kennedy.

Foreman's reference to these records may have been a warning shot to the King camp that a trial might cause their martyred leader's dirty laundry to be subpoenaed, declassified and made public. Certainly, in those days, the civil rights leader's associates wanted the file kept hidden. In 1976, they and others collaborated to convince the courts to keep the file locked away in the National Archives for 50 years, because they knew that the file contained embarrassing information on Dr. King's private life—information sought out and amassed by the FBI as part of its domestic counterintelligence program, known as COINTELPRO, directed by Cartha DeLoach.

Cartha DeLoach

COINTELPRO, bureaucratese for Counter Intelligence Program, was a surreptitious FBI operation where agents went undercover, infiltrating black groups and using other tactics to provoke and disrupt these organizations. One FBI memo admitted the use of agents and provocateurs "in harassing and impelling criminal activities." During the late 1960s, FBI operatives in the black movement repeatedly urged and initiated violent acts. In the Memphis setting, turning a nonviolent march into a race riot would have furthered the FBI's goal of undermining King's peaceful approach.

COINTELPRO was under the control of Cartha D. De-Loach. The bureau had been tapping Dr. King's telephone since the 1950s, when he came to prominence in Birmingham, Alabama. Convinced that King was a threat to internal security, FBI chief J. Edgar Hoover ordered the taps, but for years nothing incriminating turned up. In 1961, when William Sullivan took over as head of the bureau's intelligence division, he suggested that Hoover have King in for a chat. As an up-and-coming civil rights leader, Sullivan told Hoover in a memo, King "could be of great assistance to the bureau in the future."

Hoover agreed to the idea, provided his protégé, Cartha DeLoach, sat in on the conversation. King rejected the invitation, angering Hoover—who came to believe that Dr. King was a Communist. Others at the bureau were reluctant to accept Hoover's notion of Martin Luther King Jr. as a red, but Hoover ran the store, and they knew he could always hire more clerks. Several years later, after Hoover had declared King "the most notorious liar in the world," they did meet— but afterward, in a monitored telephone call, King told a friend, "The old man talks too much." Word of this got back to Hoover, and that was all she wrote. Hoover sicked De-Loach onto King's case for the rest of the civil rights leader's life and beyond.

DeLoach had used his proximity to Hoover to wiggle his way into a position as FBI liaison to the Johnson White House. Once ensconced, DeLoach went back and forth between LBJ and the FBI, tilting each in the direction he favored and keeping both off-balance. After overseeing the FBI's bugging of Martin Luther King and his associates trying to challenge the Mississippi delegation to the 1964 Democratic National Convention in Atlantic City, DeLoach was instrumental in keeping a scandal from erupting in Washington. That fall Johnson aide Walter Jenkins was arrested for propositioning an undercover cop in the restroom of Washington's downtown YMCA. DeLoach's dirty work in the Jenkins scandal put him in tight with Johnson and one up on Hoover, helping him to move into the uppermost echelons of the bureau.

William Sullivan ran the the Domestic Intelligence Division until he resigned in 1971, and then wrote a book titled *My Thirty Years in Hoover's FBI*. According to Sullivan, DeLoach used the mandatory retirement age of 65 for FBI directors, unless waived by President Johnson, to manipulate Hoover. (Hoover turned 70 in 1965.) Sullivan noted that DeLoach would skillfully play on Hoover's fear of forced retirement by subtly suggesting that his close association with President Johnson could forestall mandatory retirement.

According to Sullivan, DeLoach used the bureau to gather political information for Johnson, including dirt on Senator Barry Goldwater, Johnson's 1964 opponent.

DeLoach dabbled in the chief's pet projects, such as bugging Dr. King—not merely his telephone calls, but his hotel rooms, resulting in tapes of King's sexual escapades. Sullivan recounts how Hoover, who insisted that any pornography confiscated by his agents be sent straight to the director's office for personal attention, insisted on getting copies of King's bedroom tapes. In late 1964, Hoover had samples of his agents' handiwork sent to King's wife, in hopes of breaking up their marriage and weakening his stature among blacks.

That obviously didn't work, but DeLoach kept up the pressure—making tapes, recruiting SCLC informants, sowing the seeds of discord inside King's organization, even trying to get associates of King's such as National Association for the Advancement of Colored People executive secretary Roy Wilkins to come over to the bureau's side.

But the overtures to Wilkins were only the thin edge of the FBI's wedge. In Mark Lane's book, *Code Name Zorro*, veteran FBI agent Arthur Murtagh reveals that in an informal conversation held after working hours, he was asked to steal SCLC stationery and handwriting samples of top SCLC officials, presumably to forge incriminating notes and letters.

Long before Dr. King died bureau agents engaged in harassment, grand and petty. Besides collecting and mailing bedroom tapes—*in one instance including a letter urging King to kill himself or risk exposure*—they would monitor his comings and goings, sometimes waiting until he entered a friend's house, then calling the fire department and reporting a blaze at that address to disrupt King.

In an apartment not far from the SCLC's Atlanta headquarters, the FBI ran a full-tilt wiretapping operation, using the latest electronic equipment and stationing agents on the headphones 24 hours a day. The bureau took its act on the road, too—when Dr. King went to Sweden to accept the Nobel Peace Prize, his wiretappers went along with him.

From the FBI's paranoid outlook, nearly any citizen could appear to be a threat to American security. An outspoken citizen activist such as Dr. King sent the bureau into apoplexy. Hoover and DeLoach egged one another along in their insistence that Dr. King was, if not a Communist himself, then the tool of Communists inside and outside the SCLC. In addition to the COINTELPRO tactics, the FBI also kept the SCLC under surveillance as a part of the FBI's COMINFIL—short for "Communist Infiltration"—program. The bureau added Dr. King's name to "Section A of the Reserve Index." This was a polite tag for the list of Americans to be rounded up and imprisoned in the event of a national emergency.

William Sullivan was in the loop with DeLoach and Hoover concerning the bureau's actions to neutralize Martin Luther King. In a December 1, 1964 memorandum to Sullivan, FBI operative J. A. Sizoo stated:

[censored] stated to DeLoach that *he was faced with the difficult problem of taking steps to remove King from the national picture.* He indicates in his comments that he, alone, could be successful. It is, therefore, suggested that considerations be given to the following course of action: That DeLoach have a further discussion with [censored] and offer to be helpful to [censored] *in connection with the problem of the removal of King from the national scene.*

A copy of the entire memorandum is included in the appendix to this book. The censorship was done by the FBI.

Zorro

The bureau assigned King the code name "Zorro," from the Spanish for "fox," which reflects the perspective of Hoover, DeLoach and company. To them Dr. King was a brown animal, to be chased, hunted and run into the ground by a pack of FBI operatives.

After King's earlier visits to Memphis in 1968, the bureau floated a "news" story calling him a hypocrite for encouraging blacks to boycott white Memphis businesses but staying at the posh, white-owned Holiday Inn instead of using a black-owned establishment like the Lorraine Motel. This all but guaranteed that when he came back to the city at the beginning of April that he would register himself and his associates at the Lorraine, perhaps unwittingly fitting into a pattern of behavior designed by those who wanted him dead.

And just before Dr. King's last visit to Memphis, the FBI drafted a speech for Senator Robert Byrd (D., W.Va.). Delivered on the floor of the Senate on March 29, the Byrd speech repeated the FBI party line on King, even deriding him as a phony "messiah"—a word that appears repeatedly in FBI memoranda on the civil rights leader.

Frank Holloman

There is strong evidence that the bureau's long arm reached beyond its jurisdiction, thanks to the placement of former agents in key local law enforcement offices. For example, Frank Holloman, who was in charge of the Memphis police *and* fire departments in 1968, had spent 25 years in the FBI. Holloman rose through the ranks to become the inspector in charge of the office of Director Hoover, and the two became quite close. In addition to working in the Washington headquarters Holloman was the agent in charge of the Atlanta office, the nerve center for King harassment and wiretapping.

The day before King was shot two black Memphis firemen, who had been stationed at Fire Station Two, which offered a fine view of the Lorraine Motel across the street, were transferred without explanation. Floyd Newsum was one of the relocated firemen. He was later told that he was moved because of unspecified threats on his life. Mark Lane questioned Holloman about the transfers, but was given evasive, vague answers.

Similar unsubstantiated threats were the reason given for pulling Memphis Detective Ed Redditt, also black, from the city police squad operating out of Fire Station Two. At about 2 p.m., on April 4, four hours before the assassination, Holloman summoned Redditt away from his position protecting King to a meeting. The U.S. Secret Service had learned of a "contract" to kill Redditt, the police and fire chief said. Redditt told Mark Lane:

> It was like a meeting of the Joint Chiefs of Staff. In this room, just before Dr. King was murdered, were the heads and seconds in command of I guess every law enforcement operation in this area you could think of. I had never seen anything like it before. The Sheriff, the Highway Patrol, Army Intelligence, the National Guard. You name it. It was in the room.

Redditt protested that he wanted to stay on the job, but Holloman ordered him to his home, with guards from the police department who were supposed to stay with him. "I thought they might stay outside in unmarked cars, maintaining radio contact with each other and with me, and in that way provide some protection," Redditt told Lane. "But their orders apparently were to stay in the house with me. *That way they could watch me, but they couldn't protect me.*" Redditt continued:

> If someone threw a bomb in a window those two officers would just have been two more casualties. Then I really knew something was wrong. I sat in the car, and thought about Dr. King. I had been with him so much, every time he came to Memphis, I had heard him speak so often that I was practically one of his disciples. I didn't want to leave the car, to go into the house, because I thought the presence of the other officers was going to upset my mother-in-law. So we sat in the car for a few minutes and then the radio announced that Dr. King had been shot.

Three days later Redditt was ordered back to work, with no more mention of the "contract" on him. In subsequent interviews with Lane, Holloman couldn't provide any substantiation for the alleged threats on Redditt or Newsum.

After the Shooting

The FBI's performance after the King shooting is also mysterious. There has been no explanation for the 30-minute delay in getting the bureau into the King case—which might have closed exits from Memphis to the killer or killers. There has also been no explanation of Hoover's crack crimesolving organization taking 14 days to get my name from the evidence collected at Bessie's flophouse. I left behind belongings including my radio from prison days. The radio was labeled with my ID number—00416—and should have tipped the bureau to my escapee status immediately, but the first wave of "Wanted" posters identified me as "Eric Starvo Gault," the name that Raoul knew me by.

And along the chain of odd events in the FBI's pursuit of me there is the record of the bureau's continued efforts to keep a wire on the King household and SCLC leaders even after the murder. Supposedly the wiretapping ended in June 1966 at the direction of Attorney General Ramsey Clark. But DeLoach kept some bugs running until the year after King was shot. These wiretaps provided him with ammunition to use against King's heirs and successors. King had been dead only two days when DeLoach wrote Hoover a memo suggesting that the bureau "quietly sponsor" a book that would tell the "true story" of the King case, adding that he wanted to see the bureau advise a friendly newspaperman "on a strictly confidential basis" that Coretta Scott King and Ralph Abernathy were "deliberately plotting to keep King's assassination in the news by pulling the ruse of maintaining the King murder was definitely a conspiracy, and not committed by one man, in order to keep the money coming to Mrs. King . . . we can do this without attribution to the FBI and without anyone knowing that the information came from a wiretap."

DeLoach had his moment in the Select Committee spotlight, and he used it to perpetuate the lies about me, calling me a racist, a loner, a bigot and so forth. To hear him talk about Rev. King, you'd think he'd been a Freedom Rider, but when panel members posed hard questions about his hostile actions against King, he seemed to catch amnesia. And when the committee produced copies of documents that he'd signed, authorizing moves against King, DeLoach practically rolled over and piddled, protesting that he'd done these things only out of fear that the all-powerful Hoover would sack him. No one on the panel challenged this posing, and all in all, DeLoach played the Select Committee the way he'd played the rest of the Washington bureaucracy.

A Special Prosecutor Is Needed

No special prosecutor was appointed to investigate the FBI's activities concerning the King case. Back then there was no special prosecutor law. Since then special prosecutors have been appointed to investigate all allegations of law violations in the executive branch, from Watergate to the Iran-Contra scandals. If an incarcerated man can find the evidence described in this chapter of FBI involvement in a political murder, then a truly independent special prosecutor, with a team of skilled investigators and a multi-million dollar budget, can smoke out the real plotters. If the country is serious about finding out the whole truth of the King assassination, then appointment of an independent special prosecutor is necessary. And the special prosecutor must be authorized to unlock the FBI's and the Select Committee's sealed files, which have been hidden from public view for far too long.

Chapter Twenty-Five

David Graiver and the Parole Board

Since 1968 I'd been researching photographs dating to the period before and just after my arrest. I was looking for new evidence that would back up my side of the story and help convince the parole board that I was innocent. I had many sources: reporters, Select Committee investigators, files from the office of Representative Richard H. Ichord (D., Mo.), who chaired the House Internal Security Committee before that panel was disbanded.

By 1978 my research had narrowed to two categories, which often overlapped: drug traffickers and those with records of criminal ventures in Mexico or Argentina. The drug trafficking criterion arose from Raoul's apparent ties to that sector, exemplified by Randolph Erwin Rosenson. Another reason was Percy Foreman's declaration, back when a trial still looked likely, that he planned to use the Lansky mob to look into those mysterious telephone numbers.

The Argentina tie-in didn't jell until 1979, although it was foreshadowed far earlier in Jerry's conversations with George McMillan. Once, trying to pooh-pooh the idea of a King murder conspiracy, McMillan offhandedly said, "Maybe Argentine Nazis did it."

Taken alone, the comment wouldn't have aroused any interest—McMillan is phobic about Nazis. But he also might have been fishing to see if Jerry knew whether I'd ever raised the subject.

The next time Argentina surfaced was in November 1977, during an extremely suspicious visit to Brushy Mountain by newspaper columnist Jack Anderson and a polygraph operator named Chris Gugas. Anderson had asked me to undergo polygraph testing for a television program he planned to air at the end of the year. When I agreed, he hired Gugas to handle the technical side.

Anderson is an old hand at promoting the government's version of the King killing—he's been doing it since he was an apprentice to Washington opinion-maker Drew Pearson, another adherent of the party line—but I viewed the project as a chance to learn more about Anderson's game. The polygraph request puzzled me—the *Playboy* interview had just appeared, backing the official story. Why put out another set of polygraph results echoing the party line?

But I decided to go through with it. I was back in segregation, thanks to my June escape attempt. The authorities let me out of segregation for the examination, held in the prison hospital. Afterward, I was to be escorted downstairs to a secure room, where Anderson and his film crew would conduct the interview.

Polygraph examiner Gugas is a veteran of that business. At first he seemed satisfied with the hospital ward as a setting in which to do his work. But we'd only started when he said he was having a hard time evaluating my answers to his questions. I could see his temper rising. Once he implied that I was trying to manipulate the polygraph.

Several times during our two hours together, Gugas would go downstairs to confer with Anderson, as though things weren't going according to some plan. Once Anderson came back with a question: "Did Raoul ever mention an association with an Argentinian named 'Javier'?"

He pronounced the name "HAH-vee-yer."

"No," I said.

Anderson's program had two segments, mine and one on fugitive financier Robert Vesco, who also underwent a Gugas polygraph test in Costa Rica. When the show aired, Anderson was on-camera telling viewers Vesco had come through Gugas' questioning as an honest man, but I'd been deceptive. It didn't surprise me anymore. Very little does.

But the polygrapher's reference to "Javier" came back to haunt me. In 1979, another convict lent me a book titled *Dope, Inc.* by Jeffrey Steinberg, on the international trade in illicit drugs. Several names in it interested me. I had my brother Jerry obtain pictures to match the names, including that of David Graiver, an Argentine national. Graiver, Javier—they sound similar enough that Gugas could have been stumbling over "Graiver" when asking me about "Javier."

When I got the photo of Graiver, it strongly reminded me of someone I'd seen with Raoul: the man who'd been sitting in Raoul's car outside the motel in Nuevo Laredo back in October 1967. There were a few cosmetic differences. The current picture had Graiver sporting a heavy beard, mustache and long hair. I remembered the man in Mexico as having a more conservative hair style and less pronounced beard. But I was certain they were the same individual.

Graiver's Return

In 1980, I applied for clemency. After a massive scandal in the Tennessee parole program, recently elected Governor Lamar Alexander had ordered a new standard for consideration of requests for clemency. To obtain release, a prisoner had to provide "substantial evidence of innocence." I believed I had such evidence, in the form of even more information on the elusive David Graiver.

For if the person I saw in October 1967 in Nuevo Laredo with Raoul was Graiver it would indicate that Raoul had an associate, which could verify my story. While this alone would not establish my innocence the Parole Board had the resources and authority, if it chose to use it, to discover Graiver's role in the assassination conspiracy by requesting classified documents from the FBI.

None of what I collected on Graiver dated to the time of Dr. King's death, but in the early 1970s he was reported to be a bagman for an Argentine terrorist organization. Other reports have Graiver laundering dirty money in some capacity with Meyer Lansky's organization. In the mid-1970s Graiver reportedly used loot extorted by the Monteneros to invest in the American Bank & Trust (ABT) in New York City, gaining control of that institution and emptying its coffers. While Graiver was sucking as much as $30 million out of ABT, state and federal bank examiners were voicing concern over the bank's solvency. However, no one acted until Graiver had moved on—or perhaps passed on. On August 7, 1976, a Falcon 20 jet Graiver had chartered in New York City for a weekend trip to Acapulco, Mexico, exploded in midair or crashed into a mountain 40 miles north of its destination. However, no one can say for sure that Graiver was on board. His family quickly retrieved his supposed remains and had them cremated.

After the crash and ABT's collapse, bank examiners found that several of the bank's officers had been in on Graiver's swindle. However, no serious effort was made to prosecute. A few lower-level employees were convicted of relatively minor violations, but none of the big boys was even close to doing time.

I included a summary of the Graiver story, along with other material, when I applied for clemency. I wrote to the Justice Department requesting that the Board of Paroles get access to classified King case documents.

The board turned me down flat, but offered one hope: I might get a hearing if I answered several questions about the King case. I agreed.

Questions

The parole board wanted to know:

☐ Did I or did I not shoot or participate in the shooting of Dr. King?

☐ If I claimed innocence, what "evidence, alibi, etc." could I cite to support that claim? And the board asked, "Further, what information do you have about the offense—who committed it—your participation in it— the names, addresses and any other evidence which you may have concerning the actual perpetrators— and your whereabouts when the offense was committed."

☐ If my guilty plea was coerced, under what circumstances did that coercion take place? What was I offered to take the fall? Who participated in conversations about the plea bargain? Exactly how was I "coerced" into signing that agreement when I hadn't committed the offense?

☐ If I did participate in the King shooting, what was the nature of the participation? Who were my accomplices? How did I know them? How did I contact them? Where were they now? What other evidence did I have regarding any conspiracy to kill Dr. King? How was that evidence relevant to his murder?

☐ Finally, the board asked me to describe how materials that I have not been able to obtain—such as FBI documents and other items sealed under the 50-year order—might be relevant to my application for parole.

It took me until March 1981 to assemble the materials needed to corroborate my answers. I sent these along and wrote to Senator Howard W. Baker Jr. and Governor Alexander asking them to petition the Justice Department to release classified King case documents to the Tennessee Board of Paroles.

I was turned down again.

More Leads

In 1981, after discovering that an Argentina newspaper, *La Nueva Provincia*, was interested in Graiver, I wrote to the publishers, who said in reply that they wanted to speak with me. Through this connection the Buenos Aires-based magazine *Gente* assigned Alberto Oliva, a Manhattan correspondent for Argentine Atlantic Network, to interview me about Graiver.

Oliva and I corresponded. With one of my letters I enclosed a copy of an FBI response to one of my FOIA requests on Graiver saying that another requester already had obtained copies of the bureau's file on Graiver. The price of obtaining a copy of Graiver's FBI file was $47.90. I hadn't mentioned that sum to Oliva, but he sent me a check in that amount drawn on the Chase Manhattan Bank. I worried that this might alert the FBI to our project, but sent it along anyway, only to run into a four-month stall. When I contacted the bureau to ask about the delay, I got a letter saying because of "new classification guidelines, the file would need to be reviewed prior to release."

Eventually, I did receive the FBI file on Graiver—some 500 heavily censored pages, revealing among other things that Graiver's full name was David Graiver Gitnacht. One entry mentioned that Graiver sometimes altered his appearance by changing hair styles. Another chronicled his "last" flight to Mexico, which was to include a stop in New Orleans. However, that flight plan wasn't followed. Instead, the plane stopped in Memphis, then Houston, where the pilot left the plane, in the FBI's words, to "contact one of his homosexual friends." Finally, after mentioning the supposed cremation of Graiver's remains, *the FBI memorandum notes that after the crash a Bureau source claimed to have spotted Graiver in Ft. Lauderdale, Florida.*

All of these fragments promised to be the makings of a grand portrait of Graiver and his many-splendored activities, which in some way might have included the shooting of Martin Luther King Jr. But the story is still waiting to be written. Perhaps the FBI mentioned the pending article on Graiver to the CIA, which then pressured *Gente* into spiking the story. It wouldn't be the first time a government intelligence agency interfered with the press.

Chapter Twenty-Six

Spica's Payoff

In the spring of 1979, my brother Jerry decided to move to Des Moines, Iowa. Before doing so, he visited me at Brushy Mountain. I asked him to look up John Paul Spica the next time he was in St. Louis. That was Spica's hometown. He'd been paroled there after ten years in prison. There was talk that he was still connected. I was interested in him because the Select Committee had brought up his name, claiming that while he and I were in prison together, he'd told me about Sutherland's $50,000 offer. I asked Jerry to find out from John Paul what the committee investigators had questioned him about.

That summer, Jerry drove to St. Louis and found Spica operating a produce store. He spoke freely about his experiences with committee investigators, recalling that in late spring or early summer 1974, committee investigator Conrad Baetz and "another dude" had approached him, identified themselves and asked if he'd answer questions about the King assassination.

Before Spica could reply, Baetz suggested that it would be in his best interest to cooperate, considering his parolee status. Baetz added that the committee had other "legal remedies" with which to obtain Spica's cooperation.

Assuming Baetz was threatening him with jail, Spica paused, then asked if he could think on Baetz's proposition for a few days. Baetz agreed and gave Spica a phone number where he could be contacted.

Spica decided to go through the interrogation but to protect himself by wearing a wire. Familiar with the ways of St. Louis area politics, he bought a tape recorder small enough to conceal under his clothing.

"The Madison County politicians play rough," he later told Jerry.

When he had his rig assembled, Spica called Baetz and suggested they meet at an after-hours club in East St. Louis patronized by mob figures. Baetz set a date and time, but didn't show. Instead, he phoned Spica at the club and said he'd moved the meeting to a parking lot out of town. It took Spica 20 minutes to reach the spot and sit in Baetz's car, tape recorder rolling, listening to Baetz's proposition.

The investigator began by saying the Select Committee knew it couldn't sell the public "a goofy-ass story about a lone nut killing King." This meant linking me to Sutherland's supposed $50,000 offer. All Spica had to do was tell the committee in public session that he'd told me about the bounty on King while we were in prison together, and that I asked how much the offer was.

Spica stalled again, saying he'd have to think about it. Baetz gave him a few days' grace time. When they met again, Spica handed the investigator a copy of the tape he'd made of their last conversation and told Baetz to get lost.

Upon hearing this, my brother eagerly asked Spica if he could have a copy of the tape. Spica shook his head no. If a third party made the recording public, he'd have no protection.

"If there's to be any blackmailing, it will be by me, and not those bastards!" he told Jerry.

But John Paul Spica's worries about blackmail are over. On the morning of November 8, 1979, he left his apartment in the St. Louis suburb of Richmond Heights and got into his Cadillac. When he hit the starter, the car exploded, ripping off Spica's legs. By the time the ambulance reached the hospital, he was dead. His murder remains unsolved.

Chapter Twenty-Seven.

Talking Mustangs and Courts of Last Resort

In prison, the last thing you think about is your car, especially if you haven't been behind a steering wheel in two decades. But in 1985, I almost got to go to court to keep the title of my now famous pale yellow—unless it's been repainted—1966 Mustang.

I wasn't averse to a trial. I'd welcome any opportunity to get in front of a judge and jury and hash out the circumstances that brought me to where I am today. Over the years I've tried civil suits, libel suits, defamation suits—against everyone from Conrad Baetz to members of the House Select Committee on Assassinations.

What happened in the mid 1980s was that William Morris, mayor of Shelby County (in which Memphis is located), told a reporter the state ought to sell off my car, which the county had been stabling for 17 years. Morris had had that Mustang around almost as long as it had been in my name; before he became mayor, he was sheriff, and presided over my stint in the midnight sun.

When I read about the mayor's proposal, I sued in Memphis U.S. District Court, contending that the Mustang should be returned to me, taking care to include a clause stating that if the state could produce credible evidence connecting the automobile to the murder of Dr. King, I'd waive my claim to ownership.

Surprisingly, Judge Julia Smith Gibbons didn't brush me off. She ruled against the state's motion for summary dismissal and set the case down for trial.

At last, a trial—or maybe not. To sell off my car the state needed to have title to it, and to get the title, Tennessee would have to risk opening the prosecutor's file on the murder of Martin Luther King Jr. Apparently, that price was too high. The state returned the car to me without a trial. I sold it at an auction, and I understand that a car dealer bought it.

There are two remaining possibilities for a trial in the King murder, one rooted in a glaring error by the original judge and the other based in international law.

In the 1970s there was talk that before he named public defender Hugh W. Stanton Sr. to be my attorney, Judge Preston Battle had appointed Stanton Sr. to represent Charles Quitman Stephens, the state's star witness in the King case. The American Bar Association's Code of Professional Responsibility proscribes lawyers from representing multiple clients with differing interests in the same litigation. If he put Stanton in the position of violating ABA canon, Judge Battle had committed reversible error—a mistake serious enough to require a retrial—in my case a real first trial.

In 1982 I inquired about these rumors in a letter to the Shelby County Criminal Court Clerk, J.A. Blackwell. His office responded in a letter dated November 29, 1982. "There was never a hearing held in criminal court in reference to Charles Quitman Stephens," the letter said. I assumed this to be a truthful communication, but still contacted the Circuit Court Clerk, Clint Crabtree, to see if that body was involved. My curiosity paid off.

Documents showed there had been a legal proceeding in circuit court relating to the appointment. The clerk's records indicated that the legal proceeding came about when segments of a criminal court record had been transferred to the circuit court for a habeas corpus hearing for Mr. Stephens. These records disclosed that Judge Battle had appointed Stanton Sr. to represent Stephens as a material witness in the King murder *before* naming him to defend me in the same case.

Besides confirming the conflicted appointment, the documents showed that Judge Battle ordered Stephens jailed as a material witness in the case *on the same day* he appointed Stanton Sr. to represent Stephens. Some representation! Stephens stayed in jail until August 1968, when he hired attorney Harvey L. Gipson, who got Stephens sprung with the aforementioned habeas corpus petition. Then he signed a contract with Stephens for half of any reward money Stephens might receive for testifying against me in the King case.

These documents spurred me to sue in Memphis federal court for access to the entire criminal court record of the Stanton appointment to defend Stephens. I cited as defendants Judge Battle's successor, Judge William H. Williams, and Criminal Court Clerk Blackwell. I should have known better than to keep expecting justice from the judicial system. My suit was dismissed without the defendants even having to answer it—obviously an attempt by Judge Odell Horton to keep me from officially discovering any record of the Stanton appointment to represent Stephens in criminal court. If I could do that, I could obtain those documents and use them as the basis to petition for a trial in the King case.

Judge Horton's ruling sent me back to my old battleground, the Sixth Circuit Court of Appeals, which reversed his decision in March 1985. Afterward, the defendants, who now had to answer the lawsuit, conceded that Judge Battle had appointed Stanton Sr. to represent Stephens as a material witness in the King case, and that the court had a transcript of the appointment proceedings. I took steps to obtain that document. My case is still pending but may be sent into legal limbo on some technicality or other.

Universal Jurisdiction

But if the U.S. court system should rule, finally, that there will be no public trial for the murder of Rev. Martin Luther King, Jr., there is a venue left. Under the doctrine of "universal jurisdiction" doctrine, I may be able to seek relief.

The United States subscribes to this doctrine, and has created the Office of Special Investigations within the Justice Department to prosecutes these cases. Under the Universal Jurisdiction Law the OSI can seek revocation of U.S. citizenship if an alleged criminal must be tried in a foreign country and the crime involved is one of "universal concern." Into this category fall "crimes against humanity," "war crimes" and "terrorism."

In light of its continuing resonance in America and the world, the murder of Martin Luther King Jr. would seem to fit the bill.

The Universal Jurisdiction Law came into being to devise a legal mechanism for extraditing natives of republics in the U.S.S.R.—in particular the Baltic nations—who allegedly committed heinous crimes during World War II. In recent years, the law's application has been broadened to use against émigré Palestinians.

In my personal case, the law has a unique applicability based on the federal courts' interpretation of it—namely, that the deportee need not have committed the alleged crime in the demanding country.

Can you see how it would work? I could be deported to another country to stand trial for Dr. King's murder. The prosecutors could demand access to all federal and state records on the case. The killing of Dr. King could finally get the airing it has deserved since April 4, 1968.

But if such a scenario unfolded, no doubt I'd suddenly have zealous protectors at the Justice Deparment and in the federal courts and among the politicians of Tennessee.

"Double jeopardy!" they'd wail, asserting my right not to be tried twice for the same offense. But that would be a smoke screen. Case law says that for a repeat indictment to be valid, it need only be reworded slightly and filed in a different jurisdiction.

Anyway, I wouldn't care to have the government go to any more trouble "protecting" me. A dude could get hurt with that type of protection. So, if a foreign country should set in motion an effort to have me extradited there for trial, I would consider waiving all of my rights just to get my day in court.

Remaining Questions

As long as I live, I'll never be far from thoughts of the many questions raised by the murder of Martin Luther King. The main question, of course, is the one used in the title of this book. But there are many more questions that need to be answered, not just to show my innocence but for historians as well:

☐ What links existed between Raoul, the tramp arrested after John F. Kennedy was killed and David Graiver Gitnacht?

☐ Where is Randall Erwin Rosenson, and what story does he tell about shadowing me as I supposedly stalked Martin Luther King? What hidden role did Rosenson have in Raoul's directing me around the country, into Mexico and back across the U.S. border in time to be on hand in Memphis on April 4, 1968?

☐ What role did Memphis police and fire chief Frank Holloman—a 25-year veteran of the FBI—have in pulling that city's only two black firemen away from a post near the Lorraine Motel the day before Dr. King was shot? What was the real story behind Holloman's removal of Ed Redditt from the security detail protecting Martin Luther King?

☐ What role did Cartha DeLoach, the number three man in the FBI at the time, play in the assassination? DeLoach, a coordinator of the campaign to purge Martin

Luther King from public life, is now living in South Carolina.

☐ Who was involved in the second Mustang hoax, drawing Memphis police to the north side of town in the hour after Dr. King was shot?

☐ Why did the authorities work so hard to muzzle and even punish Grace Stephens for challenging the accuracy of the her husband's identification of me as the lone gunman?

☐ Why, considering that my fingerprints were discovered minutes after the King shooting, did it take the FBI more than two weeks to get out a bulletin of my alleged involvement in the King shooting?

☐ Why did the first wanted posters name me as "Eric S. Galt," the name known by Raoul but not used at Bessie Brewer's rooming house?

☐ What are the contents of the FBI and Select Committee files ordered sealed for 50 years? It has been 25 years since Dr. King's death—why should 25 more years pass before the American public can view evidence collected in this case?

☐ And finally, why, if official America is so firmly convinced that I pulled the trigger of the rifle that killed Martin Luther King, is there so much reluctance to allow me to have a trial and fully air the evidence? Instead of letting this cloud hang over the assassination, and over me, why not allow 12 citizens on a jury to decide, once and for all, whether I am guilty of killing Martin Luther King?

I call upon the nation to urge the president and the attorney general to appoint a special prosecutor to investigate the FBI's involvement in this case. If a special prosecutor can be appointed to investigate and prosecute those involved in the Iran-Contra scandal, certainly the assassination of Dr. Martin Luther King deserves the same independent examination. The evidence is overwhelming that the murder involved more than one person. And the conspiracy can only be uncovered by a vigorous prosecutor armed with the power to subpoena.

As we near the 21st century this generation's manipulations will come into focus for historians and truth seekers. We should not have to wait until the year 2027 for the truth to be revealed when the FBI's records are finally opened to public view—assuming that the records have not been destroyed by then or "lost" in some manner.

The KGB is now declassifying its records pertaining to political murders committed in the former Soviet Union. So why can't the land of "democracy" and the "open society" do the same?

Date: December 1, 1964

To: Mr. W. C. Sullivan

From: J. A. Sizoo

Subject: MARTIN LUTHER KING, JR.

Reference is made to the attached memorandum DeLoach to Mohr dated 11/27/64 concerning DeLoach's interview with ▓▓▓ and to your informal memo, also attached.

▓▓▓▓▓▓▓▓▓ stated to DeLoach that he was faced with the difficult problem of taking steps to remove King from the national picture. He indicates in his comments a lack of confidence that he, alone, could be successful. It is, therefore, suggested that consideration be given to the following course of action:

That DeLoach have a further discussion with ▓▓▓▓ and offer to be helpful to ▓▓▓ in connection with the problem of the removal of King from the national scene;

That DeLoach suggest that ▓▓▓▓▓ might desire to call a meeting of Negro leaders in the country which might include, for instance, 2 or 3 top leaders in the civil rights movement such as James Farmer and A. Philip Randolph; 2 or 3 top Negro judges such as Judge Parsons and Judge Hasty; 2 or 3 top reputable ministers such as Robert Johnson, Moderator of the Washington City Presbytery; 2 or 3 other selected Negro officials from public life such as the Negro Attorney General from one of the New England states. These men could be called for the purpose of learning the facts as to the Bureau's performance in the fulfillment of its responsibilities under the Civil Rights statute, and this could well be done at such a meeting. In addition, the Bureau, on a highly confidential basis, could brief such a group on the security background of King ▓▓▓▓▓▓▓▓▓▓▓▓▓▓ The use of a tape, such as contemplated in your memorandum, together with a transcript for convenience in following the tape, should be most convincing.

The inclusion of U.S. Government officials, such as Carl Rowan or Ralph Bunche, is not suggested as they might feel a duty to advise the White House of such a contemplated meeting. It is believed this would give us an opportunity to outline to a group of influential Negro leaders what our record in the enforcement of civil rights has been. It would also give them, on a confidential

jns/mls

enclosures

#3

FBI document showing DeLoach's involvement in "removing" Martin Luther King "from the national scene."

Memo to Mr. Sullivan
RE: MARTIN LUTHER KING, JR.

basis, information concerning King which would convince them of
the danger of King to the over-all civil rights movement.
is already well aware of this. This group should include such
leadership as would be capable of removing King from the scene
if they, of their own volition, decided this was the thing to do
after such a briefing. The group should include strong enough men
to control a man like James Farmer and make him see the light of
day. This might have the effect of increasing the stature of
who is a capable person and is ambitious.

There are refinements which, of course, could be added
to the above which is set forth in outline form for possible
consideration.

- 2 -

EXHIBIT-A-14,p,2.

FEDERAL. BUREAU OF INVESTIGATION 6

REPORTING OFFICE	OFFICE OF ORIGIN	DATE	INVESTIGATIVE PERIOD	
MEMPHIS	MEMPHIS	4/30/68	4/4-30/68	
TITLE OF CASE		REPORT MADE BY		TYPED BY
CHANGED		SA JOE C. HESTER		wp

TITLE OF CASE
CHANGED
JAMES EARL RAY, aka
Eric Starvo Galt,
W. C. Herron,
Harvey Lowmyer,
James McBride,
James O'Conner,
James Walton,
James Walyon,
John Willard,
Jim - FUGITIVE
IO # 4182,
WF # 442-A;
Dr. MARTIN LUTHER KING, JR. - VICTIM

CHARACTER OF CASE

CR - CONSPIRACY;
UFAC - ROBBERY

Title marked changed to reflect the subject's true name of JAMES EARL RAY and to reflect additional aliases of the subject.

REFERENCE

Report of SA JOE C. HESTER dated 4/17/68 at Memphis.

-P-

ENCLOSURES

TO CHICAGO AND KANSAS CITY:

One copy of referenced report.

APPROVED ____ SPECIAL AGENT IN CHARGE

DO NOT WRITE IN SPACES BELOW

44 - 38861 2634   REC- 97

COPIES MADE:
5-Bureau (44-38861)
3-Atlanta (44-2386)
3-Birmingham (44-1740)
3-Chicago (Enc. 1) (44-1114)
1-Jackson
3-Kansas City (44-760)(Enc. 1)
3-Los Angeles (44-1574)
3-Mobile (157-2627)
3-New Orleans
3-St. Louis (44-775)
3-Springfield
5-Memphis (44-1987)

1 COPIES DESTROYED

2 3 SEP 25 1974

14 MAY 2 1969

PROPERTY OF FBI.—This report is loaned to you by the FBI, and neither it nor its contents are to be distributed outside the agency to which loaned.

FBI document showing charge against Ray was initially "conspiracy," which means that more than one man was involved. The conspiracy charge was sole basis for Ray's extradition from England; therefore the legality of the extradition is highly questionable.

FD-302 (Rev. 4-15-64)

FEDERAL BUREAU OF INVESTIGATION

<u>1</u>

Date ___April 25, 1968___

      Photographs of JAMES EARL RAY taken in 1955, 1960, and 1966, and of the bedspread recovered at Memphis on April 4, 1968, were shown to Mr. CHARLIE QUITMAN STEPHENS, Apartment 6B, 422½ South Main Street, Memphis, Tennessee. STEPHENS said the 1955 and 1960 photographs of RAY were not familiar to him, but he advised the 1966 profile photograph of RAY appearing in Wanted Flyer 442-A, April 19, 1968, and Identification Order 4182 dated April 20, 1968, looked like the man he saw in Apartment 5B on April 4, 1968, talking to Mrs. BESSIE BREWER. STEPHENS said he only saw the man's profile in the boarding house and as a result could only say the profile photograph of RAY in 1966 looked very much like the above mentioned man in Room 5B.

      STEPHENS said he had never seen the bedspread or any similar bedspread either at the rooming house or anywhere else.

5

On ___4/24/68___ at ___Memphis, Tennessee___ File # ___Memphis 44-1987___

by ___SA ▮▮▮▮▮▮▮▮▮▮▮▮▮▮▮▮▮▮___ Date dictated ___4/25/68___

This document contains neither recommendations nor conclusions of the FBI. It is the property of the FBI and is loaned to your agency; it and its contents are not to be distributed outside your agency.

FBI report proving that eyewitness Charlie Quitman Stephens was shown old photographs of Ray, which were taken before he underwent plastic surgery on ears and nose.

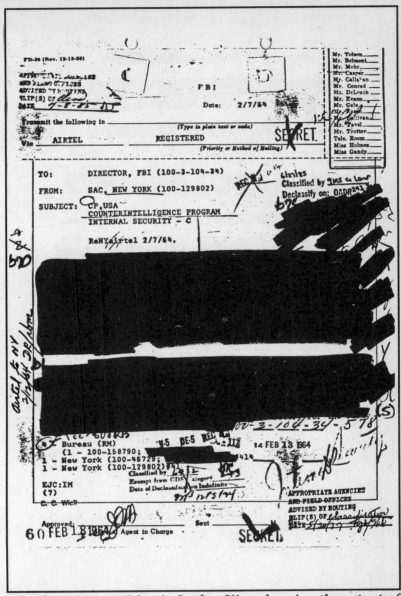

FBI document on Martin Luther King showing the extent of the bureau's censorship.

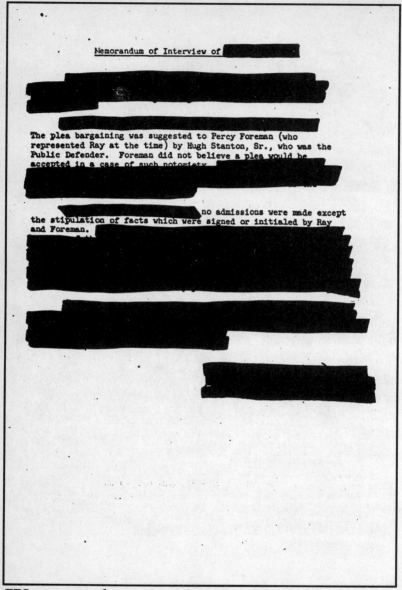

Memorandum of Interview of ▮▮▮▮▮▮▮▮▮▮

The plea bargaining was suggested to Percy Foreman (who represented Ray at the time) by Hugh Stanton, Sr., who was the Public Defender. Foreman did not believe a plea would be accepted in a case of such notoriety.

...no admissions were made except the stipulation of facts which were signed or initialed by Ray and Foreman.

FBI memorandum concerning interview which was contained in bureau's files on Percy Foreman.

Memorandum of Interview of

Second page of FBI material on Percy Foreman showing extent of censorship.

said he had no conversations with defense lawyers Hanes or Percy Foreman.

Third page of FBI file on Percy Foreman.

LAW OFFICES OF
PERCY FOREMAN
804 SOUTH COAST BUILDING
HOUSTON, TEXAS 77002

MAIN AT RUSK

CA 4-9321

March 9, 1969

Mr. James Earl Ray,
Shelby County Jail,
Memphis, Texas.

Dear James Earl:

You have asked that I advance to Jerry Ray five
($500.00) of the "$5,000.00", referring to the first five
thousand dollars paid by Wm. Bradford Huie. On January
29th, Mr. Huie advanced an additional $5,000.00. At that
time I had spent in excess of $9,500.00 on your case.
Since then, I have spent in excess of $4,000.00 additional.

But I am willing to advance Jerry $500.00 and add
it to the $165,000.00 mentioned in my other letter to you
today. In other words, I would receive the first $165,500.00.
But I would not make any other advances - just this one $500.00.

And this advance, also, is contingent upon the plea
of guilty and sentence going through on March 10, 1969, without
any unseemly conduct on your part in court.

Yours truly,

Percy Foreman

PF-4

P.S.   The rifle and the white mustang are tied up in the
suit filed by Renfro Hays. Court costs and attorneys
fees will be necessary, perhaps, to get them released.
I will credit the $165,500.00 with whatever they bring
over the cost of obtaining them, if any.

James Earl Ray   *Percy Foreman*
                                    Percy Foreman

*Fee arrangement between Percy Foreman and James Earl Ray
which was contingent upon a guilty plea.*

A

Abel, Rudolph, 49
Abernathy, Ralph, 250
Aeromarine Supply, 91, 92
Agca, Mehmet Ali, 165
Air Force, 111
Alcatraz, 49
Alexander, Lamar, 254, 257
Alhambra, 84
Alke-Bulan Society, 229, 230, 231
Alliluyeva, Svetlana, 168
Alton, Illinois, 17, 18, 19, 22, 30, 124,
    182, 216, 217, 219
American Bank & Trust (ABT), 255
American Bar Association (ABA), 263
American Civil Liberties Union
    (ACLU), 174, 175
Anderson, Jack, 253, 254
Anderson, William R., 151
Andrew Johnson Hotel, 238
Angola, 102
Argentina, 257
Argentine Atlantic Network, 257
Arnstein, Bobbie, 171
Asbury, Lee, 210
Atlanta Journal, 215
Atlanta, Georgia, 85, 89, 90, 96, 97, 106,
    171, 190, 191
Auble, John, 185
Avery, Harry, 137, 138, 139, 140, 142

B

Bad Neuheim, Germany, 23
Baetz, Conrad, 183, 184, 185, 219, 220,
    221, 259, 260, 262
Bailey, F. Lee, 107
Baker, Howard, 151, 152, 257
Bank of Alton, 193, 214, 215, 218
Bantam Books, 161, 204
Barry, William L., 142
Baton Rouge, Louisiana, 71, 72, 73, 130,
    154, 155, 156
Battle, Preston, 116, 118, 121, 122, 123,
    124, 131, 132, 133, 134, 139, 140, 141,
    162, 163, 199, 263, 264
Bauman, Robert, 178
Beasley, James, 140
Belgium, 104
Biggs, Ronald, 109
Birmingham Trust National Bank, 71,
    72

Birmingham, Alabama, 65, 67, 69, 73,
    75, 85, 89, 91, 100, 107, 120, 240, 244
Blackwell, J.A., 263
Blakey, G. Robert, 177, 181, 187, 189,
    204, 240
Blanton, Ray, 173, 187, 201, 210, 238
Boston Strangler, 126
Bowman, David A., 239
Boyle, W.A., 174
Boystown, 76
Bradley, Harold, 228
Bremen, Germany, 23
Brewer, Bessie, 94, 95, 96, 100, 109, 199,
    249, 267
Bridgman, Paul, 99
Brinton, Larry, 230
British Broadcasting Company, 100
British Overseas Airways, 101
Brownsville, Texas, 39
Brushy Mountain State Prison, 143,
    144, 149, 155, 173, 176, 186, 188, 189,
    194, 201, 205, 226, 228, 229, 230, 232,
    238, 253, 259
Brussels, Belgium, 106
Bryn Mawr, 167
Burch, Lucius, 131
Burnett, Hamilton, 141
Butler, Thomas, 106, 108, 109
Byers, Russell G., 180, 181
Byrd, Robert, 247

C

Callahan, Lawrence, 32, 154, 155
Camp Kilmer, 22, 23
Canale, Philip M., 116, 120, 130, 132,
    133, 139, 160, 199, 200
Cannon Row, 106
Capitol Homes, 97
Carson, Arzo, 210
Carter, Jimmy, 210
Catman, see Jack Gawron.
CBS, 203
Cedar Rapids, Iowa, 27
Celebrezze, Anthony, 154, 164
Central Intelligence Agency (CIA), 49,
    166, 204, 241, 242, 258
Chamorro, Pedro J., 166
Chandler, Wyeth, 174, 175
Chase Manhattan Bank, 257
Chattanooga, Tennessee, 155, 156
Cherpes, Peter, 69, 71, 85
Chicago Tribune, 58

Chicago, Illinois, 27, 28, 58, 59, 60, 69, 72, 177
Chisca Hotel, 95
Churchill, Winston, 134
Cincinnati, Ohio, 98
Citizen's Committee on Inquiry, 174
Clark, Chris, 231
Clark, Ramsey, 110, 250
Cloud, Boyd, 238
Code Name Zorro, 194, 202, 246
COINTELPRO, 160, 243, 246
Colvin, Ian, 103, 104, 106
COMINFIL, 246
Committee to Investigate Assassinations, 158
Conrad, Walter, 193
Corinth, Mississippi, 92, 191
Cosa Nostra, 34
Costa Rica, 180, 254
Cowden, Dean, 194, 195, 202, 203
Cowles Communication, Inc., 127
Crowley, Ted, 18, 59

D

Dalitz, Morris, 177
Dallas, Texas, 125
David Rogers, 183
Davis, Herman, 227, 228, 229, 230
Davis, Mendel J., 187
Davis, Wayne, 220
Decatur, Alabama, 92
DeLoach, Cartha, 160, 243, 244, 245, 246, 247, 250
DePaolo, Ron, 105
Department of Justice, 107, 108, 109, 174, 175, 185, 187, 198, 216, 218, 239, 255, 257, 265
Des Moines, Iowa, 259
Desoto Motel, 92, 192
Detroit, Michigan, 60, 65, 66, 67, 98
Devine, Samuel L., 187, 192, 222, 223, 225
Dirty John, 39
Dope, Inc., 254
Dorion, Canada, 61
Dowling, Thomas H., 174
Drake, Carl, 185
Duncan, John J. Jr., 232
Dunn, Winfield, 148, 149, 150, 152, 153
Dwyer, Robert, 130

E

East St. Louis, Missouri, 60
Eastern Airlines, 241
Eberhardt, Michael C., 225
Ebony, 226
Edgar, Robert W., 187, 225
Edmondson, Charles, 122, 127
Eist, Alexander, 192, 193, 202, 218, 222, 223, 224, 225
Ellington, Buford, 137, 138, 142, 200
Ellis, Howard M., 239, 240
Eric S. Galt, 62
Eugene, Michael, 107, 110, 123
Evening Telegraph, 98, 99
Ewing School, 104, 105
Ewing, Missouri, 18
Examiner, The, 190

F

Fabie River, 18
Face the Nation, 203
Farmers Bank of Liberty, 219
Fauntroy, Walter, 218
Federal Bureau of Investigation (FBI), 59, 100, 109, 110, 111, 125, 126, 138, 139, 158, 160, 168, 175, 180, 182, 183, 191, 192, 196, 199, 200, 209, 215, 216, 217, 218, 219, 220, 224, 242, 243, 244, 246, 247, 248, 249, 250, 251, 255, 256, 257, 258, 266, 267
Federal Bureau of Prisons, 152, 153
Fensterwald, Bernard, 150, 158, 159, 215
Ferrie, David, 241, 242
Final Assassinations Report, The, 204
Fithian, Floyd J., 193
Five Points Travel Lodge, 91
Flamingo Motel, 89
Ford Madison Prison, 17
Ford, Harold, 194, 195
Foreman, Percy, 118, 119, 120, 121, 122, 123, 124, 125, 126, 127, 128, 130, 131, 132, 133, 134, 135, 138, 139, 140, 150, 158, 160, 161, 162, 164, 195, 196, 197, 198, 199, 200, 202, 243, 252
Fort Leavenworth Penitentiary, 32, 33, 35, 36, 73, 154
Fort Leavenworth, Kansas, 33
Frank, Gerold, 126
Franklin, Joseph P., 220
Fuller, Frank, 21, 29
Fulton, Missouri, 52

G

Galt, Eric S., 63, 64, 67, 70, 71, 84, 85, 91, 99, 100, 104, 250, 267
Gant, Isaiah, 232
Garner, Jimmy, 89, 90, 91, 97
Garrison, Jim, 191, 242
Gaston Hospital, 110
Gawron, Jack (Catman), 58, 60, 182, 183, 217
Gibbons, Julia S., 263
Gill, G. Wray, 241, 242
Gipson, Harvey L., 264
Goins, Charles, 151
Goldwater, Barry, 245
Gonzalez, Henry B., 174, 176, 177
Grafenhor, Germany, 23
Graiver, David, 252, 254, 255, 257, 258, 266
Gravel, Camille F., 241
Great Train Robbery of 1963, 109
Greyhound, 98
Greyrocks, 64, 65
Grooms, Junior, 155, 156, 157
Grzegorek, Stephen, 188, 189
Gugas, Chris, 253, 254

H

Hacker, Larry, 209, 210
Hadley, Russell C., 84, 85, 110
Haggerty, Jim, 183
Haile, Henry, 158, 159, 160, 161, 169
Hanes, Arthur J. Sr., 107, 108, 110, 115, 116, 117, 119, 120, 123, 126, 134, 160, 161, 194
Hannibal, Missouri, 32
Har-K Apartments, 62, 65
Harrison, James E., 191
Hartford, Illinois, 22
Hartselle, Alabama, 117
Harvard, 167
Hays, Renfro, 134, 194, 195
He Slew The Dreamer, 124
Hearns,Thomas, 49
Heathrow Airport, 102, 106, 108
Heathrow House, 103
Hefner, Hugh, 171
Hendrix, Ernest L., 228
Hill, Earl, 207, 227
Hill, Robert, 140, 156
Hoffa, James, 155, 156
Holloman, Frank, 248, 249, 266

Hooker, John J. Jr., 124, 128, 139
Hooker, John J. Sr., 123, 124, 128, 197
Hooks, Benjamin, 131
Hoover, J. Edgar, 110, 224, 244, 245, 246, 247, 248, 250
Horrock, Nicholas, 185, 203
Horton, Odell, 264
Hotel Portugal, 102
Hotel Rio, 78
House of Representatives, 167, 168, 174, 175, 176, 177, 178, 179, 180, 182, 183, 185, 186, 187, 188, 191, 194, 195, 196, 202, 204, 205, 215, 219, 223, 224, 226, 237, 238, 240, 250, 251, 252, 259, 260, 262, 267
Houston, Texas, 122, 124, 133, 158, 257
Huie, William B., 108, 116, 117, 118, 119, 120, 123, 124, 126, 127, 130, 133, 135, 154, 159, 160, 161, 200, 201, 202
Hunt Co., 198
Hunt, H.L., 197
Hunt, Nelson, 197
Hunt, William, 197
Hyatt-Regency Hotel, 184

I

Ichord, Richard H., 252
Indian Trails Restaurant, 58, 59
Indianapolis, Indiana, 60
Internal Revenue Service (IRS), 80
International Color Council, 105
International Shoe Company, 22
Iowa River, 27
Iran-Contra scandal, 251, 267

J

J.A. Blackwell, 264
Jacksonville, Florida, 32
Jacobson, Stanley F., 183
Jefferson City Prison, 41, 42, 45, 48, 49, 54, 126, 137, 169, 181, 182
Jefferson City, Missouri, 40, 41
Jenkins, Walter, 245
Jennings, Tom, 179
Jensen, Robert G., 138, 139
Jim's Belmont Cafe, 93
Jim's Grill, 93, 94, 96, 129, 180
Johnson, Lyndon B., 244, 245
Joliet, Illinois, 29
Jolly, Robert, 232
Joplin, Missouri, 22
Jordon, Vernon, 219, 220

K

Kalb, Marvin, 165, 166
Kangaroo Alley, 103, 104
Kansas City District Court, 32
Kansas City, Kansas, 36
Kansas City, Missouri, 32
Kauffman, John R., 180-182
Kellerville, Illinois, 30
Kelly, Jon J., 197
Kennedy Travel Bureau, 100, 101
Kennedy, John F., 124, 125, 167, 168, 174, 203, 241, 242, 266
Kennedy, Robert F., 32, 124, 139, 199, 241, 243
Kershaw, Jack, 170-172, 201
King, Correta Scott, 250
King, Martin Luther Jr., 95, 97, 100, 106-111, 116, 118, 120, 122, 124, 125, 127-131, 133, 137-139, 141, 143, 152-158, 160, 163,165-169, 171, 174-181, 186, 187, 189-197, 210-212, 214-216, 218, 222, 223, 225, 226, 232, 237, 240, 241, 244-251, 253, 255-260, 263-267
KITV-TV, 185
Knoxville News Sentinel, 161, 203
Knoxville, Tennessee, 166, 188, 232, 238
Korean War, 28

L

La Nueva Provincia, 257
Lane, Mark, 95, 110, 172, 174, 178, 184 185, 187, 189, 190, 192-195, 201, 203 210-212, 223, 225, 228, 246, 248, 249
Lansky, Meyer, 130, 177, 199, 252, 255
Lardner, George, 187
Laredo, Texas, 74
Las Vegas, Nevada, 26
Laventhal Marine Supply, 155
Law Enforcement Assistance Admin. 171
Lawson, James, 212
LeBunny Lounge, 82
Leeming, Frank, Jr. 105
Legal Services Corp., 151
Lehner, Robert, 176

Lesar, James H., 150, 159, 215,-218
Lewisburg, Pennsylvania, 155
LIFE, 104-106, 124, 125, 127, 131, 163
Lisbon, Portugal, 102
Livingston, Robert, 150, 159
London, England, 101, 103, 106, 107, 162, 189, 192, 222, 224
Look, 117, 126, 127, 139
Lorraine Motel, 100, 190, 247, 248, 266
Los Angeles County Jail, 26, 27
Los Angeles, California, 25, 27, 80, 81, 83, 85, 190
Lowmeyer, Harvey, 91

M

MacDonnell, Herbert, 100
MacNeil/Lehrer Report, 203
Maddix, Tom, 20
Madison, Illinois, 38
Maher, Lucille, 17
Maher, Mary, 22
Maher, William, 22
Making of an Assassin, The, 163, 167
Managua, Nicaragua, 166
Marcello, Carlos, 155, 241, 242
Marro, Anthony J., 185
Martin, Jack S., 242
Martin, Marie, 80, 81, 84
Matamoros, Mexico, 39
Maxey, Hugh, 54, 181
McCraw, James, 128, 129, 159, 160
McFall, Lance, 193-195
McFall, Phillip, 193, 195
McMillan, George, 163, 166-170, 176, 210, 213, 214, 216, 253
McMillan, Priscilla, 167, 168
McRae, Robert, 150, 154, 158, 159, 161-, 163, 175
McVickar, John, 167
McWirter, William A., 105
Memphis Commercial Appeal, 109, 122, 202, 203
Memphis, Tennessee, 92-94, 96, 97 100, 109-111, 117, 120, 122, 124-126, 131, 133, 136, 138, 150, 159,

161, 162, 168, 169, 174, 175, 189, 190, 191, 193, 195, 196, 198, 214, 237, 243, 244, 247, 248, 257, 263, 264
Metropol Hotel, 167
Mexicali, Mexico, 79
Mexico, 254, 255, 266
Mexico City, Mexico, 77
Miami, Florida, 90, 237
Michael Dresden & Co., 107
Miller's Mutual Insurance Co., 30
Miller, Johnny, 73
Miller, William E., 142, 143, 150, 151, 153, 154, 156, 162, 163, 164
Millington Airforce Base, 111
Milnor Hotel, 59
Mississippi, 48
Missouri Hospital for the Criminally Insane, 52, 53
Missouri State Prison, 40, 169
Mobile Register, 180
Mobile, Alabama, 65, 179
Montedonico, Eddie, 97
Montreal, Canada, 40, 61, 62, 64, 65, 101
Moore, Gerald, 105
Moore, Robert, 148, 149
Morelock, Jake, 145, 146, 147, 148
Morris, William N., 160, 262
Morton, L. Clure, 151, 152, 153, 154, 161
Moscow, USSR, 167
Murtagh, Arthur, 246
My Thirty Years in Hoover's FBI, 245
Myszak, John J., 181

N

Nash, E.V., 41, 42, 47, 49
Nashville Banner, 230
Nashville Tennessean, 139, 154, 202, 231, 232
Nashville, Tennessee, 123, 136, 149, 151, 152, 156, 170, 173, 230, 231
Nat'l Ass. Defense Lawyers in Criminal Cases, 197
National Archives, 175
National Enquirer, 194
National Guard, 248
National States Rights Party, 183
NBC, 165
Neff, Chuck, 185
Neptune Tavern, 63, 64, 65
New Earls Court, 104
New Franklin, Missouri, 58

New Orleans, Louisiana, 38, 68, 71, 72, 77, 79, 80, 81, 82, 85, 89, 92, 96, 130, 154, 155, 171, 198, 237, 238, 241, 242, 257
New Rebel Motel, 92
New York Times, 166, 175, 182, 185, 187, 193, 203, 204
New York, New York, 255, 257
Newark, New Jersey, 171
Newsum, Floyd, 248
Nigeria, 102, 104
Nixon, Richard, 152, 240
Northbrook, Illinois, 59, 69
Notre Dame University, 177
Nuevo Laredo, Mexico, 72, 73, 74
Nuremberg, Germany, 23

O

O'Neill, Thomas, 177
Office of War Information, 166
Oliva, Alberto, 257
Osborn, Z.T., 155
Oswald, Lee Harvey, 167
Oswald, Marina, 168
Ottawa, Canada, 65, 66
Owens, James, 40, 41
Owens-Illinois, 17

P

Pack, David, 153
Paisley, William, 70
Palace of Justice, 23
Parton, Edward G., 155, 156
Patterson, Oliver B., 183, 184, 185, 186, 187
Peabody Motel, 122, 134
Peacock, Robey, 104, 105
Pearson, Drew, 253
Pekkanen, John, 105
Penthouse, 177
Petros, Tennessee, 143
Phillips, Harry, 164
Playboy, 165, 170, 171, 205, 253
Plot to Kill the President, 204
Pontiac, Illinois, 29
Pope John Paul II, 165
Pope Paul VII, 185
Powers, Francis Gary, 49
Preyer, Richard, 190
Preyer, Richardson, 203
Progressive, The, 167
Prohibition, 20

Provencal Motel, 82
Pursell, Dick, 20

Q
Quarter Master Corps, 22
Quincy, Illinois, 17, 19, 21, 24, 29, 30, 32, 48, 59

R
Rabbit's Foot Club, 83
Randall, Murray L., 181
Raoul, 61, 63, 64, 65, 66, 67, 68, 70, 71, 72, 73, 74, 75, 76, 77, 81, 82, 85, 89, 90, 91, 92, 93, 94, 95, 96, 98, 125, 126, 130, 154, 179, 191, 240, 241, 250, 252, 254, 255, 266, 267
Ray, Carol, 18, 166
Ray, Earl, 18, 19, 20, 21, 30
Ray, Frank, 18
Ray, George Ellis, 17, 18
Ray, James E., 100, 104, 106, 109, 110, 116, 120, 126, 127, 133, 166, 187, 192, 195, 202, 203, 217, 220, 224, 231, 240
Ray, James W., 119
Ray, Jerry, 18, 59, 69, 91, 117, 118, 131, 140, 154, 155, 156, 158, 166, 168, 183, 184, 186, 193, 196, 201, 213, 214, 215, 217, 229, 237, 238, 253, 259
Ray, Jim, 18, 20, 21
Ray, John, 18, 132, 179, 193, 213, 215, 216, 217, 218, 219, 220, 221
Ray, Lillian, 18
Ray, Marjorie, 18
Ray, Michael, 156
Rayns, James Earl, 18, 58
Rayns, John L., 63, 67, 71
Reader's Digest, 127
Redditt, Ed, 248, 249, 266
Remington, 92
Rhodes, John, 177
Rife, Walter, 30, 31, 32
River Bend, 136, 137, 140
Rockefeller Foundation, 167
Rockefeller, Nelson, 152, 164
Rose, Jim, 150
Rosen, Randy, 79, 237
Rosenson, Randolph E., 237, 238, 239, 240, 241, 252, 266
Rubin, Ben, 238

Rumbaut, Carlos H., 179, 180
Ryan, Richard J., 139, 140, 141, 238

S
Saint Jovite, Canada, 64
Sally Jesse Raphael, 229
Salt Lake City, Utah, 27
San Diego, California, 79
San Fransisco Motel, 77
San Quentin, 80
Sandhu, Anna, 211, 212, 229, 231, 239
Santa Ana, Mexico, 78
Sarro, Ron, 187
Sawyer, Harold, 187, 189, 190, 203
Schoolfield, Raulston 32, 33, 139, 156, 158, 237
Scotland Yard, 106, 107, 108, 111, 192, 218, 224
Secret Service, 242, 248
Selma, Alabama, 89, 190
Sentinella, Alan G., 191
Shaheen, Michael, 175, 176
Shaw, Robert, 103
Shelby County Jail, 111, 115, 118, 136, 159, 160
Shelton, Doug, 205, 206, 207, 209, 227
Siegenthaler, John, 154, 164
Sizoo, J.A., 246
Smith, Billy, 122
Sneyd, Ramon G., 99, 100, 106
Southern Christian Leadership Conference, 131, 171, 191, 201, 246, 250
Southhaven, Mississippi, 192
Spencer, Lillian, 100
Spica, John Paul, 54, 181, 182, 259, 260, 261
Sportman's Country Club, 69
Sprague, Richard A., 174, 176, 177
Springfield, Missouri, 153
St. Francis Hotel, 80, 84, 85
St. Louis Steamfitters Union, 32
St. Louis, Missouri, 31, 37, 38, 39, 54, 58, 117, 130, 179, 180, 181, 183, 185, 203, 215, 218, 219, 237, 259, 260
St. Mary's Elementary School, 18
Stalin, Joseph, 168
Stanley, David A., 240
Stanley, Gene A., 239
Stanton, Hugh W. Jr., 132, 134, 159
Stanton, Hugh W. Sr., 121, 122, 132,

159, 200, 263, 264
Starlight Club, 70, 71, 89, 91
Stein, Charlie, 80, 81, 82
Steinberg, Jeffrey, 254
Stephens, Charles Q., 109, 110, 127, 129, 160, 263, 264
Stephens, Grace, 110, 267, 199
Stokes, Louis, 177, 186, 187, 190, 191, 197, 198, 202, 203, 215, 217, 218, 224, 226, 240
Stoner, J.B., 140, 183
Sudbury, Ontario, 100
Sullivan, William, 244, 245, 246
Sultan Club, 80, 81
Summers, Owen, 224
Sutherland, John H., 180, 181, 203, 259, 260
Swenson, Harold, 49, 51
Szapowski, 98, 99

T

Tadaro, Dominic, 31, 34
Taylor, Robert, 239
Teamsters Union, 32, 139, 140, 155, 156
Telegraph, 103
Thompson, Herman A., 73, 130, 155
Tijuana, Mexico, 79
Time, 134, 163, 165, 166, 168, 169, 170, 177, 210
Timkin, Victor, 161
Tollett, Lewis, 143, 148
Toronto, Canada, 84, 98, 99, 100, 101, 102
Town & Country Motel, 155
Trailways, 58
TWA, 111
Twain, Mark, 17, 32
Twenty Letters to a Friend, 168

U

Union Planters Bank of Memphis, 130
United Mine Workers, 174
United Press International, 161
Universal Jurisdiction Law, 265
Urban League, 219
US Army, 22, 23, 24, 248
US Congress, 20
US Customs House, 74
US Post Office, 30
US Senate, 175
US Surpeme Court, 163

V

Veracruz, Mexico, 39
Vesco, Robert, 254
Vietnam, 151
Vinson, Fred M., 107

W

Wachtel, Harry, 200
Walden, Grace, 128
Wallace, George, 81, 218
Wandsworth Prison, 107, 111
Ward, Jerry, 207, 209
Wartburg, Tennessee, 210
Washington Post, 175, 187
Washington Star, 174, 176, 187
Washington, D.C., 84, 150, 158, 184, 188, 189, 196, 218, 245, 248, 250
Watergate, 251
Watts, Clyde, 237
Waxman, Mel, 183
Webster, William H., 219, 220
Wellford, Harry, 169, 170
Western State Hospital, 110
Wilkins, Roy, 245, 246
Wilkinson, Fred, 49
Willard, John, 93, 94
Williams, Evan, 223
Williams, Hosea, 229
Williams, William H., 264
Windsor, Canada, 60, 65, 66, 67, 74, 98
Winnetka, Illinois, 58, 60
Wood, Donald, 91, 92
Woodbury, Richard, 105
Woodriver, Illinois, 184
Works Progress Administration, 54
World War II, 22
World's Fair Expo '67, 62
Wynn, William, 230, 231, 232

Y

Yablonski, Joseph A., 174
YMCA, 245
York Arms Co., 95